HOW TO FINANCE YOUR SMALL BUSINESS WITH GOVERNMENT MONEY

Wiley Series on Small Business Management

Rick Stephan Hayes, Editor

Simplified Accounting for Non-Accountants
by Rick Stephan Hayes and C. Richard Baker

Accounting for Small Manufacturers
by C. Richard Baker and Rick Stephan Hayes

Simplified Accounting for Engineering and Technical Consultants
by Rick Stephan Hayes and C. Richard Baker

Simplified Accounting for the Computer Industry
by Rick Stephan Hayes and C. Richard Baker

The Complete Legal Guide for Your Small Business
by Paul Adams

Running Your Own Show: Mastering Basics of Small Business
by Richard T. Curtin

Up Front Financing
by A. David Silver

How to Finance Your Small Business with Government Money: SBA and Other Loans, Second Edition
by Rick Stephan Hayes and John Cotton Howell

HOW TO FINANCE YOUR SMALL BUSINESS WITH GOVERNMENT MONEY

SBA and Other Loans

RICK STEPHAN HAYES

JOHN COTTON HOWELL
Attorney at Law

Second Edition

A Ronald Press Publication

JOHN WILEY & SONS

New York • Chichester • Brisbane • Toronto • Singapore

Copyright © 1983 by John Wiley & Sons, Inc.

All rights reserved. Published simultaneously in Canada.

Reproduction or translation of any part of this work beyond that permitted by Section 107 or 108 of the 1976 United States Copyright Act without the permission of the copyright owner is unlawful. Requests for permission or further information should be addressed to the Permissions Department, John Wiley & Sons, Inc.

A portion of the material on SBA Loans in this book was excerpted and abridged from *Business Loans*, Second Edition by Rick Stephan Hayes, published by CBI Publishing Company, Inc., 51 Sleeper Street, Boston, MA 02210. Permission to use this material is gratefully acknowledged.

This publication is designed to provide accurate and authoritative information in regard to the subject matter covered. It is sold with the understanding that the publisher is not engaged in rendering legal, accounting, or other professional service. If legal advice or other expert assistance is required, the services of a competent professional person should be sought. *From a Declaration of Principles jointly adopted by a Committee of the American Bar Association and a Committee of Publishers.*

Library of Congress Cataloging in Publication Data:

Hayes, Rick Stephan, 1946–
How to finance your small business with government money.

(Wiley series on small business management)
"A Ronald Press publication."
Bibloiography: p.
Includes index.
1. Small business—United States—Finance. 2. Government lending—United States. I. Howell, John Cotton, 1926– II. Title. III. Series.

HG4027.7.H39 1982 658.1′5224 82-16060
ISBN 0-471-86563-X

Printed in the United States of America

10 9 8 7 6 5 4 3 2 1

Preface

Government programs can change without warning! Since the first edition of this book, many government loan programs have been eliminated, all programs have been changed somewhat, and a few programs have been added. The new edition now includes government loan programs of the Farmer's Home Administration, Export-Import Bank, Economic Development Administration, Maritime Administration, and other agencies. Also newly featured are sample forms of loan proposals and expert guidance in coping with the present administration.

Because government loan programs are subject to change with each new administration, people who apply for loans must have a standard procedure that will allow them to apply to any agency, at any time. This book provides a detailed, step-by-step guide for applying to any government agency for a loan. This book discusses Small Business Administration (SBA) loan programs in particular because the SBA is a long-running source of loans that has changed little from administration to administration. Firms eligible under SBA criteria are also eligible for most of the other government loan programs.

This book presumes no knowledge of business finance or accounting. You learn how to pick the best bank and how to do a complete loan proposal from projected cash flow to presentation format. You are taken through the necessary financial information by use of many examples. Whether you need money to start a new business or to expand an existing firm, this book helps you complete a proposal by actually showing you how. It takes you through all the necessary calculations using your own data for your own business.

This book is above all practical. When you have reached the end, you will have a completed loan proposal you have prepared while reading. And you can use the proposal you've prepared for many other sources of financing and equity: banks, insurance companies, trusts, individual investors, small offerings, small business investment companies, and so on. The format and financing taught in this book can be used to make a presentation to *all* sources of money.

The first part of the book (Chapters 1 through 7) tells you how to prepare a standard venture proposal that may be presented to any lender. All information you are required to have is explained here. All financial knowledge necessary to submit a loan is outlined in detail. These chapters give a general explanation of concepts, detailed examples illustrating the concepts, and a format for using the concept on your own business and in gathering your own data.

The second part of the book (Chapters 8 through 12) explains all the government loan programs as they existed when this book was written. There is a thoroughly updated list of the government programs, eligibility requirements, minimum and maximum amounts that can be borrowed, where to apply, and how each program works.

The appendixes include an SBA business plan questionnaire (Appendix I), a sample loan proposal for Yourcompany (Appendix II), and a glossary.

This book tells you everything you need to know to get the money.

RICK STEPHAN HAYES
JOHN COTTON HOWELL

Topanga Canyon, California
October 1982

Contents

HOW TO FINANCE YOUR SMALL BUSINESS WITH GOVERNMENT MONEY

Chapter One
The Financial Gambit

A business cannot survive without loans. A company as large as Exxon borrows money. The local convenience store borrows money. A business may operate for many years without borrowing, but eventually getting a loan is the only alternative that makes sense.

Today borrowing money is a complex proposition. Lenders get many applications for loans even at high interest rates. Generally lenders can pick and chose which businesses they want to lend to. "We don't have any trouble lending money," an independent banker in Southern California told us. "If we just loaned to everyone who comes in here asking for a loan, we could get rid of all our cash in a few weeks. What we need is *qualified* borrowers. We need to loan to people who will make us money."

But who qualifies?

BORROWING CRITERIA

When people lend you money, they are primarily interested in how you'll repay them. All lenders want to be repaid, even the government lending agencies. Therefore, to receive a loan, you have to convince the lender that you can and will repay. No one can predict the future, so a lender must judge your abilities by the way you present yourself and your business.

The lender is convinced of your repayment ability in three ways:

1. The strength of your financial condition.
2. The way you conduct yourself in your personal communications with the bank.
3. The thoughtfulness, accuracy, and completeness of your loan application.

For traditional commercial bank lending these three are listed in order of importance: Financial condition is most important, followed by the interview and then the loan application. For *government loans*, the three are listed in order of ascending importance: The application is the most important, then personal contact, and finally financial condition.

The major advantage of government loans is that they are often given to high-risk businesses. *High-risk businesses* include businesses that are:

New.

Building a new plant.

Expanding rapidly (having more than a 100% sales increase per year).
Oriented toward research and development.
Involved in commerce with third-world countries.
Damaged by imports.
Damaged by natural disaster.

These high-risk businesses have a difficult time getting money from traditional lenders. Banks, for example, are interested in low-risk business loans to established, profitable bank customers with large dollar sales or net worth.

Company Financial Condition

Assets are things that a company or an individual owns. For a company, assets include equipment, inventory, cash, accounts receivable, leasehold improvements, and real estate. For an individual, assets include house, car, furniture, cash surrender value of life insurance, stocks, bonds, cash, and art.

Liabilities are the amounts owed on assets. Mortgages on real estate, loans on your car or furniture, amounts owed on credit cards, and other loans are *personal liabilities*. Accounts payable (amounts owed for inventory and supplies purchased on credit), loans, and expenses owed but not paid are *business liabilities*.

Net worth is the difference between what you have (assets) and what you owe (liabilities). Net worth is one of the most crucial factors in qualifying for a loan.

The strength of your financial condition is determined primarily by your personal and business net worth and by your liquidity. *Liquidity* is the amount of your cash and current assets relative to your liabilities.

Firms or individuals with high net worth and good liquidity have the best chance of being successful in their loan request. A *high net worth* means that your assets are well above your liabilities. *Good liquidity* means you have a lot of cash and things that can be turned into cash such as inventory and accounts receivable. Furthermore, liquid companies do not have so much debt due and payable this year that it equals or exceeds their cash, inventory, and accounts receivable.

If you or your company has high net worth or good liquidity, or both, you are considered a low-risk business, and banks will lend money to you. If your company has low net worth or bad liquidity, banks may still lend to you, but the loan is much more difficult to get. If you have both a low net worth and bad liquidity, you are considered a high risk, and the bank will not lend to you.

If you are a high-risk company, don't despair. High-risk companies can sometimes get the money they need from a government-guaranteed loan program.

Personal Contact with the Lender

The most subjective of what lenders call the "three Cs of credit"—character, collateral, and capacity—is character. Lenders will judge a loan by the criteria of whether the company has the capacity (financial and market strength) to repay the loan and whether it has sufficient collateral. These two Cs of credit, capacity and collateral, are objective measures, but a banker must make some subjective evaluations; otherwise, very few loans would be made.

The lender's judgments about the applicant's character take into consideration management's general knowledge of the industry and the degree of planning and control exercised in the business. What a lender thinks about the company's management makes or breaks a loan application's chance of success. Lenders often make loans that are weak financially if they are strongly convinced of management's competence and good character.

Business owners generally have few chances to convince the banker of their competence. It is important that when they do meet the banker face to face, they make the most of the opportunity. Wise businesspeople will expend effort to establish and maintain good relationships with their bankers. They will introduce themselves when they open a checking account, say hello whenever they see the manager of the bank, and talk to the manager about their business. In short, wise businesspeople involve the bank in their everyday business activity by being friendly and open about their business.

If a lender knows nothing of the management's character, a loan must be approved on the strength of the company's financial position alone. If your financial condition could be improved, be nice to your banker, or you'll never see that loan money.

A Complete and Competent Loan Application

A lender, whether government or private, spends a lot of time writing reports. A large California bank recently ran a survey to determine how much time each bank officer spends preparing reports. The survey found that on average, branch managers spent fully 60% of their total work time writing reports. Unless your loan request is small, chances are good that the lender must write a report on your loan application. That report is then passed to a higher-up to make the final decision.

The more you help a lender in this report process by making the loan application complete, the better your chances of getting the loan. Government loans require more documentation than do standard loans. Helping bankers in all their paperwork will help you get the loan.

THE BASICS OF FINANCE

Eavesdropping on two computer professionals, you might hear a conversation like this:

"DEC has a nice massbus, but for some reason we're having IO problems," the first person said.

"Well," was the response "could it be the disk controller? Did you check the backplane? Is this IO under volatile control from the CPU or does it use ROM?"

Does this conversation make sense to you? It does to computer programmers. Computers have their own special language, and people who know it can talk for hours using words and concepts unintelligible to the layperson.

Finance has its own language, too. The majority of phrases used by bankers regarding finance are accounting phrases. Therefore, just to communicate with your bank you need to understand accounting, the language of finance.

Understanding Accounting

Accounting is simple, but people get confused because they don't understand how it works. Accounting has been around for a long time, about 5,000 years. The earliest writings discovered are cuneiform clay tablets from Sumaria (modern Iran and Iraq) enscribed with a stylus. Of the early fragments of cuneiform found, the great majority was not literature, as one might expect, but accounting records.

Nothing changed in accounting until AD 1340. At that time a commune in Genoa, Italy, developed a better accounting system, double-entry accounting.

The double-entry accounting system recognizes that when you make a payment, you are not just making a payment; you are also reducing your cash. Paying rent with a check, for instance, does two things: It increases the cumulative amount of rent you have paid to date, and it simultaneously decreases the cash in your checking account. To record these transactions properly in accounting, two entries are made in the books. One entry shows an increase (debit) in the cumulative rent account, and the other entry shows a decrease (credit) in the cash account.

Accounting, then, is a balanced, binary (two-state) system. An action in one account produces an equal reaction in the other. A $1,000 payment of rent causes a $1,000 reduction in cash. Since each accounting action is actually two actions, the cumulative total of one set of actions should equal the cumulative total of the other. If $12,000 is spent on rent for one year, $12,000 in cash will be gone.

This idea of the balance of two parts is the primary concept behind accounting. All accounts in accounting fit into two groups: (1) sources of money and (2) uses of money.

Circle of Accounts

The best way to illustrate the components of accounting is to start with a circle representing the total, closed accounting system (see Figure 1.1).

Let's divide that circle into two parts: sources of money and uses of money (see Figure 1.2).

What are the sources of money for a business? One obvious source of money is *income*, or money from gross sales, rents, or investments. Income is the first piece of the accounting pie (see Figure 1.3).

Where else does a company get money? The reader of this book is well aware of another source—loans. Loans (notes payable), along with accounts payable (money owed trade suppliers) and accruals (taxes, etc., owed but not yet paid), comprise the group of accounts called liabilities. If you borrow money or you get inventory, services, or supplies on credit or you owe the Internal Revenue Service (IRS), you have liabilities. Liabilities are a source of money that has to be repaid. Liabilities form the second important piece in the accounting puzzle (see Figure 1.4).

There is one and only one remaining source of money. That source is the money that comes out of the business owner's pocket to start and build the company. It is

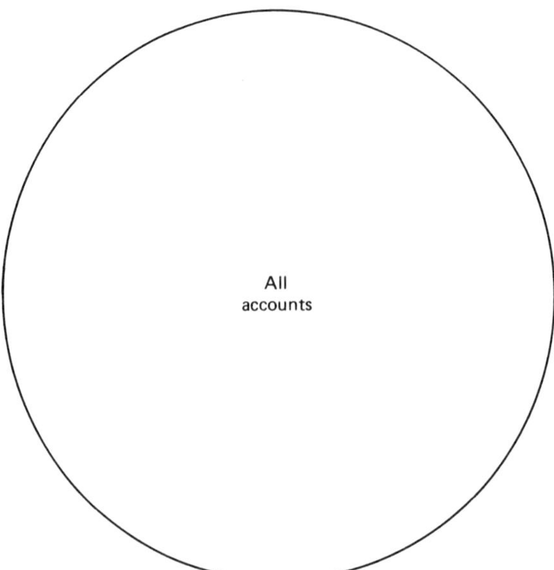

Figure 1.1 Accounting circle.

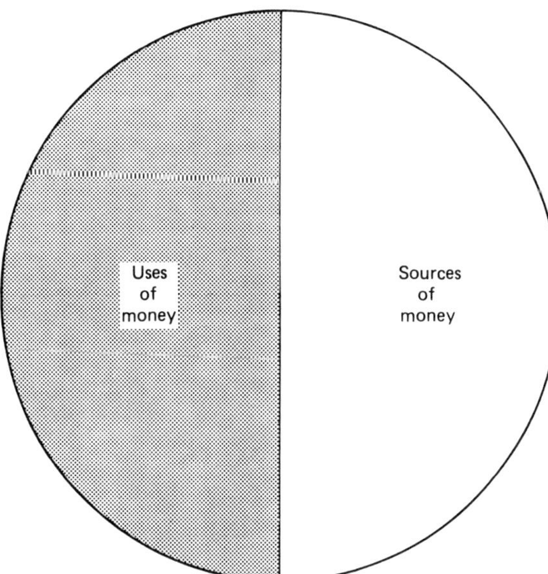

Figure 1.2 Sources and uses of funds.

called owners' equity, net worth, or just plain equity (see Figure 1.5). In a corporation, owners' equity is stocks and retained earnings. Equity is the third piece of the accounting circle, and it is the last component of all sources of money available to a company.

"Well, how about profit?" you may ask. "Isn't profit a source of money?" Yes, it is a source of money, but here's the catch: it is considered part of owners' equity. Net profit after taxes and owners' withdrawals or dividends are retained in the business. *Retained earnings* represent the new equity contributed to the business by the business's earnings during the last accounting period.

Owners' equity has two parts (see Figure 1.6):

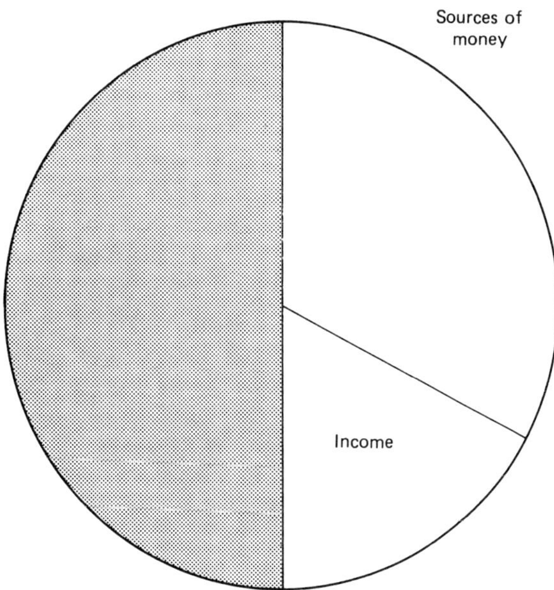

Figure 1.3 Income—a source of money.

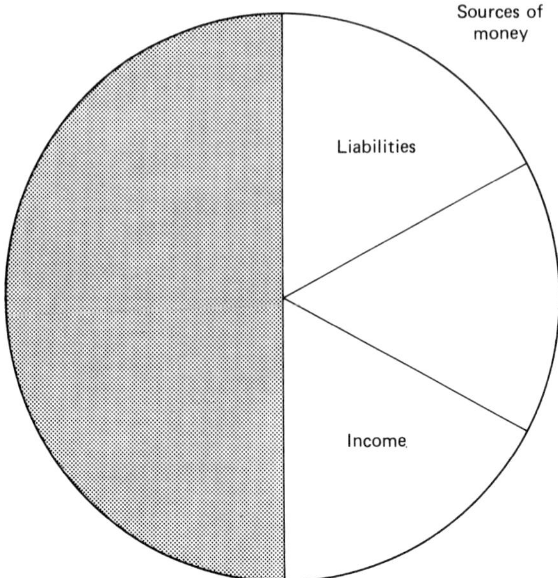

Figure 1.4 Liabilities—a source of money that must be repaid.

1. The money the owners put into the business from their own pockets.
2. The money that is left from profits after they are reduced by taxes and owners' withdrawals.

Uses of Money

Money comes from three sources: income, liabilities, and equity. How is the money used in the business?

One obvious answer is that the money is used to pay business *expenses:* rent, salaries, supplies, utilities, insurance, automobile costs, entertainment, postage, and

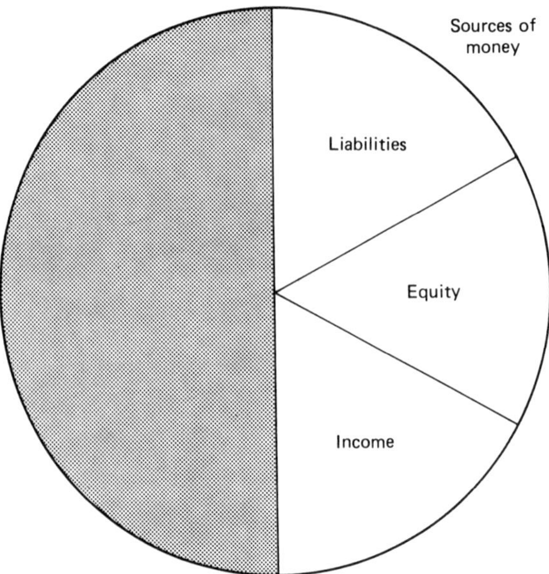

Figure 1.5 Equity—the owner's share.

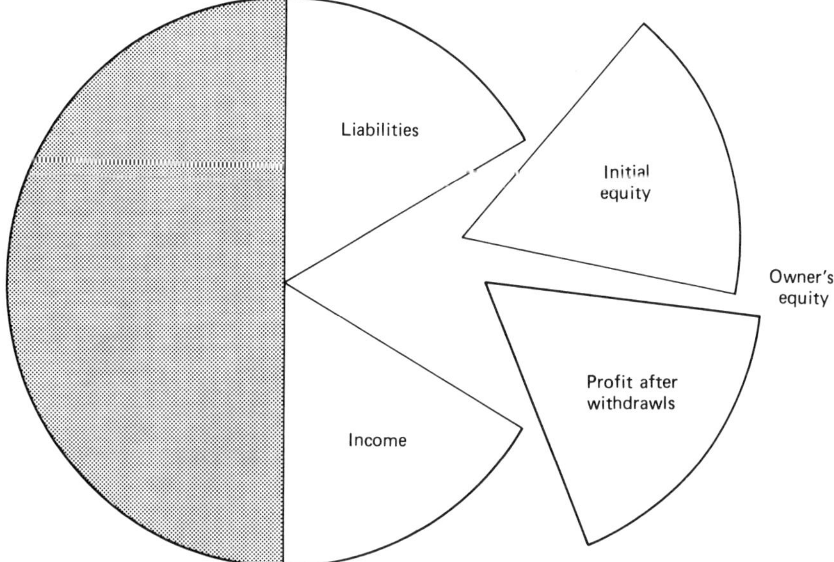

Figure 1.6 What makes up equity.

so on. Since uses of money are the opposite of sources of money, let's put expense on the left-hand (uses) side of the accounts circle (see Figure 1.7).

Another use of money is the cost of the merchandise that is sold. In retail and wholesale businesses this merchandise is the goods purchased from manufacturers or distributors and resold. A man's coat may cost you $100 in a retail clothing store. That retailer bought the coat for $60. The wholesaler, who sold the man's coat to the retailer for $60, paid $40 for it. The coat cost the manufacturer $20 for the material and labor to make it, and the manufacturer adds overhead and profit and sells it to the wholesaler for $30. In this case the cost of sales of each business is the direct cost of the coat, either as merchandise or as materials and labor. The cost of

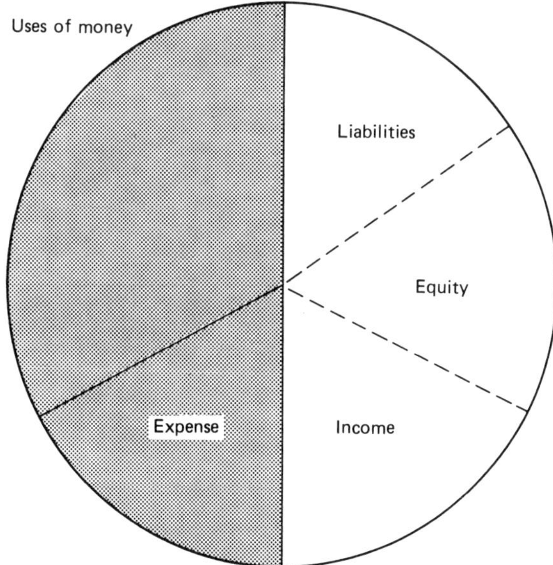

Figure 1.7 Expense—a use of money.

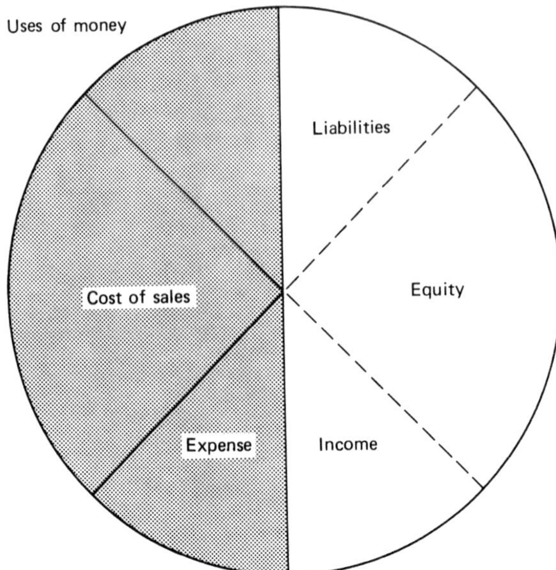

Figure 1.8 Cost of sales—a direct cost of what is sold.

the merchandise, the goods, that is sold is called *cost of goods sold* or *cost of sales*. Cost of sales is the second use of funds and the fifth piece in the accounting pie.

There is only one use of funds that we have not discussed, and it completes the circle of accounts. A business uses money to pay expenses and to purchase merchandise (cost of sales). What else does a business spend money for?—equipment, buildings and improvements; inventory, fixtures, investments. All these items taken together are called assets. Assets are what a company owns. The sixth and last group of accounts in all of accounting is assets, and assets is the third and last use of funds.

So the circle is complete. All accounts in accounting are included in these six groups: assets, liabilities, equity, income, expense, and cost of sales.

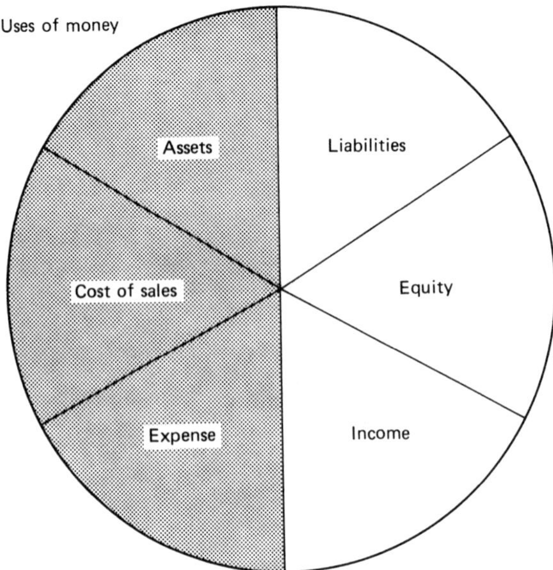

Figure 1.9 Assets—what you own.

Summary

Lenders are convinced of a company's repayment ability in three ways: (1) The strength of the company's and its owners' financial condition, (2) how impressed the lender is with the company's management, and (3) the accuracy and completeness of the loan presentation.

How well you communicate with the lender and how well you prepare your loan application depends on your understanding of finance and accounting. The language of finance is accounting. Understanding accounting terms is of the upmost importance.

Accounting can be divided into two groups of accounts: sources of money and uses of money. All individual accounts in accounting fall into these two groups. These two groups can be further divided into six smaller and more specific groups. The three *sources* of money are liabilities, equity, and income. The three groups of accounts that are *uses* of money are assets, expenses, and cost of sales.

ORGANIZATION OF THIS BOOK

The remainder of this book is divided into two parts. The first part explains how to prepare a loan proposal and fill out government forms. The second part discusses the various government lending programs and explains qualifications, special programs, and management assistance. Appendix I is a sample loan proposal, and Appendix II presents a fill-in-the-blank loan proposal that you can copy and use for your own business loan application.

Chapter Two

Steps for Preparing a Loan Proposal

Submitting a loan proposal for a government loan is not difficult. It involves four simple steps:

1. Collect the necessary data.
2. Use the data to do the necessary financial calculations.
3. Write up the proposal.
4. Present the proposal to a bank.

If your business needs a Small Business Administration (SBA) loan, you must either prepare a loan proposal yourself or have one prepared by a competent financial analyst. Analysts' fees range from $500 to $10,000.

The loan proposal that has the best chance of success is the one you prepare yourself. There are good reasons for this: When you prepare the proposal yourself, you gain an understanding of all the financial and managerial implications that receiving a loan implies. When you prepare all the market and financial work yourself, you know what is in the loan proposal. If someone else prepares the proposal for you, you do not. A proposal you have prepared impresses the lender that you can do it yourself. And preparing the loan proposal yourself is cheaper; often it is several thousand dollars cheaper.

The only advantage to paying someone to prepare the proposal is that it saves time, but reading this book should give you all the technical expertise you need to do it yourself.

Each of the four steps in preparing a loan proposal consists of other, smaller steps.

Acquiring the necessary data is the first step in preparing a loan application and generally is very time-consuming. Some of the information, such as income tax, leases, and business financial statements, is available from your files. Some data are found from library research, such as interest rates, industry data, and seasonal adjustments. Some data come from interviews with businesspeople in similar areas, with customers, and others. It takes from 10 to 60 hours of research time to get the proper data.

Doing the necessary financial calculations requires only this book and a calculator. The calculations require that you determine the business expenses and cash costs, the sales, and the financial future of the business when the loan is approved. The financial calculations result in a series of projections. These projections show how the business will perform financially in the coming years. From the lender's standpoint, this step is the heart of the proposal. The financial projections have to look right. From 15 to 30 hours is required for this work.

Writing up the proposal is the easiest and least time-consuming of the steps. When you get to this point, most of the work has already been done. You simply put everything in its proper place. Much of the write-up is composed of standard phrases. In this step you footnote the financial calculations, use standard wording for the proposal, complete government forms, and organize the exhibits. The time required for this step is between 5 and 20 hours.

Presenting the proposal to the lenders, watching the loan's progress, and making necessary changes is the most frustrating and time-consuming of the steps. This is not work time, but waiting time. At this point how the loan proceeds is beyond your personal control. This step takes from one month to three years.

For three of these steps we have given the time requirement in hours because it represents actual hours of work expended. Twenty hours' work, for instance, may be spread over one day or several months, depending on your schedule. Time estimates vary widely; some people are fast learners, and others learn slowly. The type of business you have greatly influences the time required to prepare the proposal. The newer the business (especially start-ups) and the larger the amount of money requested, the more time the proposal involves. The more established the business, the more profitable and financially secure it is, and the smaller the amount of money requested, the shorter the time from research to approval.

This brings up one of the crucial points in preparing the loan proposal yourself. Although the steps are simple, the time required is great. If time is extremely important or if you absolutely must have the money in three to four months, we suggest you hire someone to do the work. You should not even consider an SBA loan if you require the money in less than three months. Remember, SBA loans take *a lot of time*. It is possible to get a loan prepared, presented, and disbursed in less than three months, but we have seen this happen only *once* in 10 years of experience. In this instance the applicant, who wanted to buy a grocery store, was the largest depositor at the bank where the loan was submitted. The man selling the grocery store owned the property on which the bank stood. The applicant had the proposal prepared by the best loan packager in the country, and the bank was the largest SBA lender in California. In other words, if you absolutely cannot wait at least three months to get your money, *don't request an SBA loan*.

Chapter Three
What Data Are Required

Three types of information are needed to prepare a government loan proposal:

1. Financial data.
2. Market data.
3. Other documentation required by SBA regulations or the bank.

FINANCIAL DATA

The financial data are the most important information required for an SBA or government loan. The lender's decisions are based primarily on financial data. The business should be strong enough financially to repay the debt. The financial data show the sales, profitability, and strength of the company. An existing business is required to have financial data showing its history and its present situation. These include the business's income statement and balance sheet as well as an aging of accounts receivable and accounts payable. A new business does not have a financial history. It must therefore locate financial information on similar enterprises and obtain information from an independent source to make financial projections for the upcoming years.

Looking at Figure 3.1 you can see what financial data are required. The information comes from the existing or proposed business, personally from the owner(s), or from research.

Business Data

From an *existing business* the following financial data are needed:

Income statement or business income tax for the last three years and the current income statement. The current statement should not be more than two months old.

Balance sheets for the last three years and a current balance sheet. The current balance sheet should not be more than two months old.

An aging of accounts receivable and accounts payable.

The historical and current income statement and balance sheets not only are required by the SBA and the government, but are absolutely necessary for the financial calculations.

From Business	Personal	From Research
Last 3 years and current income statement*	Personal income tax (last 3 years)	Interest rate
Last 3 years and current balance sheet*	Personal financial statement	Seasonal adjustment for sales
Age accounts receivable and payable*	Percentage ownership of company	
Statement of use of funds		
Expected next year expense		

*For existing businesses only

Figure 3.1 Financial data.

For *all businesses* the following financial information is required:

Use of funds statement. This is a summary of how you will spend the borrowed money, including equipment, debt repayment, inventory, and so on.

Expected expenses for the next years.

It is obvious why banks need to know how you are going to spend their money. They want to see what collateral, among other things, you have to secure the loan. They also want to determine if the proposed expenditures are legitimate. Estimates of the worth of equipment, improvements, deposits, buildings, and land should be furnished *in writing*. For instance, if you are borrowing $40,000 to purchase a winepress, the lender will want to see a written estimate from Sonoma Winepress Company, or whomever, stating that you can purchase that machine for the amount of $40,000, including taxes.

If you are intending to use some of the loan proceeds to repay debt, you should describe the debt you are paying. Include original balance, present balance, to whom the debt is owed, terms, and interest.

Example. If Yourcompany wants an SBA loan, and a portion of that loan—say, $43,500—is used to pay existing debt, the repayment would be footnoted as follows:

Debt repayment of $43,500 is for the following loan:

Present Balance	Owed To	Original Balance	Terms	Interest
$43,500	Gold Bank 20 Tops Drive Jewel, Minn.	$55,000	4 years	14%

You should have a general idea of what your rent, utilities, supplies, salaries, and so on, will run next year. Determining the expected expenses for the next year is easier for an existing business than for a start-up. An existing business can use its historical experience to determine future expenses. A start-up business will have to research this question using industry data and relying on interviews with appropriate personnel from similar companies.

Calculation Example—Aging of Accounts. Many lenders require that the company prepare, in addition to its financial statements, an aging of accounts receivable and accounts payable. This is a very simple process. Take all your accounts receivable or accounts payable and divide them into piles labeled "up to 30 days old," "between 30 and 60 days old," "between 60 and 90 days old," and so on.

Example. Yourcompany has $100,000 in accounts receivable at its last balance sheet period. Some are not due yet, some are past due, and some are just becoming due. Yourcompany has five customers that constitute these accounts receivable. John Your, the owner of Yourcompany, takes the invoices and sorts them into three piles on his desk. The date is January 30. All invoices that are dated from January 1 through January 31 go in the 30-day pile. All invoices dated December 1 through December 31 go in the 60-day pile, and all the rest go in the 60-day-plus pile. John then takes each pile and records each invoice under the appropriate heading, as follows:

Date	Company	Invoice No.	30 Days	60 Days	60+ Days
9/15	Teleview	4201	$	$	$21,200
9/30	Rolston	4205			5,300
10/15	Thompson	4210			10,700
11/06	Ball	4213			1,002
12/01	Teleview	4216		2,300	
12/10	Jacks	4217		25,402	
12/14	Thompson	4218	13,160		
1/10	Rolston	4220	15,920		
1/25	Teleview	4221	5,016		
Totals			$34,096	$27,702	$38,202

To age accounts payable (the amounts you owe to your suppliers), you use a similar procedure.

Now try aging you own accounts receivable. First, get all the billings that are outstanding and enter them according to the following form.

Aging of Accounts Receivable for ________ *(Company Name)*

Billing Date	Name of Company	Invoice No.	Less than 30 Days	30–60 Days	More than 60 Days
____	______	________	________	____	________
____	______	________	________	____	________
____	______	________	________	____	________
____	______	________	________	____	________
____	______	________	________	____	________
____	______	________	________	____	________
____	______	________	________	____	________
____	______	________	________	____	________
____	______	________	________	____	________
____	______	________	________	____	________

Use of Funds

The amount of money you need is of primary importance. You should therefore consider how much you are going to need to keep your business running for the upcoming year. Make your estimate high; government loans take some time and prices inevitably go up.

Some items that you might include in the use of funds needed are:

1. Deposits (for rent, insurance, lease, association dues, etc.).
2. Licenses.
3. Inventory.
4. Equipment (a *written* estimate is generally required).
5. Leasehold improvements (carpets, counters, shelves) and buildings.
6. Furniture.
7. Debt repayment (retire debt).
8. Working capital (cash you need to cover at least two months of expenses).
9. Automobile and truck.

Note. You *cannot* borrow money to buy out a partner or stockholder.

What is your use of funds for your loan? Get written estimates on the equipment you plan to buy. Be very sure of your costs because once you get the loan approved for the requested amount, that's it. You can't change your mind in midstream.

Here is a sample list of use of funds items with blanks. Copy this form to fill in your own information:

Use of Funds

Inventory	$________
Deposits	________
Licenses	________
Equipment	
Shop	________
Office	________
Factory	________
Automobile	________
Leasehold improvements	________
Furniture	________
Debt repayment	________
Working capital	________
Other	________
Total funds needed	________
Less: Owners' cash*	________
Government loan required	$________

*New businesses are required to put up cash equal to at least 25% of the total funds needed.

Example. The following uses of funds is from the loan proposal sample in Appendix I:

Purchase fixed assets		
Equipment	$35,000	
Furniture	5,000	
Improvements	10,000	$ 50,000
Create current assets		
Working capital	46,000	
Inventory	60,000	
Prepayments	1,450	107,450
Repay debt		42,550
Total requirements		$200,000

Personal Data

From all business owners, shareholders, or partners, the following personal financial data are needed:

Personal income tax records for the last three years.

A personal financial statement.

A schedule of ownership showing who owns what percentage of the business.

Records of the last three years' personal income tax are required by the SBA. They also serve as a guide to the banker to see if taxes have been paid.

If the business is or will be a sole proprietorship (that is, you are the only owner), you will *not* have to prepare a schedule of ownership. If the business is a partnership or corporation, then you will need a schedule of what each person owns and how much each contributed. The schedule would look like the following:

Partner (Shareholder)	Percentage Ownership	Amount Contributed	Position
John Your 85 Ole Fifty-five Trail Chevy, Minn.	50%	$50,000	President
Tath Tacki 1222 Fromp Avenue Chevy, Minn.	30%	$30,000	Vice president
Ed Syrup 7211 Last Street Chevy, Minn.	20%	$20,000	Secretary

Calculation Example—Personal Financial Statement. One of the first things any lender looks at when appraising company management is the personal financial statement of the owners. A strong personal financial statement is important in motivating the lender to give you a loan.

A personal financial statement is really a personal balance sheet. It lists all the things you own (your automobile, home, furniture, savings accounts), what you owe (your home mortgage, auto loan, credit card debts, and so on), and the difference between the two, which is your personal net worth.

Example. Figure 3.2 is John Your's personal financial statement. It shows what he owes, what he owns, and his net worth. The illustrated personal financial statement is on SBA Form 413. It could just as easily be on a bank personal financial statement form or on a plain piece of paper.

Photocopy SBA Form 413, a blank personal financial statement, from Figure 3.3, and fill it out for the owners of your company who own 20% or more of the stock.

Start with cash, which includes cash in checking and savings accounts. Accounts and notes receivable may be some amount of money owed you because of a second mortgage you hold on a house, a note from a relative, and so on. The cash value of your life insurance is the cash value that you can borrow on a whole life policy. There is a schedule of what this amount is inside your life insurance policy. The market value of your stocks and bonds should be listed in the blank on the first page and explained in section 3 on the second page of Form 413.

Real estate includes the *market value* of all the real estate you own. The second page of Form 413, section 4, gives a complete description of the real estate including who owns the title, the address, and the name and address of the bank that holds the mortgage. Other information requested is the original cost of the property, when it was purchased, the present market value (the value you use when you list real estate value on page 1 of Form 413), and the tax-assessed value. You also are asked to supply the date of the present mortgage, the original amount of the mortgage, the balance owed (which goes on the first page after Mortgages on Real Estate), the maturity of the note (number of years until paid), and the terms of payment (dollars per month).

The assets section of the personal financial statement is completed with the present value of your automobiles and other personal property (including furniture, appliances, antiques, and art).

On the liability side accounts payable is the present balance owed on credit cards. Notes payable to banks and others are listed in section 2 on the first page and include unsecured loans, boat loans, pool loans, and the like. Section 2 asks for name and address of the note holder, original and present balance, terms (dollars per month), maturity of loans, and whether they are secured or unsecured.

Installment accounts on automobile payments and mortgage on home are self-explanatory.

Your net worth is the difference between the total assets and total liabilities. Assets minus liabilities equals net worth.

Please stop your reading right now, and complete the personal financial statement, Figure 3.3.

Researched Data

From research, the following financial information is needed:

Interest rate of the loan, monthly loan payments, annual interest, and annual principal loan repayment.

Seasonal monthly adjustments for industry sales.

To find the current interest rate for SBA-guaranteed or other SBA loans, contact the SBA office nearest you or call your banker. Once you know the interest rate being charged, you must use an amortization table to find what interest and principal payments you'll make each month.

Form Approved
OMB No. 100-R-0081 121

PERSONAL FINANCIAL STATEMENT	Return to: Small Business Administration	For SBA Use Only SBA Loan No.
As of March 30, 19 79.		

Name and Address, Including ZIP Code (*of person and spouse submitting Statement*)	This statement is submitted in connection with S.B.A. loan requested or granted to the individual or firm, whose name appears below:
John Your 85 Ole Fifty-five Trail Chevy, Minn. 56785	Name and Address of Applicant or Borrower, Including ZIP Code Yourcompany 38 Gerry Avenue Everywhere, Minn. 56785
SOCIAL SECURITY NO.	
Business (*of person submitting Statement*) Retail Computer	

Please answer all questions using "No" or "None" where necessary

ASSETS		LIABILITIES	
Cash on Hand & In Banks	$ 4,800	Accounts Payable Charge Cards	$ 2,200
Savings Account in Banks	12,000	Notes Payable to Banks (*Describe below - Section 2*)	
U. S. Government Bonds	-0-	Notes Payable to Others (*Describe below - Section 2*)	3,000
Accounts & Notes Receivable	-0-	Installment Account (Auto)	2,600
Life Insurance-Cash Surrender Value Only	3,000	Monthly Payments $	
Other Stocks and Bonds (*Describe - reverse side - Section 3*)	4,200	Installment Accounts (Other)	
Real Estate (*Describe - reverse side - Section 4*)	140 140,000	Monthly Payments $ 125	
Automobile - Present Value	8,000	Loans on Life Insurance	
Other Personal Property (*Describe - reverse side - Section 5*)	20,000	Mortgages on Real Estate (*Describe reverse side Section 4*)	65,000
Other Assets (*Describe - reverse side - Section 6*)		Unpaid Taxes (*Describe - reverse side - Section 7*)	
		Other Liabilities (*Describe - reverse side - Section 8*)	
		Total Liabilities	72,800
		Net Worth	119,200
Total	$ 192,000	Total	$ 192,000

Section 1. Source of Income (*Describe below all items listed in this Section*)		CONTINGENT LIABILITIES	
Salary	$	As Endorser or Co-Maker	$
Net Investment Income		Legal Claims and Judgments	
Real Estate Income		Provision for Federal Income Tax	
Other Income (*Describe*)		Other Special Debt	

Description of items listed in Section I

Life Insurance Held (*Give face amount of policies - name of company and beneficiaries*)

SUPPLEMENTARY SCHEDULES

Section 2. Notes Payable to Banks and Others

Name and Address of Holder of Note	Amount of Loan: Original Bal.	Amount of Loan: Present Bal.	Terms of Repayments	Maturity of Loan	How Endorsed, Guaranteed, or Secured
Ace Finance Company	$ 4,000	$ 3,000	$ 144.61	3 yrs.	Secured-Furniture

SBA FORM 413 (8-67) REF: ND 520-1 EDITION OF 1-67 MAY BE USED UNTIL STOCK IS EXHAUSTED (OVER)

Figure 3.2 John Your's personal financial statement.

Section 3. Other Stocks and Bonds: Give listed and unlisted Stocks and Bonds *(Use separate sheet if necessary)*

No. of Shares	Names of Securities	Cost	Market Value Statement Date Quotation	Amount
100	Slop Labs	$35/share	$42/share	$4,200

Section 4. Real Estate Owned. *(List each parcel separately. Use supplemental sheets if necessary. Each sheet must be identified as a supplement to this statement and signed). (Also advises whether property is covered by title insurance, abstract of title, or both).*

Title is in name of John and Joan Your	Type of property Residential
Address of property (City and State) 85 Ole Fifty-Five Trail Chevy, Minn. 56785	Original Cost to (me) (us) $ 90,000 Date Purchased 1977 Present Market Value $ 140,000 Tax Assessment Value $ 90,000
Name and Address of Holder of Mortgage (City and State) Gold Bank 20 Tops Drive Jewel, Minn.	Date of Mortgage 12/1/79 Original Amount $ 70,000 Balance $ 65,000 Maturity 20 yrs. Terms of Payment $722.53/Month

Status of Mortgage, i.e., current or delinquent. If delinquent describe delinquencies

Current

Section 5. Other Personal Property. *(Describe and if any is mortgaged, state name and address of mortgage holder and amount of mortgage, terms of payment and if delinquent, describe delinquency.)*

Appliances, jewelry, furniture, clothing

Section 6. Other Assets. *(Describe)*

Section 7. Unpaid Taxes. *(Describe in detail, as to type, to whom payable, when due, amount, and what, if any, property a tax lien, if any, attaches)*

Section 8. Other Liabilities. *(Describe in detail)*

(I) or (We) certify the above and the statements contained in the schedules herein is a true and accurate statement of (my) or (our) financial condition as of the date stated herein. This statement is given for the purpose of: *(Check one of the following)*

☐ Inducing S.B.A. to grant a loan as requested in application, of the individual or firm whose name appears herein, in connection with which this statement is submitted.

☐ Furnishing a statement of (my) or (our) financial condition, pursuant to the terms of the guaranty executed by (me) or (us) at the time S.B.A. granted a loan to the individual or firm, whose name appears herein.

Signature   Signature   Date

Page 2

GPO : 1977 O - 244-581

Figure 3.2 *(Continued)*

Form Approved
OMB No. 100-R-0081

PERSONAL FINANCIAL STATEMENT As of __________, 19___.	Return to: Small Business Administration	For SBA Use Only SBA Loan No.

Complete this form if 1) a sole proprietorship by the proprietor; 2) a partnership by each partner; 3) a corporation by each officer and each stockholder with 20% or more ownership; 4) any other person or entity providing a guaranty on the loan.

Name and Address, Including ZIP Code *(of person and spouse submitting Statement)* SOCIAL SECURITY NO. ________ Business *(of person submitting Statement)*	This statement is submitted in connection with S.B.A. loan requested or granted to the individual or firm, whose name appears below: Name and Address of Applicant or Borrower, Including ZIP Code

Please answer all questions using "No" or "None" where necessary

ASSETS		LIABILITIES	
Cash on Hand & In Banks	$	Accounts Payable	$
Savings Account in Banks		Notes Payable to Banks	
U. S. Government Bonds		*(Describe below - Section 2)*	
Accounts & Notes Receivable		Notes Payable to Others	
Life Insurance-Cash Surrender Value Only		*(Describe below - Section 2)*	
Other Stocks and Bonds		Installment Account (Auto)	
(Describe - reverse side - Section 3)		Monthly Payments $	
Real Estate		Installment Accounts (Other)	
(Describe - reverse side - Section 4)		Monthly Payments $	
Automobile - Present Value		Loans on Life Insurance	
Other Personal Property		Mortgages on Real Estate	
(Describe - reverse side - Section 5)		*(Describe - reverse side - Section 4)*	
Other Assets		Unpaid Taxes	
(Describe - reverse side - Section 6)		*(Describe - reverse side - Section 7)*	
		Other Liabilities	
		(Describe - reverse side - Section 8)	
		Total Liabilities	
		Net Worth	
Total	$	Total	$

Section I. Source of Income *(Describe below all items listed in this Section)*		**CONTINGENT LIABILITIES**	
Salary	$	As Endorser or Co-Maker	$
Net Investment Income		Legal Claims and Judgments	
Real Estate Income		Provision for Federal Income Tax	
Other Income (Describe)*		Other Special Debt	

Description of items listed in Section I ________

*Not necessary to disclose alimony or child support payments in "Other Income" unless it is desired to have such payments counted toward total income.

Life Insurance Held *(Give face amount of policies - name of company and beneficiaries)* ________

SUPPLEMENTARY SCHEDULES

Section 2. Notes Payable to Banks and Others

Name and Address of Holder of Note	Amount of Loan Original Bal.	Amount of Loan Present Bal.	Terms of Repayments	Maturity of Loan	How Endorsed, Guaranteed, or Secured
	$	$	$		

SBA FORM 413 (12-78) REF: SOP 50 50 Edition of 8-67 May Be Used Until Stock Is Exhausted

Figure 3.3 Blank personal financial statement.

Section 3. Other Stocks and Bonds: Give listed and unlisted Stocks and Bonds *(Use separate sheet if necessary)*

No. of Shares	Names of Securities	Cost	Market Value Statement Date Quotation	Amount

Section 4. Real Estate Owned. *(List each parcel separately. Use supplemental sheets if necessary. Each sheet must be identified as a supplement to this statement and signed). (Also advises whether property is covered by title insurance, abstract of title, or both).*

Title is in name of	Type of property
Address of property (City and State)	Original Cost to (me) (us) $ ______ Date Purchased ______ Present Market Value $ ______ Tax Assessment Value $ ______
Name and Address of Holder of Mortgage (City and State)	Date of Mortgage ______ Original Amount $ ______ Balance $ ______ Maturity ______ Terms of Payment ______
Status of Mortgage, i.e., current or delinquent. If delinquent describe delinquencies	

Section 5. Other Personal Property. *(Describe and if any is mortgaged, state name and address of mortgage holder and amount of mortgage, terms of payment and if delinquent, describe delinquency.)*

Section 6. Other Assets. *(Describe)*

Section 7. Unpaid Taxes. *(Describe in detail, as to type, to whom payable, when due, amount, and what, if any, property a tax lien, if any, attaches)*

Section 8. Other Liabilities. *(Describe in detail)*

(I) or (We) certify the above and the statements contained in the schedules herein is a true and accurate statement of (my) or (our) financial condition as of the date stated herein. This statement is given for the purpose of: *(Check one of the following)*

☐ Inducing S.B.A. to grant a loan as requested in application, of the individual or firm whose name appears herein, in connection with which this statement is submitted.

☐ Furnishing a statement of (my) or (our) financial condition, pursuant to the terms of the guaranty executed by (me) or (us) at the time S.B.A. granted a loan to the individual or firm, whose name appears herein.

______ Signature ______ Signature ______ Date

SBA FORM 413 (12-78) REF: SOP 50 50 Page 2 GPO : 1979 O - 286-301

Figure 3.3 (*Continued*)

Calculation Example—Finding Interest and Principal Payments. When you borrow money, you repay it at so much per month. The monthly payment includes both interest and principal. Interest is an expense and is the amount you pay the bank as its fee. Principal payments are that part of your total payment which is used to reduce the debt.

You can get interest rates and monthly payments from a bank, or you can calculate monthly payments by using an amortization table like that shown in Figure 3.4.

Amortization tables can be found at any library and at all banks, real estate agencies, and savings and loan associations. Most title companies, such as Title Insurance Company, Transamerica Title, and so on, give away amortization booklets.

Figure 3.4 shows a typical amortization table, in this case for 10%.

Example. Yourcompany wants to borrow $200,000 for 10 years. What will be the amount of its monthly payments? The current SBA interest rate is 10%.

To determine the payments:

1. Find the amortization table for the appropriate interest rate (10%). Figure 3.4 shows a portion of the page for 10%.
2. Find the term (number of years to pay back) of the loan. On Figure 3.4 follow the top row, which starts with 8 Years, until you find the correct number (10 years). Circle it.
3. Find the term amount (dollar amount of the loan). The far left side of the table starts with $55,000 and increases to $100,000. The amount we are looking for is $200,000. Since the highest the table goes is $100,000, circle that figure.
4. Find the monthly payments. If a line is drawn straight down from the 10-year column to the $100,000 row, you find that the interest and principal monthly payment is $1,321.51. This is the monthly payment for $100,000 for 10 years at 10% interest. In our example the loan is for $200,000, so you therefore double the monthly payment to $2,643.02 (2 × 1,321.51 = $2,643.02). To find out how much the payment will be for one year, multiply the monthly figure by 12 months (12 × $2,643.02 = $31,716.24).

How much of this annual payment of $31,716.24 is interest, and how much is prin-

	Monthly Payment Necessary to Amortize a Loan		
10%	8 Years	10 Years	12 Years
$ 55,000	834.58	726.83	657.30
60,000	910.45	792.91	717.05
65,000	986.33	858.98	776.81
70,000	1062.20	925.06	836.56
75,000	1138.07	991.14	896.31
80,000	1213.94	1057.21	956.07
85,000	1289.81	1123.29	1015.82
90,000	1365.68	1189.36	1075.58
95,000	1441.55	1255.44	1135.33
100,000	1517.42	1321.51	1195.08

Figure 3.4 Monthly payment necessary to amortize a loan.

cipal? The interest is an expense and can be written off for income tax purposes. The principal portion of the loan repayment is the amount by which loan is reduced and is *not* tax deductible. For example, you borrow $200,000 and in the first year repay $11,716 principal. At the end of the year, you will owe $188,284 on the loan ($200,000 – $11,716).

Yourcompany's annual loan repayment is $31,716. How much of this is interest, and how much is principal? Some amortization tables give this information. If the one you use does not, you can find the interest for the first year by multiplying the loan amount by the interest. This will give you a rough idea. For instance, $200,000 (the loan amount) times 0.10 (the interest amount) equals $20,000. So interest for the first year is $20,000.

If you know what the interest is for the year ($20,000), you can find the principal by simply taking the full amount of repayment ($31,716), which includes both interest and principal, and subtracting the interest ($20,000). The principal portion of the annual loan repayment is therefore $11,716. For subsequent years' interest and principal, you use the same process, but reduce the loan balance each time. For instance, at the end of the first year (which is the beginning of the second year), the loan balance is $188,284 ($200,000 original balance minus $11,716 principal payment that year). Next you multiply that balance of $188,284 by the interest rate (0.10). This gives you $18,828, which is the interest portion of the loan repayment for the second year. To find the principal portion, you take the total repayment ($31,716) and subtract the second-year interest ($18,828). This will give you the second-year principal of $13,888. This is summarized as follows:

	Previous loan balance	$200,000
Less:	Principal loan repayment	11,716
Equals:	New loan balance	$188,284
Times:	Interest rate	× 0.10
Equals:	Interest for second year	$ 18,828
	Total loan repayment	$ 31,716
Less:	Second year interest	– 18,828
Equals:	Second year principals	$ 13,888

Notice that as you calculate subsequent years, the amount of *interest declines* and the amount of *principal increases*, but the total loan repayment remains the same.

Interest Calculation Example. You know how much money you need. Now you can find out how much it costs.

Before you do any calculation, call the local SBA or government lender office to find what the correct loan-guarantee rate is.

Proceed as follows:

1. Find what the loan amount and current interest rates are, calling the loan amount *A* and the current interest rate *B*.
   Loan amount = ____________(*A*)
   Current interest rate = ____________(*B*)
2. Find the term of the loan according to the following table:

Item	Cost	× Term Allowed	= Term Adjusted Cost
Equipment	____	7 years	____________
Leasehold Improvement	____	10 years	____________
Furniture	____	10 years	____________
Working Capital	____	6 years	____________
Inventory	____	6 years	____________
Total Term Adjusted Cost			____________(*C*)

Divide total term adjusted cost ____________(*C*) by total loan amount ______ (*A*), which equals the term of the loan ____________(*D*).

3. Find the factor on the amortization table that is for the interest rate *B* and term *D* and the loan dollar amount *A*. This factor is the monthly interest and principal payment ____________(*E*).

   Note: Monthly interest and principal payment may also be calculated by using the formula in Figure 3.5, or by using 'business' calculators such as Texas Instruments MBA or programable calculators.
4. Multiply monthly payment ____________(*E*) by twelve months, which equals the total annual interest and principal payment ____________(*F*).
5. Multiply loan dollar amount ____________(*A*) times interest rate (in decimal equivalent) ____________(*B*), which equals annual interest costs ____________ (*G*).
6. From annual principal and interest payment ____________(*F*) subtract the annual interest cost ____________(*G*) to give you the annual principal payment ____________(*H*).

Annual principal and interest payment = ____________(*F*)
Annual interest payment = ____________(*G*)
Annual principal payment = ____________(*H*)

Where: PV = present value or loan amount
PMT = payment per period (month)
N = number of periods (months) loan is to be repaid in
i = interest rate in decimal form (11% is 0.11)

To find monthly payment:

$$\text{PMT} = \text{PV}\,\frac{i}{1-(1+i)^{-N}}$$

Example. What is the monthly principal and interest payment (PMT) for a \$100,000 loan (PV) for 5 years or 60 months (*N*) at 20 percent per annum or 20/12 = 1.667 percent per month (*i*)?

Substituting:

$$\text{PMT} = 100{,}000\,\frac{0.01667}{1-(1+0.01667)^{-60}}$$

PMT = \$2,649.39 principal and interest per month.

Figure 3.5. Formula for calculating monthly loan repayment

Industry Seasonal Adjustments

Industry seasonal adjustments are the record of what certain businesses experience in monthly sales fluctuations each year. For instance, most retail businesses do 15–35% of their total yearly business in December. Toy manufacturers have their greatest sales in late summer and fall and their lowest sales in December and January.

If you are preparing a loan application for the SBA and you have a monthly sales projection, do not use the same sales amounts for every month. It is unrealistic to divide the annual sales by 12 to arrive at a monthly sales figure. It also shows the bank or SBA that you are ignorant of your own business.

Existing businesses can look at past monthly sales and see how their sales fluctuate each month. Take the sales of each month of last year and find out how much they are as a *percentage* of total yearly sales.

Example. Yourcompany had total sales of $600,000 last year. Monthly sales were as follows:

January	$40,000	May	$44,000	September	$55,000
February	35,000	June	48,000	October	61,000
March	40,000	July	40,000	November	63,000
April	41,000	August	43,000	December	90,000

Each month's sales figure is divided by the total sales for the year ($600,000) to find that month's sales as a percentage of total yearly sales. For instance:

$$\frac{\text{Sales for January } \$40{,}000}{\text{total sales } \$600{,}000} = 0.0625, \text{ or } 6.25\% \text{ of total sales}$$

January sales of $40,000 is 6.25% of the total sales for the year ($600,000). Using the same procedure for each month results in the following figures:

Month	Sales ($)	Total Sales (%)
January	40,000	6.25
February	35,000	5.21
March	40,000	6.25
April	41,000	6.46
May	44,000	7.08
June	48,000	7.92
July	40,000	6.25
August	43,000	6.88
September	55,000	9.37
October	61,000	10.62
November	63,000	11.04
December	90,000	16.67

When you do your sales projections for the upcoming year, use these percentages to determine monthly sales.

If your *business is new*, you need to use outside information to determine seasonal sales. The best source is the Department of Commerce's *Survey of Current Business*, "Retail Monthly Sales" and "Manufacturer's Sales" indexes (see Figures 3.6 and 3.7). Trade associations also have this information. If your business is not retail and you cannot find trade association materials, you might have to interview similar businesses.

The information from the Department of Commerce, trade associations, and personal discussions are used later when you prepare monthly sales projections.

INDUSTRY MARKET DATA

To prepare the loan application and to appear competent to the lender, it is a good idea to find out information about your industry.

If your business is new (less than one year old) or a start-up, you *must* do research. It is necessary to get reliable expense estimates and sales projections. When you project sales for the repayment period, you have to support your sales assumptions (what you base sales projections on).

Industry information falls into the following four groups:

1. Ratios.
2. Percentages.
3. General industry information.
4. Your business resources.

If yours is a new or start-up business, you should also do research for a breakdown of operating expenses as a percentage of sales.

The most common sources for this information include Dun and Bradstreet reports. These include "Cost of Doing Business" and "Key Business Ratios," both published as pamphlets or in their monthly magazine, *Dun's Review*. These reports are available in libraries, or they may be purchased at the local Dun and Bradstreet office. Figure 3.8 is a page from "Key Business Ratios" and Figure 3.9 is a page from "Cost of Doing Business." "Key Business Ratios" gives the debt-to-worth and current ratios (current assets to current liabilities), as well as 14 other ratios. The "Cost of Doing Business" gives operating expense as a percentage of sales.

National Cash Register Company publishes yearly the *Expenses in Retailing* booklet, which examines the cost of operations in other 50 lines of business. For start-up retail businesses this is an excellent guide. The booklet, a page of which is illustrated in Figure 3.10, may be acquired at any National Cash Register Company branch. Many libraries also have this information. The booklet gives operating expenses as a percentage of sales. If you know what your expected sales will be, you can use this booklet to determine what expenses will run, provided your business is similar to the rest of the industry.

Almost every industry has a *trade association*. These associations publish excellent material for their industries. The following associations have published material in the past:

Air-Conditioning and Refrigeration Wholesalers, 22371 Newman Avenue, Dearborn, Mich. 48124

Air Transport Association of America, 1000 Connecticut Avenue NW, Washington, D.C. 20036

American Bankers Association, 90 Park Avenue, New York, N.Y. 10016

GENERAL BUSINESS INDICATORS—Continued

Unless otherwise stated in footnotes below, data through 1974 and descriptive notes are as shown in the 1975 edition of BUSINESS STATISTICS	1976	1977	1977							1978						
	Annual		June	July	Aug.	Sept.	Oct.	Nov.	Dec.	Jan.	Feb.	Mar.	Apr.	May	June ᵖ	July ¹
INDUSTRIAL PRODUCTION♂																
Federal Reserve Board Index of Quantity Output																
Not Seasonally Adjusted																
Total index....1967=100..	129.8	137.1	141.5	134.1	138.2	142.4	142.7	139.5	134.9	134.8	139.6	141.4	ʳ144.2	ʳ144.1	148.3	141.0
By market groupings:																
Products, total....do....	129.3	137.1	141.5	135.0	139.5	145.1	144.3	139.5	133.8	133.5	139.0	141.0	ʳ143.2	ʳ142.1	147.7	141.1
Final products....do....	127.2	134.9	139.4	132.5	136.4	142.9	142.0	136.9	131.1	131.0	136.6	138.6	ʳ140.7	ʳ138.9	144.7	137.7
Consumer goods....do....	136.2	143.4	149.2	140.0	145.9	152.9	152.4	144.4	135.8	136.7	143.4	145.3	ʳ148.4	ʳ145.2	151.9	142.0
Durable consumer goods....do....	141.4	153.1	164.2	142.3	140.0	158.8	168.1	157.6	144.4	142.7	155.7	162.4	ʳ169.7	ʳ164.1	167.9	144.0
Nondurable consumer goods....do....	134.1	139.6	143.3	139.1	148.2	150.5	146.2	139.1	132.4	134.3	138.5	138.4	ʳ140.0	ʳ137.6	145.5	141.2
Equipment....do....	114.6	123.2	126.0	122.1	123.5	129.2	127.7	126.6	124.6	123.1	127.1	129.3	ʳ130.1	ʳ130.2	134.8	131.7
Intermediate products....do....	137.2	145.1	149.2	144.5	150.9	153.2	152.7	149.0	144.1	142.5	148.0	150.3	ʳ152.6	ʳ154.1	158.9	153.7
Materials....do....	130.6	136.9	141.4	132.6	136.3	138.0	140.5	139.4	136.5	137.0	140.6	142.1	ʳ146.1	ʳ147.0	149.2	140.6
By industry groupings:																
Mining and utilities....do....	131.6	136.2	136.9	140.6	138.8	137.3	134.1	132.9	135.0	142.0	139.9	136.3	ʳ137.0	ʳ136.9	141.2	144.8
Manufacturing....do....	129.5	137.1	141.9	133.2	138.2	142.8	144.1	140.3	134.8	133.9	139.6	142.1	ʳ145.1	ʳ145.0	148.9	140.1
Nondurable manufactures....do....	140.9	148.1	152.8	144.1	154.1	156.2	155.8	151.0	143.0	142.8	148.7	150.5	ʳ153.3	ʳ153.4	158.6	149.5
Durable manufactures....do....	121.7	129.5	134.3	125.6	127.2	133.7	136.0	132.9	129.2	127.8	133.2	136.3	ʳ139.5	ʳ139.2	142.4	133.5
Seasonally Adjusted																
Total index....1967=100..	129.8	137.1	137.8	138.7	138.1	138.5	138.9	139.3	139.7	138.8	139.2	140.9	ʳ143.2	ʳ143.9	144.6	145.3
By market groupings:																
Products, total....do....	129.3	137.1	137.3	138.7	138.4	138.8	138.9	139.5	140.3	138.5	139.6	141.6	ʳ143.0	ʳ143.1	143.7	144.3
Final products....do....	127.2	134.9	135.4	136.8	136.3	136.8	136.5	137.0	137.6	134.9	136.4	138.9	ʳ140.5	ʳ140.5	140.9	141.6
Consumer goods....do....	136.2	143.4	143.8	145.4	144.7	144.9	144.9	145.2	145.8	141.8	143.8	145.9	ʳ147.5	147.1	146.9	147.3
Durable consumer goods....do....	141.4	153.1	155.8	158.0	154.7	155.6	156.8	155.2	155.8	146.5	151.2	157.5	ʳ161.8	ʳ160.3	161.2	161.6
Automotive products....do....	154.8	174.2	179.8	184.8	177.2	177.0	179.4	173.6	172.4	157.5	162.8	175.8	184.3	ʳ180.0	180.3	180.8
Autos and utility vehicles....do....	149.8	169.2	177.4	184.1	173.1	172.6	176.1	167.6	165.5	145.5	153.9	171.0	ʳ182.7	ʳ175.6	175.3	175.7
Autos....do....	132.0	148.4	156.8	161.4	150.9	151.6	154.3	147.5	143.6	127.4	131.5	149.7	159.1	ʳ151.6	150.1	152.7
Auto parts and allied goods....do....	167.6	186.8	185.8	186.6	187.3	188.1	187.6	188.7	190.4	187.8	185.3	188.5	ʳ188.2	ʳ191.2	192.9	193.5
Home goods....do....	133.9	141.3	142.3	142.9	142.1	143.6	144.2	145.0	146.6	140.3	144.6	147.2	ʳ149.2	ʳ149.3	150.4	150.8
Appliances, air cond., and TV....do....	114.6	127.3	133.1	130.1	129.6	129.4	128.6	131.4	132.8	116.1	133.3	135.4	ʳ142.2	ʳ139.6	141.1	140.9
Carpeting and furniture....do....	144.1	152.2	151.2	154.1	154.8	159.0	160.5	160.0	161.5	159.1	160.2	159.3	158.9	ʳ163.4	165.2	....
Nondurable consumer goods....do....	134.1	139.6	139.1	140.3	140.6	140.7	140.1	141.2	141.8	139.9	140.8	141.3	ʳ141.8	ʳ141.7	141.1	141.6
Clothing....do....	124.0	125.2	125.7	124.1	126.4	128.3	128.0	126.4	126.9	118.3	121.1	122.4	124.9	125.4	....	
Consumer staples....do....	136.9	143.6	142.9	144.8	144.6	144.1	143.5	145.3	145.9	145.9	146.3	146.4	146.6	ʳ146.2	145.6	146.2
Consumer foods and tobacco....do....	130.7	135.5	135.4	137.1	137.9	137.1	135.2	136.7	137.9	136.5	138.3	138.7	140.8	ʳ139.9	139.0	....
Nonfood staples....do....	144.1	152.9	151.7	153.8	152.4	152.4	153.4	155.1	155.2	156.6	155.8	155.3	ʳ153.3	153.4	153.4	154.6
Equipment....do....	114.6	123.2	124.1	124.8	124.9	125.6	125.0	125.8	126.2	125.4	126.2	129.1	ʳ130.8	ʳ131.6	132.5	133.8
Business equipment....do....	136.3	149.2	150.1	151.2	151.1	152.1	152.6	153.5	154.0	152.6	154.2	157.4	ʳ159.3	ʳ160.2	161.3	162.8
Industrial equipment ♀....do....	128.0	138.5	140.0	140.7	140.4	141.4	141.8	142.6	143.0	144.3	144.6	146.9	ʳ147.8	ʳ149.6	150.4	151.8
Building and mining equipment.do....	177.7	202.5	208.1	210.6	203.9	204.5	205.7	206.7	208.3	211.1	214.9	221.7	225.1	ʳ225.1	226.5	228.2
Manufacturing equipment....do....	106.5	113.9	115.0	114.3	115.3	117.6	118.5	118.7	118.2	118.8	117.7	118.3	119.0	ʳ121.4	122.1	123.3
Commercial, transit, farm eq. ♀....do....	145.8	161.6	161.9	163.3	163.4	164.4	165.1	165.9	166.9	162.2	165.5	169.4	172.6	ʳ172.3	173.9	175.5
Commercial equipment....do....	173.5	191.6	191.4	191.7	193.0	193.7	195.4	197.4	198.8	198.5	200.9	202.0	203.8	ʳ204.2	206.6	208.1
Transit equipment....do....	104.1	117.8	118.5	121.5	121.9	125.1	122.3	118.9	121.1	111.1	115.9	126.1	ʳ133.7	ʳ132.2	131.8	132.7
Defense and space equipment....do....	78.4	79.6	80.3	80.4	80.8	80.9	78.9	79.3	79.5	79.7	79.2	81.9	82.9	ʳ83.2	84.1	85.5
Intermediate products....do....	137.2	145.1	144.7	146.3	146.1	146.5	147.8	148.4	150.4	151.6	151.4	151.4	ʳ152.1	ʳ152.9	154.3	154.8
Construction supplies....do....	132.6	140.8	139.9	141.2	141.7	143.2	144.9	146.5	148.3	149.2	148.6	147.9	ʳ148.5	150.4	151.3	152.4
Business supplies....do....	141.8	149.5	149.6	151.3	150.6	149.7	150.5	150.1	152.6	153.8	154.2	155.0	ʳ155.6	ʳ155.3	157.1	....
Materials....do....	130.6	136.9	138.7	138.9	137.6	137.9	138.9	139.0	138.8	139.2	138.6	139.9	ʳ143.7	ʳ145.2	146.2	146.9
Durable goods materials ♀....do....	126.8	134.5	136.4	136.8	135.4	135.7	137.1	137.2	138.7	138.2	137.0	138.6	ʳ142.7	ʳ144.0	145.0	146.4
Durable consumer parts....do....	121.6	132.0	134.5	137.2	135.2	135.8	135.4	136.5	135.7	133.0	131.1	133.1	ʳ136.8	ʳ138.3	139.0	140.5
Equipment parts....do....	133.9	143.1	143.0	145.0	145.6	146.8	147.6	147.2	149.2	148.7	146.6	151.3	ʳ154.8	ʳ155.8	157.7	159.2
Nondurable goods materials ♀....do....	146.3	153.5	154.7	154.1	155.1	153.9	154.4	155.4	155.3	155.0	158.5	160.5	ʳ162.0	ʳ163.4	164.0	164.0
Textile, paper, and chemical....do....	151.1	158.3	160.1	158.9	159.6	159.0	160.0	159.3	159.3	160.7	162.8	165.7	166.4	ʳ168.0	168.9	168.7
Energy materials....do....	120.2	122.4	124.3	125.2	121.4	123.5	124.0	123.0	118.7	122.2	117.7	117.5	ʳ123.9	ʳ125.9	126.7	127.5
By industry groupings.																
Mining and utilities....do....	131.6	136.2	138.8	139.4	134.4	135.1	135.8	135.5	133.9	137.4	137.7	138.2	ʳ140.9	ʳ141.6	142.1	142.8
Mining....do....	114.2	117.8	122.8	119.8	115.4	118.0	119.6	118.8	113.4	115.0	114.4	119.3	ʳ127.2	ʳ128.1	128.9	129.3
Metal mining....do....	122.8	105.4	121.3	101.9	70.0	71.4	80.0	84.8	104.3	121.4	119.9	127.6	122.3	ʳ120.1	121.1	....
Coal....do....	117.2	118.0	133.4	120.7	113.6	133.0	141.4	140.6	74.6	54.8	56.5	78.4	ʳ129.5	ʳ132.7	136.8	137.4
Oil and gas extraction ♀....do....	112.0	118.0	121.3	120.6	119.3	119.6	119.4	117.8	118.4	121.1	120.4	123.3	ʳ127.3	ʳ128.0	128.5	128.7
Crude oil....do....	92.2	92.4	93.9	94.3	92.8	94.7	94.4	92.9	93.4	96.9	92.7	94.0	ʳ99.4	ʳ98.5	99.1	....
Natural gas....do....	109.5	110.4	114.0	112.6	111.0	105.4	108.5	107.1	109.6	108.8	108.7	109.9	107.6	....	....	....
Stone and earth minerals....do....	118.3	124.9	122.5	126.7	125.0	126.7	128.1	127.2	126.5	130.0	129.1	128.2	128.9	129.6	130.0	....
Utilities....do....	151.0	156.5	156.8	161.4	155.7	154.1	154.0	154.2	156.7	162.3	163.5	159.5	ʳ156.0	ʳ156.7	156.9	157.9
Electric....do....	167.6	175.5	176.8	183.9	175.4	173.7	173.6	173.3	175.9	183.6	184.3	178.8	ʳ175.0	176.9	....	....
Manufacturing....do....	129.5	137.1	137.8	138.5	138.6	139.0	139.4	139.9	140.5	138.7	139.4	141.4	143.5	ʳ144.2	144.9	145.6
Nondurable manufactures....do....	140.9	148.1	148.4	148.6	149.4	149.5	149.6	150.1	150.9	149.8	150.6	151.4	ʳ153.2	ʳ153.8	154.3	154.3
Foods ♀....do....	132.3	137.9	136.9	138.3	139.3	138.3	137.3	139.4	140.4	139.3	140.8	141.1	ʳ143.1	ʳ142.5	141.9	....
Meat products....do....	111.2	114.0	114.5	111.6	116.1	116.1	112.0	114.8	111.6	109.2	117.9	113.8	116.1	ʳ113.6	111.4	....
Dairy products....do....	113.8	117.4	115.5	117.0	118.2	118.9	118.9	119.9	119.2	119.0	118.7	119.7	119.8	118.9	119.4	....
Beverages....do....	156.7	167.6	166.2	172.4	168.0	166.0	168.1	168.4	167.6	174.5	176.0	172.6	181.1	ʳ177.8	176.4	....
Tobacco products....do....	117.9	114.3	119.2	114.5	117.0	113.5	113.8	117.5	120.6	113.4	117.7	115.6	121.0	120.2	....	....
Textile mill products....do....	136.4	137.1	135.4	137.2	136.6	140.7	142.4	141.6	143.7	137.1	136.4	135.1	ʳ138.1	ʳ138.5	139.1	....
Apparel products....do....	122.2	124.2	122.1	121.1	124.1	127.7	129.0	125.1	125.8	118.6	121.1	122.8	126.1	125.9		
Paper and products....do....	133.0	137.4	139.3	139.2	140.3	139.1	137.9	137.8	138.6	139.9	143.9	144.9	ʳ145.7	146.6	147.8	144.4
Printing and publishing....do....	120.6	124.7	124.1	124.9	125.0	124.2	125.7	126.2	127.5	129.9	128.3	129.1	128.6	ʳ128.2	128.0	128.6
Chemicals and products....do....	169.3	180.7	183.5	182.6	182.6	181.3	182.3	183.1	183.0	184.4	183.7	185.2	185.5	ʳ188.1	190.2	....
Basic chemicals....do....	158.6	165.3	170.2	166.7	168.7	164.3	163.9	164.3	164.1	165.1	163.0	167.3	171.0	ʳ174.9	179.1	....
Petroleum products....do....	133.1	141.0	140.0	140.4	139.9	141.9	141.4	140.5	139.3	139.7	139.0	140.1	ʳ141.7	ʳ142.3	141.6	142.4
Rubber and plastics products....do....	200.2	232.2	235.2	235.2	237.4	239.5	236.3	238.5	240.1	238.7	240.0	243.1	ʳ249.1	ʳ253.0	253.4	....
Leather and products....do....	80.9	75.3	74.1	74.1	74.5	74.9	77.0	78.1	77.3	74.5	73.0	72.1	76.0	75.7	74.4	....

ʳ Revised. ᵖ Preliminary. ¹ Estimated. ♂ Monthly revisions back to 1967 will be shown later; effective Sept. 1977 SURVEY, indexes revised to reflect more up-to-date information. ♀ Includes data for items not shown separately.

NOTE FOR P. S-5:
⊙ Revised back to Jan. 1975 to reflect corrections in reporting errors in the machinery industry, and corrections in classifications in the aircraft and machinery industries; revisions prior to Apr. 1976 are available from the Bur. of the Census, Wash., D.C. 20233.

Figure 3.6 Survey of Current Business (from Department of Commerce).

March 1982 SURVEY OF CURRENT BUSINESS S–9

Unless otherwise stated in footnotes below, data through 1978 and descriptive notes are as shown in the 1979 edition of BUSINESS STATISTICS	1980	1981	1981												1982	
	Annual		Jan.	Feb	Mar.	Apr.	May	June	July	Aug	Sept.	Oct	Nov	Dec	Jan	Feb
CONSTRUCTION AND REAL ESTATE—Continued																
CONSTRUCTION COST INDEXES																
Dept. of Commerce composite ... 1977 = 100	143.3	152.7	149.2	149.7	152.1	151.1	150.6	150.2	152.2	153.0	154.5	155.5	156.0	158.2	159.1	
American Appraisal Co., The:																
Average, 30 cities ... 1913 = 100	2,495	2,643	2,578	2,581	2,576	2,600	2,635	2,655	2,678	2,679	2,676	2,678	2,678	2,700		
Atlanta ... do	2,660	2,841	2,773	2,781	2,788	2,807	2,805	2,784	2,894	2,896	2,898	2,892	2,878	2,893		
New York ... do	2,553	2,645	2,621	2,639	2,629	2,644	2,640	2,631	2,653	2,668	2,658	2,655	2,646	2,659		
San Francisco ... do	2,671	2,873	2,820	2,821	2,834	2,855	2,855	2,821	2,915	2,909	2,893	2,896	2,918	2,934		
St. Louis ... do	2,343	2,453	2,396	2,357	2,346	2,361	2,485	2,476	2,467	2,505	2,494	2,491	2,523	2,535		
Boeckh indexes:																
Average, 20 cities:																
Apartments, hotels, office buildings 1977 = 100	125.1	137.4	131.1		132.6		135.4		139.7		142.1		143.2		144.1	
Commercial and factory buildings ... do	127.7	140.1	133.9		135.3		138.1		141.9		145.3		145.9		146.3	
Residences ... do	128.9	136.0	129.7		131.3		134.4		138.3		140.4		141.6		142.1	
Engineering News-Record:																
Building ... 1967 = 100	287.7	310.3	298.2	298.4	298.0	305.5	307.3	308.3	312.1	313.5	316.6	319.1	323.6	323.3	324.7	[1]325.7
Construction ... do	301.4	328.9	313.9	314.0	315.0	321.4	323.3	326.8	331.6	332.8	336.1	341.9	345.4	344.9	346.8	[1]347.8
Federal Highway Adm.—Highway construction:																
Composite (avg. for year or qtr.) ... 1977 = 100	163.0	156.7			160.0			152.4			157.3			156.8		
CONSTRUCTION MATERIALS																
Output indexes:																
Iron and steel products ... 1947-49 = 100																
Lumber and wood products ... do																
Portland cement ... do																
REAL ESTATE ¶																
Mortgage applications for new home construction:																
FHA net applications ... thous. units	141.4	92.3	7.4	8.3	13.0	11.3	8.8	7.4	6.2	7.2	5.4	4.5	4.6	8.2	7.5	8.6
Seasonally adjusted annual rates ... do			128	121	144	120	88	84	65	84	58	50	61	126	136	126
Requests for VA appraisals ... do	202.2	153.8	12.5	14.9	17.3	18.2	[r]15.4	14.2	13.8	11.9	8.5	9.0	8.7	9.1	9.3	9.1
Seasonally adjusted annual rates ... do			[r]182	[r]196	[r]192	[r]192	[r]180	[r]156	[r]150	[r]135	[r]99	[r]100	[r]123	141	142	119
Home mortgages insured or guaranteed by:																
Fed. Hous. Adm.: Face amount ... mil. $	16,458.53	10,278.14	955.33	849.36	983.70	1,121.55	983.42	978.02	793.47	622.98	1,014.78	654.28	727.94	593.31	443.87	606.52
Vet. Adm.: Face amount § ... do	13,855.54	7,905.93	917.26	745.20	706.41	769.70	583.44	875.83	644.07	696.21	660.19	485.73	464.19	357.69	327.39	393.60
Federal Home Loan Banks, outstanding advances to member institutions, end of period ... mil. $	48,963	65,194	48,581	48,206	49,175	51,530	53,148	56,095	59,475	62,471	64,347	64,662	64,409	65,194	65,099	65,089
New mortgage loans of all savings and loan associations, estimated total ... mil. $	72,537	53,283	[r]4,288	[r]3,679	[r]4,927	[r]5,537	[r]5,734	[r]6,052	[r]4,987	[r]4,055	[r]3,865	[r]3,465	[r]2,934	[r]3,760	2,369	
By purpose of loan:																
Home construction ... do	14,946	11,599	[r]1,030	[r]889	[r]1,226	[r]1,367	[r]1,248	[r]1,187	1,003	772	[r]803	[r]650	[r]600	[r]824	412	
Home purchase ... do	42,957	28,299	[r]2,317	[r]1,967	[r]2,540	[r]2,828	[r]3,130	[r]3,435	[r]2,771	[r]2,323	[r]1,970	[r]1,838	[r]1,498	[r]1,682	1,094	
All other purposes ... do	14,634	13,385	941	[r]823	1,161	[r]1,342	[r]1,356	[r]1,430	[r]1,213	[r]960	[r]1,092	[r]977	836	[r]1,254	863	
DOMESTIC TRADE																
ADVERTISING																
McCann-Erickson national advertising index, seasonally adjusted:																
Combined index ... 1967 = 100																
Network TV ... do																
Spot TV ... do																
Magazines ... do																
Newspapers ... do																
Magazine advertising (Publishers Information Bureau):																
Cost, total ... mil. $	2,846.1		184.3	225.7	268.0	288.3	297.9	267.1	196.6	210.9	284.8	330.5	393.3	275.3		
Apparel and accessories ... do	111.7		6.7	6.2	12.1	14.4	11.1	7.4	6.4	12.9	21.1	15.4	16.5	11.6		
Automotive, incl. accessories ... do	229.5		14.8	24.0	25.7	27.2	31.0	29.0	17.6	17.4	14.7	29.3	38.4	21.1		
Building materials ... do	48.3		2.3	3.2	3.2	4.8	7.4	5.3	3.6	4.8	7.2	5.4	5.4	3.8		
Drugs and toiletries ... do	284.2		18.1	24.9	27.4	31.6	31.3	27.4	21.4	22.3	30.9	28.2	31.1	23.5		
Foods, soft drinks, confectionery ... do	211.6		9.0	17.9	18.4	19.4	17.5	19.5	17.6	15.8	18.4	23.7	34.2	20.3		
Beer, wine, liquors ... do	238.9		11.5	14.4	17.8	19.6	19.0	25.7	15.0	14.3	18.1	24.8	33.7	37.9		
Houshold equip., supplies, furnishings ... do	138.8		8.9	7.8	11.6	14.8	18.4	12.3	9.9	9.5	14.6	21.1	23.5	13.0		
Industrial materials ... do	70.8		4.3	3.8	5.8	6.0	7.2	5.4	4.3	4.0	5.9	7.9	8.3	4.7		
Soaps, cleansers, etc ... do	29.8		1.9	1.9	2.1	3.0	3.4	2.0	1.4	1.9	3.2	3.6	3.5	1.7		
Smoking materials ... do	289.7		20.7	24.8	30.0	29.8	24.8	28.5	25.5	27.5	25.6	23.6	28.4	25.2		
All other ... do	1,198.0		86.0	96.8	113.9	117.8	126.8	104.5	73.4	80.7	125.1	146.8	170.3	112.7		
Newspaper advertising expenditures (Media Records Inc.):																
Total ... mil. $	8,192.3		671.2	703.8	840.3	816.6	884.5	772.2	707.3	811.7	779.3	856.7	936.7	795.0		
Automotive ... do	183.6		16.2	19.4	22.5	18.4	21.3	15.7	15.8	21.3	17.4	24.7	19.6	13.2		
Classified ... do	2,191.8		197.7	199.2	235.0	215.6	240.2	217.1	208.8	238.8	204.3	207.8	201.3	149.1		
Financial ... do	298.0		33.9	24.6	31.2	30.9	26.0	28.0	29.7	35.2	39.4	45.5	31.1	31.7		
General ... do	1,122.7		100.6	113.3	136.2	126.5	134.9	114.0	94.1	92.8	109.4	129.4	137.1	91.7		
Retail ... do	4,396.3		322.7	347.4	415.4	425.2	462.1	397.4	358.9	423.6	408.8	449.4	547.5	509.4		
WHOLESALE TRADE †																
Merchant wholesalers sales (unadj.), total ... mil. $	1,043,886		93,845	89,641	101,273	99,081	96,676	98,639	96,072	93,655	96,992	99,236	94,449	[r]97,098	87,058	
Durable goods establishments ... do	438,439		35,927	37,054	41,991	41,934	40,679	43,152	41,459	41,349	41,587	42,065	39,195	[r]39,970	34,494	
Nondurable goods establishments ... do	605,447		57,918	52,587	59,282	57,147	55,997	55,487	54,613	52,306	55,405	57,171	55,254	[r]57,128	52,564	
Merchant wholesalers inventories, book value, end of year or month (unadj.), total ... mil. $	105,449		105,446	107,209	107,907	106,420	105,985	106,915	105,556	106,603	108,134	109,555	111,930	[r]112,032	112,051	
Durable goods establishments ... do	66,716		66,230	68,251	69,208	69,673	71,113	71,821	70,729	71,487	72,348	71,958	73,432	[r]73,304	72,356	
Nondurable goods establishments ... do	38,733		39,216	38,958	38,699	36,747	34,872	35,094	34,827	35,116	35,786	37,597	38,498	[r]38,728	39,695	

See footnotes at end of tables.

Figure 3.7 Retail of Monthly Sales from Survey of Current Business.

American Book Publishers Council, One Park Avenue, New York, New York 10016

American Booksellers Association, 175 Fifth Avenue, New York, N.Y. 10010

American Carpet Institute, 350 Fifth Avenue, New York, N.Y. 10001

American Institute of Launderine, Doris and Chicago Avenues, Joliet, Ill. 60433

American Institute of Supply Associations, 1505 22d Street NW, Washington, D.C. 20037

American Meat Institute, 59 East Van Buren Street, Chicago, Ill. 60605

American Paper Institute, 260 Madison Avenue, New York, N.Y. 10016

American Society of Association Executives, 2000 K Street, NW, Washington, D.C. 20006

American Electric Association, 16223 Meyers Street, Detroit, Mich. 48235

American Supply Association, 221 North LaSalle Street, Chicago, Ill. 60601

S–10 SURVEY OF CURRENT BUSINESS March 1982

Unless otherwise stated in footnotes below, data through 1978 and descriptive notes are as shown in the 1979 edition of BUSINESS STATISTICS	1980	1981	1981												1982	
	Annual		Jan.	Feb	Mar	Apr.	May	June	July	Aug	Sept	Oct	Nov	Dec	Jan	Feb
DOMESTIC TRADE—Continued																
RETAIL TRADE																
All retail stores: †																
Estimated sales (unadj.), total † ..... mil. $	956,655		77,361	74,321	84,652	85,770	87,383	87,784	88,768	89,555	86,023	89,289	87,813	[r]106,441	[r]77,279	[r]75,693
Durable goods stores # ..... do	297,926		23,239	23,857	28,295	27,688	27,669	29,130	29,038	29,438	27,797	27,315	25,867	[r]29,045	[r]21,912	[r]23,184
Building materials, hardware, garden supply, and mobile home dealers # ..... mil. $	48,210		3,351	3,359	4,043	4,524	4,798	4,993	4,769	4,646	4,534	4,495	4,048	[r]3,689	[r]2,947	[r]2,956
Building materials and supply stores ..... do	33,682		2,360	2,360	2,785	3,038	3,221	3,463	3,361	3,298	3,225	3,198	2,850	[r]2,324	1,940	
Hardware stores ..... do	7,743		565	538	655	771	809	809	784	748	731	758	716	[r]875	626	
Automotive dealers # ..... do	167,017		13,351	14,370	17,336	16,279	15,791	16,794	16,922	17,352	15,988	15,382	13,932	[r]13,829	[r]12,690	[r]14,089
Motor vehicle dealers ..... do	148,799		11,926	13,011	15,745	14,563	14,154	15,042	15,050	15,501	14,181	13,517	12,190	[r]12,069	11,173	[r]12,648
Auto and home supply stores ..... do	18,218		1,425	1,359	1,591	1,716	1,637	1,752	1,872	1,851	1,807	1,865	1,742	[r]1,760	1,517	
Furniture, home furn., and equip # ..... do	43,198		3,616	3,351	3,716	3,608	3,662	3,819	3,779	3,915	3,873	3,920	4,016	[r]4,888	[r]3,352	[r]3,218
Furniture, home furnishings stores ..... do	26,228		2,152	2,020	2,260	2,229	2,300	2,351	2,281	2,378	2,332	2,319	2,382	[r]2,595	2,022	
Household appliance, radio, TV ..... do	13,190		1,074	976	1,088	1,047	1,043	1,154	1,182	1,211	1,204	1,264	1,296	[r]1,742	1,048	
Nondurable goods stores ..... do	658,729		54,122	50,464	56,357	58,082	59,714	58,654	59,730	60,117	58,226	61,974	61,946	[r]77,396	[r]55,367	[r]52,509
General merch. group stores ..... do	116,287		7,279	7,160	8,972	9,961	10,241	10,011	9,530	10,355	9,827	10,910	12,492	[r]19,790	[r]7,468	[r]7,376
Department stores ..... do	[2]94,185		5,873	5,783	7,337	8,093	8,359	8,220	7,757	8,467	8,099	8,909	10,203	[r]16,083	[r]6,128	[r]6,024
Variety stores ..... do	8,856		566	557	663	787	738	716	716	757	668	757	787	[r]1,440	534	
Food stores ..... do	217,511		19,195	17,477	18,837	19,383	20,387	19,792	21,038	20,234	19,597	20,779	19,562	[r]22,069	[r]19,985	[r]18,552
Grocery stores ..... do	202,065		17,830	16,133	17,410	17,839	18,941	18,338	19,557	18,840	18,243	19,407	18,218	[r]20,265	[r]18,659	[r]17,241
Gasoline service stations ..... do	94,470		8,047	7,616	8,380	8,492	8,734	8,996	9,173	8,955	8,648	8,762	8,364	[r]8,652	[r]8,185	[r]7,722
Apparel and accessory stores # ..... do	44,487		3,279	2,911	3,448	3,972	3,735	3,632	3,598	4,126	3,929	4,234	4,271	[r]6,662	[r]3,319	[r]2,909
Men's and boys' clothing ..... do	8,025		565	494	552	621	615	626	565	649	623	725	744	[r]1,238	511	
Women's clothing, spec. stores, furriers ..... do	16,991		1,258	1,141	1,355	1,532	1,470	1,404	1,439	1,592	1,561	1,654	1,639	[r]2,493	1,258	
Shoe stores ..... do	8,040		614	530	665	831	728	690	660	774	756	793	761	[r]1,073	686	
Eating and drinking places ..... do	86,612		7,065	6,742	7,710	7,897	8,344	8,264	8,524	8,588	8,073	8,271	7,653	[r]7,973	[r]7,270	[r]7,078
Drug and proprietary stores ..... do	31,557		2,722	2,530	2,701	2,769	2,810	2,758	2,769	2,756	2,714	2,880	2,843	[r]4,003	[r]2,771	[r]2,686
Liquor stores ..... do	16,556		1,275	1,195	1,247	1,285	1,381	1,367	1,448	1,422	1,343	1,403	1,383	[r]2,044	1,297	
Estimated sales (seas. adj.), total † ..... do			85,463	[r]85,961	87,608	85,855	85,501	87,384	87,350	88,591	88,699	86,660	87,222	[r]87,444	[r]86,165	[r]87,552
Durable goods stores # ..... do			27,075	[r]27,479	28,429	26,356	26,536	27,532	27,753	28,439	28,380	26,319	26,484	[r]26,694	[r]25,756	[r]26,538
Building materials, hardware, garden supply, and mobile home dealers # ..... mil. $			4,596	4,596	4,481	4,427	4,399	4,381	4,260	4,158	4,145	3,952	4,095	[r]3,920	[r]3,973	[r]3,994
Building materials and supply stores ..... do			3,246	3,233	3,126	3,087	3,127	3,040	2,910	2,850	2,834	2,712	2,827	[r]2,626	2,625	
Hardware stores ..... do			731	738	731	732	718	740	735	751	723	707	729	[r]724	806	
Automotive dealers ..... do			14,965	[r]15,466	16,330	14,572	14,786	15,603	15,998	16,726	16,630	14,937	15,067	[r]15,262	[r]14,490	[r]15,140
Motor vehicle dealers ..... do			13,355	[r]13,754	14,688	12,945	13,167	13,967	14,212	14,948	14,818	13,226	13,337	[r]13,576	12,726	[r]13,300
Auto and home supply stores ..... do			1,610	1,712	1,642	1,627	1,619	1,636	1,786	1,778	1,812	1,711	1,730	[r]1,686	1,764	
Furniture, home furn., and equip. # ..... do			4,016	3,888	3,897	3,822	3,794	3,873	3,719	3,883	3,907	3,807	3,780	[r]3,818	[r]3,671	[r]3,733
Furniture, home furnishings stores ..... do			2,404	2,319	2,313	2,286	2,323	2,337	2,215	2,336	2,372	2,251	2,220	[r]2,260	2,217	
Household appliance, radio, TV ..... do			1,201	1,163	1,185	1,166	1,103	1,170	1,163	1,212	1,197	1,227	1,238	[r]1,228	1,159	
Nondurable goods stores ..... do			58,388	58,482	59,179	59,499	58,965	59,852	59,597	60,152	60,319	60,341	60,738	[r]60,750	[r]60,409	[r]61,014
General merch. group stores ..... do			9,994	10,306	10,306	10,563	10,350	10,674	10,409	10,713	10,507	10,581	10,745	[r]10,724	[r]10,491	[r]10,637
Department stores ..... do	([2])		8,078	8,381	8,443	8,610	8,452	8,754	8,496	8,756	8,607	8,624	8,758	[r]8,708	[r]8,655	[r]8,743
Variety stores ..... do			775	770	762	792	748	763	768	781	738	750	753	[r]750	732	
Food stores ..... do			19,072	19,112	19,522	19,672	19,506	19,850	19,939	20,328	20,050	20,206	20,538	[r]20,553	[r]20,137	[r]20,374
Grocery stores ..... do			17,601	17,632	18,098	18,185	18,091	18,430	18,467	18,897	18,596	18,805	19,116	[r]19,118	[r]18,734	[r]18,946
Gasoline service stations ..... do			8,497	8,596	8,613	8,595	8,513	8,633	8,541	8,480	8,683	8,557	8,578	[r]8,558	[r]8,726	[r]8,676
Apparel and accessory stores # ..... do			3,945	4,022	3,947	3,931	3,923	4,000	4,013	4,052	4,062	3,992	3,940	[r]3,965	[r]3,996	[r]4,001
Men's and boys' clothing ..... do			642	681	660	646	666	674	662	708	706	713	634	[r]643	596	
Women's clothing, spec. stores, furriers ..... do			1,549	1,557	1,502	1,547	1,534	1,572	1,580	1,595	1,559	1,502	1,525	[r]1,517	1,549	
Shoe stores ..... do			728	755	745	734	739	750	750	746	722	734	710	[r]768	797	
Eating and drinking places ..... do			7,885	7,876	8,006	7,842	7,902	7,893	7,799	7,793	8,081	8,077	8,005	[r]7,997	[r]8,051	[r]8,250
Drug and proprietary stores ..... do			2,815	2,768	2,770	2,831	2,830	2,826	2,837	2,844	2,909	2,924	2,934	[r]2,920	[r]2,880	[r]2,945
Liquor stores ..... do			1,390	1,404	1,386	1,401	1,396	1,368	1,376	1,404	1,414	1,396	1,377	[r]1,462	1,430	
Estimated inventories, end of year or month: †																
Book value (unadjusted), total ..... mil. $	108,717	120,224	108,147	110,635	113,741	114,951	115,877	117,342	118,980	119,106	122,080	127,815	[r]130,767	120,224		
Durable goods stores # ..... do	51,159	56,168	51,904	52,409	53,018	53,868	55,033	55,969	56,238	54,680	54,663	56,654	[r]58,021	56,168		
Building materials and supply stores ..... do	8,695	9,057	8,816	9,151	9,590	9,642	9,849	9,711	9,487	9,461	9,358	9,375	[r]9,358	9,057		
Automotive dealers ..... do	24,457	27,925	24,931	24,783	24,624	25,539	26,470	27,503	27,893	25,878	25,552	26,669	27,626	27,925		
Furniture, home furn., and equip ..... do	8,008	8,472	7,975	8,146	8,374	8,358	8,431	8,472	8,382	8,480	8,553	8,887	[r]9,066	8,472		
Nondurable goods stores # ..... do	57,558	64,056	56,243	58,226	60,723	61,083	60,844	61,373	62,742	64,426	67,417	71,161	[r]72,746	64,056		
General merch. group stores ..... do	19,894	22,873	19,397	20,593	22,054	22,499	22,575	22,960	23,515	24,437	26,274	28,451	28,780	22,873		
Department stores ..... do	14,819	17,113	14,366	15,190	16,289	16,783	16,893	16,989	17,319	17,992	19,447	21,164	21,645	17,113		
Food stores ..... do	12,471	13,621	12,167	12,527	12,892	12,891	12,822	12,814	12,893	12,936	13,239	13,690	[r]13,988	13,621		
Apparel and accessory stores ..... do	9,120	9,692	8,624	9,060	9,436	9,453	9,265	9,325	9,718	10,154	10,590	11,043	[r]11,256	9,692		
Book value (seas. adj.), total ..... do	111,694	123,662	111,790	113,507	113,404	113,963	115,426	117,307	119,824	121,277	122,219	123,485	[r]123,799	123,662		
Durable goods stores # ..... do	51,853	56,970	52,234	52,374	51,791	52,306	53,529	54,880	56,199	57,121	57,124	57,492	[r]57,464	56,970		
Building materials and supply stores ..... do	9,076	9,464	9,061	9,096	9,302	9,298	9,590	9,558	9,487	9,537	9,443	9,518	[r]9,539	9,464		
Automotive dealers ..... do	24,263	27,758	24,491	24,273	23,385	24,184	25,066	26,446	27,672	28,282	28,265	28,311	28,133	27,758		
Furniture, home furn., and equip ..... do	8,163	8,645	8,196	8,346	8,450	8,316	8,423	8,447	8,458	8,463	8,468	8,562	[r]8,819	8,645		
Nondurable goods stores # ..... do	59,841	66,692	59,556	61,133	61,613	61,657	61,897	62,427	63,625	64,156	65,095	65,993	[r]66,335	66,692		
General merch. group stores ..... do	21,861	25,160	21,614	22,386	22,646	22,644	22,846	23,304	23,795	24,070	24,685	25,381	25,217	25,160		
Department stores ..... do	16,178	18,703	15,980	16,583	16,690	16,817	17,012	17,248	17,691	17,849	18,433	18,863	18,789	18,703		
Food stores ..... do	12,372	13,526	12,315	12,795	12,840	12,930	12,925	12,840	13,050	13,146	13,373	13,291	[r]13,412	13,526		
Apparel and accessory stores ..... do	9,470	10,064	9,394	9,679	9,638	9,646	9,512	9,643	9,876	9,955	9,962	9,985	[r]10,159	10,064		
Firms with 11 or more stores:																
Estimated sales (unadjusted), total ..... mil. $	324,279	357,461	25,080	23,689	27,291	28,755	29,643	29,017	29,238	29,772	28,814	31,026	[r]32,050	43,086		
Durable goods stores ..... do	23,390	25,522	1,606	1,565	1,863	2,039	2,148	2,206	2,170	2,123	2,086	2,131	[r]2,271	3,314		
Auto and home supply stores ..... do	3,501	3,733	260	250	288	324	315	343	339	324	313	332	312	333		
Nondurable goods stores # ..... do	300,889	331,939	23,474	22,124	25,428	26,716	27,495	26,811	27,068	27,649	26,728	28,895	[r]29,779	39,772		
General merchandise group stores ..... do	101,963	111,780	6,314	6,268	7,955	8,776	9,043	8,874	8,390	9,162	8,701	9,593	[r]11,040	17,664		
Department stores ..... do	89,229	97,987	5,564	5,491	6,977	7,677	7,930	7,809	7,372	8,057	7,687	8,440	[r]9,678	15,305		
Variety stores ..... do	6,627	6,983	414	416	511	593	563	548	530	572	508	570	[r]613	1,145		
Miscellaneous general stores ..... do	6,107	6,810	336	361	467	506	550	517	488	533	506	583	[r]749	1,214		

See footnotes at end of tables.

Figure 3.7 *(Continued)*

Automotive Service Industry Association, 230 North Michigan Avenue, Chicago, Ill. 60601

Bowling Proprietors' Association of America, Inc., West Higgins Road, Hoffman Estates, Ill. 60172

Florists' Telegraph Delivery Association, 900 West Lafayette Boulevard, Detroit, Mich. 48226

Food Service Equipment Industry, Inc., 332 South Michigan Avenue, Chicago, Ill. 60604

Laundry and Cleaners Allied Trades Association, 1180 Raymond Boulevard, Newark, N.J. 07102

Material Handling Equipment Distributors Association, 20 North Wacker Drive, Chicago, Ill. 60616

Line of Business (and number of concerns reporting)	Current assets to current debt	Net profits on net sales	Net profits on tangible net worth	Net profits on net working capital	Net sales to tangible net worth	Net sales to net working capital	Collection period	Net sales to inventory	Fixed assets to tangible net worth	Current debt to tangible net worth	Total debt to tangible net worth	Inventory to net working capital	Current debt to inventory	Funded debts to net working capital
	Times	Per cent	Per cent	Per cent	Times	Times	Days	Times	Per cent	Per cent	Per cent	Per cent	Per cent	Per cent
5075 & 78 Air Condtg. & Refrigtn. Equipt. & Supplies (53)	4.21	3.78	16.66	21.43	7.49	7.89	37	10.5	6.7	26.4	76.6	64.0	51.1	14.8
	2.45	**2.38**	**11.39**	**12.61**	**4.50**	**5.03**	**49**	**6.1**	**15.7**	**64.0**	**118.1**	**99.6**	**91.1**	**29.9**
	1.76	1.52	4.61	7.33	2.53	3.29	63	4.5	22.4	117.7	199.4	134.0	127.2	53.3
5013 Automotive Parts & Supplies (161)	4.47	4.73	18.01	21.99	5.33	6.54	27	7.2	8.7	26.1	49.6	66.2	36.7	10.7
	3.07	**3.03**	**12.09**	**13.95**	**3.80**	**4.54**	**33**	**4.9**	**16.4**	**48.3**	**82.9**	**87.8**	**60.2**	**23.4**
	2.16	1.19	5.18	8.36	2.66	3.25	43	3.6	39.6	98.0	144.0	116.7	91.7	46.3
5181 & 82 Beer, Wine & Alcoholic Beverages (111)	3.81	2.97	17.89	31.98	11.01	18.69	7	17.7	15.5	27.6	62.1	64.3	54.8	8.3
	2.24	**1.59**	**10.71**	**15.86**	**7.95**	**10.94**	**20**	**9.9**	**29.7**	**64.4**	**112.7**	**104.1**	**83.2**	**29.3**
	1.58	0.62	3.93	6.62	5.03	6.85	34	7.1	53.3	149.7	267.1	172.9	113.7	53.2
5161 Chemicals & Allied Products (57)	4.01	4.73	21.17	36.69	7.55	12.38	41	15.9	17.4	28.8	75.4	33.8	88.2	11.2
	2.24	**3.38**	**14.39**	**21.47**	**4.74**	**7.49**	**45**	**11.4**	**27.0**	**67.8**	**107.5**	**65.8**	**137.7**	**36.5**
	1.61	2.03	10.02	14.71	3.51	4.79	60	7.5	61.1	129.6	224.6	97.8	218.0	94.2
5137 Clothing & Accessories, Women's, Children's & Infants' (71)	3.88	4.51	19.70	29.85	9.56	11.11	25	15.5	3.2	32.6	46.3	39.8	68.0	7.1
	2.30	**1.99**	**6.97**	**15.08**	**4.56**	**5.32**	**41**	**11.4**	**8.6**	**93.3**	**136.5**	**70.7**	**116.3**	**28.0**
	1.56	0.67	0.94	4.38	2.73	3.47	59	5.2	35.9	204.7	306.3	124.6	180.9	43.8
5136 Clothing & Furnishings, Men's & Boys' (71)	4.00	5.26	19.54	24.65	7.90	8.17	21	8.7	2.6	33.6	71.3	52.6	58.9	7.8
	2.36	**2.05**	**11.55**	**14.05**	**4.98**	**5.16**	**36**	**5.0**	**8.4**	**72.4**	**103.4**	**72.8**	**98.0**	**28.4**
	1.64	0.58	4.38	4.90	2.21	3.76	54	3.7	37.4	200.0	245.7	106.5	130.6	49.9
5081 Commercial Machines & Equipment (59)	3.53	8.43	21.22	34.03	8.04	10.25	28	18.5	7.3	32.1	47.1	38.6	60.6	8.7
	2.30	**3.32**	**12.28**	**17.59**	**5.35**	**5.75**	**48**	**7.9**	**19.3**	**60.4**	**91.8**	**77.8**	**141.4**	**18.8**
	1.65	1.69	6.65	9.93	2.66	3.55	63	5.8	30.0	138.3	159.0	91.6	195.8	53.8

5145 Confectionery (43)	4.59	3.28	18.26	28.05	13.33	18.90	12	20.5	6.0	33.9	65.7	60.5	42.9	15.1
	2.63	**1.18**	**11.09**	**15.03**	**7.05**	**9.10**	**17**	**12.4**	**16.3**	**57.6**	**111.4**	**76.2**	**79.2**	**28.2**
	1.86	0.61	5.65	6.78	3.16	5.87	25	7.8	43.1	101.7	238.9	112.1	109.1	86.6
5143 Dairy Products (56)	2.68	2.86	19.86	60.58	24.29	35.98	20	102.9	16.1	28.1	86.7	12.8	140.6	23.8
	1.51	**1.42**	**12.74**	**23.23**	**9.68**	**15.21**	**25**	**39.3**	**39.6**	**97.7**	**182.6**	**40.4**	**254.4**	**84.2**
	1.17	0.49	3.12	9.73	4.12	7.93	35	18.0	78.8	200.0	377.5	143.8	443.1	225.5
5122 Drugs, Drug Proprietaries & Sundries (91)	2.93	2.70	18.59	23.69	13.29	14.44	19	9.7	10.0	46.8	69.7	74.8	52.4	11.6
	2.12	**1.61**	**10.62**	**13.33**	**6.06**	**7.87**	**34**	**7.1**	**21.0**	**76.0**	**126.9**	**97.2**	**92.3**	**28.9**
	1.55	0.95	3.83	5.29	4.12	5.31	44	6.0	49.9	163.8	245.8	143.0	129.3	64.4
5063 Electrical Apparatus & Equipment (132)	2.98	3.19	16.31	20.08	8.17	8.40	36	9.8	7.1	43.2	68.7	64.0	70.0	8.4
	2.30	**2.08**	**10.09**	**11.56**	**5.17**	**5.57**	**45**	**6.8**	**17.5**	**69.0**	**95.8**	**84.4**	**93.2**	**16.1**
	1.83	0.94	3.47	5.39	3.42	4.13	53	4.8	32.8	148.5	214.6	107.6	133.3	41.3
5064 Electrical Appliances, TV & Radio Sets (101)	2.79	4.16	17.98	19.59	8.65	8.78	27	6.5	4.6	48.0	70.9	72.5	67.4	5.4
	1.99	**1.97**	**9.38**	**11.22**	**4.89**	**6.35**	**40**	**5.6**	**11.4**	**83.7**	**110.9**	**103.5**	**94.9**	**22.1**
	1.57	0.99	4.13	5.60	3.26	3.61	58	4.4	27.1	189.8	245.4	134.8	131.2	43.0
5065 Electronic Parts & Equipment (61)	4.00	4.83	22.25	24.94	8.43	9.18	31	7.6	8.6	29.2	73.3	63.9	41.0	12.8
	2.22	**3.00**	**13.81**	**17.37**	**5.22**	**5.68**	**41**	**5.5**	**17.9**	**74.3**	**144.4**	**100.1**	**77.3**	**22.5**
	1.67	1.60	7.68	9.48	3.29	3.73	54	4.0	33.9	182.6	294.8	144.6	113.3	65.3
5083 Farm & Garden Machinery & Equipment (147)	2.75	5.36	19.09	26.77	6.76	8.64	20	6.4	9.7	46.8	88.8	80.4	64.7	10.8
	1.78	**2.70**	**10.68**	**15.21**	**4.72**	**6.07**	**32**	**4.1**	**21.6**	**104.7**	**149.5**	**116.6**	**87.1**	**26.9**
	1.44	1.44	3.14	7.67	2.76	3.44	50	2.9	39.8	169.6	223.9	194.9	106.7	69.0
5139 Footwear (69)	4.55	4.46	21.17	22.95	6.43	6.64	27	9.0	2.2	34.1	52.9	46.4	47.0	3.7
	2.63	**1.91**	**12.95**	**14.07**	**4.65**	**4.80**	**57**	**5.5**	**4.8**	**66.7**	**110.4**	**72.7**	**106.8**	**17.5**
	1.80	0.27	1.72	2.10	2.86	3.49	93	3.6	16.8	140.5	185.5	106.5	158.0	48.9
5148 Fresh Fruits & Vegetables (76)	2.78	2.49	22.33	47.76	17.28	31.05	13	108.9	16.7	30.7	60.8	10.6	133.9	28.9
	1.84	**1.03**	**10.03**	**16.59**	**10.17**	**15.17**	**21**	**65.2**	**48.0**	**78.2**	**122.6**	**40.0**	**290.3**	**72.1**
	1.28	0.13	0.66	4.39	5.00	7.66	32	16.9	92.4	175.1	266.6	81.0	586.5	95.6

Figure 3.8 Page from "Key Business Ratios."

Cost of Doing Business Ratios—Corporations

The following operating ratios for 190 lines of business have been derived to provide a guide as to the average amount spent by corporations for these items. They represent a percentage of business receipts as reported by a representative sample of the total of all Federal Income Tax returns* filed for 1974-75.

Industry	Total Number of Returns Filed	Cost of Goods Sold	Gross Margin	SELECTED OPERATING EXPENSES								
				Compen-sation of Officers	Rent Paid on Business Property	Repairs	Bad Debts	Interest Paid	Taxes Paid†	Amortiza-tion Deprecia-tion Depletion	Adver-tising	Pension & Other Employee Benefit Plans
		%	%	%	%	%	%	%	%	%	%	%
ALL INDUSTRIES	1,965,894	72.44	27.56	1.86	1.32	0.78	0.45	4.66	2.62	3.45	0.86	1.28
CONTRACT CONSTRUCTION	185,563	81.89	18.11	3.49	0.64	0.55	0.32	1.41	2.11	1.97	0.22	0.93
General Building Contractors & Operative Builders	74,694	87.46	12.54	2.67	0.44	0.30	0.22	1.83	1.46	1.23	0.24	0.54
Heavy Construction Contractors	14,895	80.12	19.88	2.25	0.79	1.14	0.31	1.54	2.14	3.96	0.10	1.10
Special Trade Contractors	95,974	76.27	23.73	5.13	0.79	0.51	0.43	0.84	2.87	1.77	0.26	1.30
RETAILERS & WHOLESALERS	602,423	78.02	21.98	1.68	1.33	0.32	0.26	1.05	1.41	0.91	0.89	0.45
RETAIL TRADE	386,772	71.37	28.63	1.81	2.26	0.43	0.30	1.23	1.81	1.21	1.54	0.52
Building Materials, Garden Supplies, & Mobile Home Dealers	31,319	73.31	26.69	2.98	1.33	0.45	0.65	1.30	1.87	1.23	1.05	0.54
General Merchandise Stores	10,996	63.46	36.54	0.38	2.66	0.46	0.55	2.47	2.31	1.39	2.62	0.64
Food Stores	26,335	78.96	21.04	0.61	1.48	0.41	0.05	0.38	1.20	0.97	0.88	0.69

Automotive Dealers & Service Stations	63,863	82.77	17.23	1.72	1.06	0.26	0.17	1.24	1.18	0.79	0.81	0.27
Motor Vehicle Dealers	32,965	84.53	15.47	1.44	0.91	0.21	0.15	1.33	0.96	0.71	0.87	0.26
Gasoline Service Stations	12,662	80.44	19.56	1.95	1.35	0.39	0.14	0.57	2.08	1.05	0.21	0.21
Other Automotive Dealers	18,236	70.71	29.29	3.86	2.00	0.43	0.37	1.34	1.83	1.16	1.17	0.44
Apparel & Accessory Stores	38,529	60.52	39.48	3.50	5.47	0.34	0.30	0.84	2.19	1.14	2.18	0.60
Furniture & Home Furnishings Stores	36,044	64.54	35.46	4.18	3.02	0.35	0.62	1.33	2.04	0.99	3.40	0.50
Eating & Drinking Places	76,601	46.12	53.88	3.54	4.94	1.23	0.13	1.35	3.81	2.81	1.73	0.44
Drug Stores & Proprietary Stores	20,316	70.31	29.69	3.01	3.05	0.28	0.11	0.66	1.67	0.88	1.12	0.51
Liquor Stores	12,074	80.10	19.90	3.04	1.68	0.32	0.06	0.52	2.03	0.77	0.50	0.18
Other Retail Stores	70,695	65.13	34.87	3.75	2.69	0.45	0.54	1.02	2.07	1.63	2.05	0.53
WHOLESALE TRADE	214,975	83.64	16.36	1.56	0.55	0.22	0.23	0.90	1.07	0.65	0.33	0.38
Groceries & Related Products	20,870	88.15	11.85	1.05	0.46	0.23	0.14	0.46	0.67	0.51	0.22	0.33
Machinery, Equipment & Supplies	45,391	74.88	25.12	2.75	0.71	0.26	0.34	1.09	1.15	1.02	0.42	0.60
Motor Vehicles & Automotive Equipment	18,292	78.86	21.14	2.02	0.91	0.19	0.23	1.21	1.12	0.64	1.03	0.40
Drugs, Chemicals & Allied Products	7,801	79.83	20.17	0.94	0.46	0.24	0.22	0.98	1.06	1.41	0.29	0.33
Apparel, Piece Goods & Notions	10,137	78.48	21.52	2.97	1.19	0.09	0.39	1.19	1.43	0.42	0.49	0.45
Farm-Product Raw Materials	7,161	93.76	6.24	0.40	0.18	0.23	0.07	0.62	0.30	0.42	0.07	0.11
Electrical Goods	13,728	76.42	23.58	2.26	0.79	0.17	0.47	1.11	1.14	0.48	0.88	0.57
Hardware, Plumbing & Heating Equipment	10,375	76.49	23.51	2.63	0.83	0.19	0.54	0.82	1.25	0.58	0.33	0.72
Alcoholic Beverages	4,619	79.02	20.98	1.37	0.50	0.20	0.10	0.45	5.15	0.52	0.55	0.50
Lumber & Construction Materials	9,956	81.57	18.43	2.09	0.55	0.29	0.50	1.17	1.15	0.90	0.29	0.43
Metals & Minerals, except Petroleum & Scrap	4,340	85.66	14.34	1.17	0.28	0.16	0.16	0.70	0.73	0.42	0.06	0.37
Petroleum & Petroleum Products	8,981	89.35	10.65	1.00	0.51	0.29	0.14	0.51	1.39	0.83	0.10	0.25
Paper & Paper Products	4,683	78.92	21.08	2.29	0.77	0.17	0.28	0.65	0.95	0.42	0.18	0.55
Other Wholesale Trade, Durable & Nondurable Goods Combined	48,641	83.96	16.04	1.68	0.57	0.22	0.25	1.43	1.05	0.55	0.37	0.37

Copyright Dun & Bradstreet, Inc. 1978 / Permission to reprint or reproduce in any form whatsoever in whole or in part should be obtained from Dun & Bradstreet, Inc. 99 Church Street, New York, N.Y. 10007, Att: Public Relations & Advertising Department

Figure 3.9 Page from "Cost of Doing Business."

PHOTOFINISHERS*

Profit and Loss (As Percent of Net Sales)	Under $1,000,000	$1,000,000-$5,000,000	Over 5,000,000
Gross Profit	42.57	44.11	41.93
Employee Salaries	13.29	13.63	11.48
Rent	1.36	2.06	3.56
Advertising	8.28	2.00	1.04
Depreciation	4.60	3.30	2.66
Total Expenses	37.30	38.59	37.75
Net Profit	5.27	5.52	4.18
Balance Sheet Ratios			
Current Ratio (times)	1.74	1.66	1.42
Quick Ratio (times)	1.20	1.14	1.07
Liabilities to Investment	44.12%	119.80%	70.08%
Inventory to Working Capital	60.65%	67.87%	74.81%
Other Operating Ratios			
Inventory Turnover (times)	10.19	9.75	12.20
Return on Net Worth (percent)	12.79	31.21	11.15
Return on Total Assets (percent)	7.13	19.54	6.55
Sales to Net Worth (times)	3.73	5.65	3.92
Sales to Working Capital (times)	10.54	11.72	15.58

**Photo Marketing Association – Master Data Report, 1976.*

SOURCE: "1977–1978 Wolfman Report"
130 East 59th Street, New York, N.Y. 10022

PHOTO DEALERS 1976*

Profit and Loss (As Percent of Net Sales)	Volume Under $500,000	Volume Over $500,000
Gross Profit	31.36	27.98
Employee Salaries	13.62	14.38
Rent and/or Depreciation	3.01	2.84
Advertising	2.11	1.76
Total Expenses	26.38	26.22
Net Profit	4.98	1.76
Balance Sheet Ratios		
Current Ratios (times)	2.08	1.94
Quick Ratio (times)	0.54	0.58
Liabilities to Investment	112.84%	140.97%
Inventory to Working Capital	137.27%	135.01%
Other Operating Ratios		
Inventory Turnover (times)	2.74	3.66
Return on Net Worth (percent)	22.8	8.72
Return on Total Assets (percent)	10.36	3.57
Sales to Net Worth (times)	4.7	6.63
Sales to Working Capital (times)	5.44	6.75

**Photo Marketing Association – Master Data Report, 1976.*

SOURCE: "1977–1978 Wolfman Report"
130 East 59th Street, New York, N.Y. 10022

Figure 3.10 Page from *Expenses in Retailing*.

Mechanical Contractors Association of America, 666 Third Avenue, Suite 1464, New York, N.Y. 10017

Menswear Retailers of America, 390 National Press Building, Washington, D.C. 20004

Motor and Equipment Manufacturers Association, 250 West 57th Street, New York, N.Y. 10019

National-American Wholesale Lumber Association, 180 Madison Avenue, New York, N.Y. 10016

National Appliance and Radio-TV Dealers Association, 1319 Merchandise Mart, Chicago, Ill. 60654

National Association of Accountants, 525 Park Avenue, New York, N.Y. 10022

National Association of Building Owners and Managers, 134 South LaSalle Street, Chicago, Ill. 60603

National Association of Electrical Distributors, 600 Madison Avenue, New York, N.Y. 10022

National Association of Food Chains, 1725 Eye Street, NW, Washington, D.C. 20006

National Association of Furniture Manufacturers, 666 North Lake Shore Drive, Chicago, Ill. 60611

National Association of Insurance Agents, 96 Fulton Street, New York, N.Y. 10038

National Association of Music Merchants, Inc., 222 West Adams Street, Chicago, Ill. 60606

National Association of Plastic Distributors, 2217 Tribune Tower, Chicago, Ill. 60611

National Association of Retail Grocers of the United States, 360 North Michigan Avenue, Chicago, Ill. 60601

National Association of Textile and Apparel Wholesalers, 350 Fifth Avenue, New York, N.Y. 10001

National Association of Tobacco Distributors, 360 Lexington Avenue, New York, N.Y. 10017

National Automatic Merchandising Association, Seven South Dearborn Street, Chicago, Ill. 60603

National Beer Wholesalers' Association of America, 6310 North Cicero Avenue, Chicago, Ill. 60646

National Builders' Hardware Association, 1290 Avenue of the Americas, New York, N.Y. 10019

National Electrical Contractors Association, 1200 18th Street, NW, Washington, D.C. 20036

National Electrical Manufacturers Association, 155 East 44th Street, New York, N.Y. 10017

National Farm and Power Equipment Dealers Association, 2340 Hampton Avenue, St. Louis, Mo. 63130

National Home Furnishing Association, 1150 Merchandise Mart, Chicago, Ill. 60654

National Kitchen Cabinet Association, 918 Commonwealth Building, 674 South 4th Street, Louisville, Ky. 40204

National Lumber and Building Material Dealers Association, Ring Building, Washington, D.C. 20036

National Office Products Association, Investment Building, 1511 K Street, NW, Washington, D.C. 20015

National Machine Tool Builders Association, 2071 East 102d Street, Cleveland, Ohio 44106

National Oil Jobbers Council, 1001 Connecticut Avenue, NW, Washington, D.C. 20036

National Paper Box Manufacturers Association, 121 North Broad Street, Suite 910, Philadelphia, Pa. 19107

National Paper Trade Association, 220 East 42d Street, New York, N.Y. 10017

National Parking Association, 1101 17th Street, NW, Washington, D.C. 20036

National Restaurant Association, 1530 North Lake Shore Drive, Chicago, Ill. 60610

National Retail Furniture Association, 1150 Merchandise Mart Plaza, Chicago, Ill. 60654

National Retail Hardware Association, 964 North Pennsylvania Avenue, Indianapolis, Ind. 46204

National Retail Merchants Association, 100 West 31st Street, New York, N.Y. 10001

National Shoe Retailers Association, 200 Madison Avenue, New York, N.Y. 10016

National Sporting Goods Association, 23 East Jackson Boulevard, Chicago, Ill. 60604

National Stationery and Office Equipment Association, Investment Building, 1511 K Street, NW, Washington, D.C. 20005

National Tire Dealers and Retreaders Association, 1343 L Street, NW, Washington, D.C. 20005

National Wholesale Druggists' Association, 220 East 42d Street, New York, N.Y. 10017

Industry association studies generally contain valuable information that help you with both market analysis and projections. Information includes sales trends in metropolitan and rural areas, distribution of state trends, and the expense and cost of sales percentages. If the association of your industry is listed here, I suggest you write to it for information.

The government is the best source of general business information, and some of their publications are very helpful.

The most current and completely developed ratio data are published jointly by the Federal Trade Commission (FTC) and the Securities and Exchange Commission (SEC) in the form of the *Quarterly Financial Report for Manufacturing Corporations*. These are available only for broadly defined industry groups. The data cover all manufacturing corporations except newspapers and related subgroups.

The SBA publishes a series called the *Starting-and-Managing Series*, available from the SBA or the U.S. Government Printing Office. Very few libraries have copies. This series has a pamphlet for each type of business. The books discuss capital requirements, competition, licenses, business terms, service requirements, operation, quality control, customers, financial reports, law, and other topics. The Department of Commerce has a more recent series of pamphlets called the *Urban Business Profile Series*, which is similar in scope.

The IRS publishes annually (with a three-year lag) the *Statistics of Income, Business Income Tax Returns*. The reports represent selected income statement, balance sheet, and tax items obtained from federal income tax returns. The Bureau of the Census publishes *The Census of Business* at five-year intervals, which provides limited ratio and dollar financial data, mostly in the wholesale trade area.

The following are publications of *The Census of Business:*

1. *Retail Trade* presents statistics by kinds of business for states, standard metropolitan statistical areas (SMSAs), counties, and cities of 2,500 or more. It includes data on the number of establishments, sales, payroll, and personnel.
2. *Wholesale Trade* presents data on the number of establishments, sales, payroll, and personnel for kinds of businesses in states, SMSAs, and counties.
3. *Selected Services* includes data on hotels, motels, barbershops, beauty parlors, and other retail service organizations. It lists the number of establishments, receipts, and payrolls for states, SMSAs, counties, and cities.
4. *County and City Data Book* is a comprehensive basic reference book giving data for counties, cities, and SMSAs. Data presented are taken from the censuses of business, manufacturers, and governments, the census of agriculture, the census of population, and other censuses.
5. *County Business Patterns* is based on Social Security tax records. It gives a series of separate reports for each state and "United States Summary" gives data on employment, size of reporting units, and taxable payrolls for various segments of the economy. It is useful for analyzing market potentials.

Census tracts are important sources of information for retail businesses selling to the public at large. A city map shows you the area from which your business will draw. Look up the following areas in the census tracts: population, income characteristics, population growth, and age characteristics.

The *local government* can also be a good source of information. Local chambers of commerce often have good general information about a town, including business areas, zoning, population growth, other population characteristics, and expected growth areas. The chamber of commerce might also provide you with contacts that could help your business marketing analysis and perhaps your future sales.

The traffic department of each local or county government has automobile traffic counts for your location. You might also study traffic counts at several different locations before you decide on a particular place to locate a business.

The *Bank of America Small Business Reporter* series is another guide to the specifics of certain industries. We have personally used these publications and suggest that if your business is one of the following, you order for $1.00 the appropriate booklet. There are booklets available on the following: apparel manufacturing, apparel stores, automobile parts and accessory stores, bars and cocktail lounges, bicycle stores, bookstores, building maintenance services, daycare centers, drugstores, coin-operated dry cleaning, equipment rental services, food stores, gift shops, handicraft businesses, health food stores, home furnishing stores, coin-operated laundries, liquor stores, mail order businesses, manufacturing, mobile home and recreation vehicle dealers, mobile home parts suppliers, retail nurseries, pet shops, plant shops, printing shops, repair services, service stations, sewing and needlecraft centers, shoe stores, and sporting goods stores.

Enquiries can be addressed to: *Small Business Reporter*, Bank of America, Department 3120, P.O. Box 37000, San Francisco, California 94137 (Phone: 415-622-2491).

Your Business Resources

From business resources, the following information can be gathered:

List of customers.

Sales history.

List of products sold.

List of major competitors.

The list of customers should certainly include the ten largest customers, and the more the better. If you are in a retail or service business, you will not have a list of major customers. A new business can provide a list of *expected* customers. This list can be compiled from research or from communication with future customers.

A sales history should show what the sales have been since the beginning of the business. Introduction of new products, marketing compaigns, and so on, should be discussed. This can be a one-page typed summary giving a brief overview. If you business is a new one, there will be no business sales history.

A list of products that your company sells or expects to sell helps a lender understand your line of merchandise. If you are already in business, you should know who your major four to six competitors are. These should be listed by name and address. If you are starting a new business, this information can be found by talking with others in the industry and doing some library research.

Figure 3.11 provides some forms you might use to report business resources.

List of Customers

Name	Address	Contract Value per Year
________	____________________	______________
________	____________________	______________
________	____________________	______________
________	____________________	______________
________	____________________	______________
________	____________________	______________
________	____________________	______________
________	____________________	______________
________	____________________	______________
________	____________________	______________

Sales History

First year in business ________

Sales, first year ________

Present annual sales ________

New products developed and dates ________

____

____

Product List

The following are our major products and sales:

Product	Price	Last Annual Sales	Expected Sales
____	___	________	________
____	___	________	________
____	___	________	________

List of Major Competitors

Name	Address	Annual Sales
____________	________________	______________
____________	________________	______________
____________	________________	______________
____________	________________	______________

Figure 3.11 Business resource reporting forms.

OTHER DOCUMENTATION

In addition to the financial and market information already discussed, certain other documents and information may be required. This information is usually not necessary as source data for the actual preparation of the loan proposal but must be part of the loan proposal to satisfy bank and SBA requirements or needs. It is usually presented as an exhibit.

Businesses Documents

From all businesses, the following documents are needed:

Corporation or partnership papers.
Copy of the premises lease or property deed.
Company brochures (optional).

Corporation and partnership papers include articles of incorporation, certification by the secretary of state, bylaws, and written partnership papers.

The lenders usually require a copy of the premises lease or, if the business property is owned by the business, a copy of the deed of trust. This is so that the bank can check rental provisions or, if the property is company owned, so that it can file the proper collateral agreements.

If your company has brochures or catalogs, it is nice to have these as part of the loan proposal, although they are not required by the lender.

Owner Documents

From the owners of the business, the following documents should be gathered:

Personal income tax records for the last three years.
A copy of the deed or trust to all personal real property.

The inclusion of copies of personal income tax records of all the business owners is required by the SBA. The copy of the deed to real property is needed by the bank so that it will have the necessary information to collateralize the property. The lender wants a secondary source of repayment for the loan.

Research Documents

You should provide photostatic copies of all the printed material you used for your financial projections and market research. This would include the seasonal adjustments data, interest tables, articles, books, and so on. The copies allow the lender to check your sources.

IMPORTANCE OF DATA

We would like to reemphasize the importance of this financial data, market data, and other documentation. Until you have this information, you cannot proceed with preparing the loan proposal. Most of this data is *required* by the government or bank and is necessary for consideration your loan application.

Library research might give you trouble at first, but if you read this book carefully, you should be able to understand it quickly.

Remember, acquiring the necessary data as described in this chapter can take you from 10 to 40 hours or more. Do not shortchange yourself on time, or you may end up with carelessly prepared and inadequate data. This will negatively affect your whole loan proposal.

SUMMARY

To prepare the loan application and get the maximum bank response, three types of data are necessary: (1) financial information, (2) market information, and (3) other documents.

The financial data are the most important and include from your business the last three years' financial statements (balance sheet and income statement), an aging of accounts receivable, and a list of what you will use the loan for (use of funds). Personal information required includes personal financial statements, income tax records, and schedule of ownership.

From research, you must find what your monthly interest and principal costs will be, what percentages the industry uses for expense, seasonal sales adjustments, and other business data.

Lenders may require other documentation such as partnership or coporation papers, leases, and company advertising material.

Chapter Four

Financial Calculations: Annual Projections

FINANCIAL STATEMENTS AND TECHNICAL TERMS

Income Statement

The most recognizable financial statement is called a profit and loss statement or income statement. The IRS requires that all businesses submit a profit and loss statement at the end of each year to show their net income for that year. Figure 4.1 is a sample profit and loss statement. Notes to explain each major term are presented immediately after the statement. For Figure 4.1, they would read as follows:

(1) *Sales or gross receipts* represent the total amount of money that a business receives from the sale of its merchandise or services.

(2) *Cost of goods sold* is, literally, the cost of the merchandise that the business sells. This cost differs with each type of business. For a retail business, the cost of sales is the cost of the merchandise bought from the wholesaler or jobber. It is calculated by taking the beginning inventory that the business has at the start of the period, adding the purchases of goods during the period, and subtracting out the ending inventory that the business has at the end of the period. This procedure will indicate exactly how many goods purchased are sold. For a manufacturing business, cost of sales includes the inventory as described for retailing and also the cost of labor to manufacture the goods, the freight charges, and the direct costs of running the factory (factory overhead).

(3) *Operating expense*, also called business expense, includes all the costs of the business not directly related to the cost of the merchandise. In other words, the operating expense is the cost of the fiscal plant (rent), salaries, and other costs that must be paid on a regular, recurring basis. Operating expense includes:

Rent on the business, including equipment rental.

Repairs on the facility or equipment and maintenance of the building and equipment.

All salaries except factory salaries (which are included in the cost of goods sold).

Payroll taxes.

Employee benefits such as shared-cost medical, pension, and profit-sharing plans.

Taxes, licenses, and fees.

Sales or gross receipts (1)		$______
Beginning inventory	$______	
Inventory purchased	______	
Less ending inventory	______	
Cost of goods sold (2)		$______
Gross profit		$______
Less business expenses		
Operating expense (3)		
Rent	$______	
Depreciation	______	
Repairs and maintenance	______	
Salaries and wages	______	
Payroll taxes and fringe Benefits@ 10%	______	
Taxes, licenses, and fees	______	
Insurance	______	
Accounting, legal, and professional fees	______	
Bad debts	______	
Telephone	______	
Utilities	______	
Supplies	______	
Security	______	
Auto and truck	______	
Advertising and promotion	______	
Interest	______	
Miscellaneous	______	
Total expenses		$______
Net profit before taxes (4)		$______
Federal income taxes (Corporation only)		$______
Net profit		$______

Figure 4.1 Sample profit and loss statement.

Insurance.
Accounting, legal, and professional fees.
Bad debts such as bounced checks.
Telephone and utilities.
Supplies for either the office or the store.
Security, alarm systems, or guards.
Automobile and truck expenses.
Advertising and promotion.
Interest on business debts.
Miscellaneous.
Entertainment.
Travel.
Depreciation.

Depreciation is an expense of the business even though it is not a cash expense. Depreciation is the money the business charges off to pay for the declining value of its machinery.

(4) *Net profit before taxes* equals the sales less the cost of sales less the operating expense.

To get some perspective on the income statement, let's take another look at the circle of accounts with the income, expense, and cost of sales pieces in place (see Figure 4.2).

Income is the source of money. Cost of sales and expense are the uses of money. When income is reduced by cost of sales, the result is gross profit. When income is further reduced by expense, net profit before tax is left.

Income − cost of sales − expense = net profit

Figure 4.3 is an illustration of a balance sheet from the *Small Business Reporter*, Vol. 7, No. 11, "Understanding Financial Statements." Refer to the figure for further clarification of the following:

1. *Current assets* are cash, accounts receivable, and inventory. Current assets also include prepaid expenses; stocks in other businesses; bonds used for investment; and notes owed the business, payable in one year. Current assets are assets that presumably could be turned into cash within one year.
2. *Fixed assets*, or long-term assets, include equipment, real estate, leasehold improvements, and sometimes long-term investments or long-term notes owed the company. Fixed assets are those possessions of the business that can't be sold quickly.
3. *Other assets* (not illustrated) include such items as money (notes) due from officers or employees and prepaid expenses (last month's rent, security deposits, association deposits).
4. *Current liabilities* are notes payable to a bank or others within a year, accounts payable to trade suppliers, and unpaid taxes. They also include accrued expenses (those not yet paid) and the current portion of long-term debt (that is, that portion of long-term debt due within one year that has to be paid in one year).
5. *Long-term liabilities* are those debts that are to be paid after this year. Besides mortgages (as illustrated), long-term liabilities also include the long-term por-

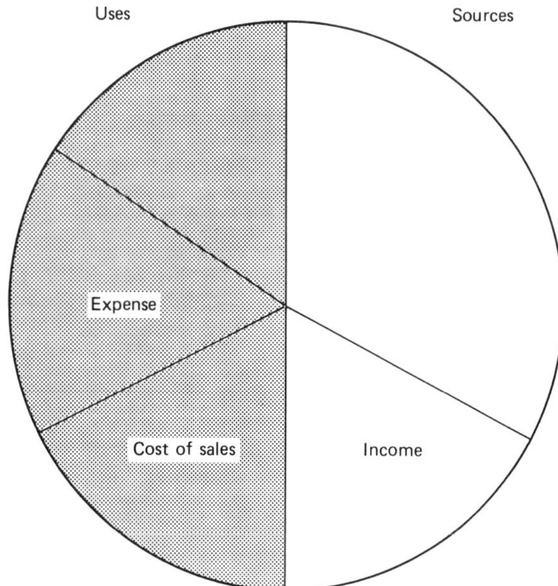

Figure 4.2 Circle of accounts.

BALANCE SHEET

This is how the business looks on a specific date.

ASSETS

What the business itself owns.

CURRENT ASSETS: In varying states of being converted into cash—within the next 12 months.

CASH: Money on hand, in the bank.

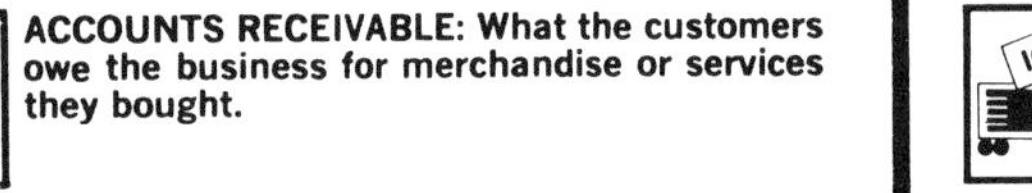

ACCOUNTS RECEIVABLE: What the customers owe the business for merchandise or services they bought.

INVENTORY: Merchandise on hand:
1) ready to be sold
2) in some stage of production
3) raw material

FIXED ASSETS: Used in the operation of the business. Not intended for resale.

REAL ESTATE: Land and buildings used by the business. Listed at original cost.

LEASEHOLD IMPROVEMENTS: Permanent installations—remodeling or refurbishing of the premises.

MACHINERY, EQUIPMENT, VEHICLES: Used by the business. Listed at original cost.

Less Accumulated Depreciation: These assets (except land) lose value through wear, tear and age. The business claims this loss of value as an expense of doing business. The running total of this expense is the accumulated depreciation.

NET FIXED ASSETS: Cost of fixed assets less depreciation = Present Value.

LIABILITIES

This side of the balance sheet shows the claims on the assets—by both creditors and owners of the business. The claims of creditors are debts of the business—the LIABILITIES. The owner's claim is the investment in the business—the NET WORTH.

CURRENT LIABILITIES: Debts owed by the business to be paid within the next 12 months.

NOTES PAYABLE: IOU Bank or Trade Creditors.

ACCOUNTS PAYABLE: IOU Trade & Suppliers.

INCOME TAXES: IOU Government.

LONG-TERM LIABILITIES: Debts owed by the business to be paid beyond the next 12 months.

MORTGAGE: On property.

NET WORTH

Owner's (or stockholders' claim on the assets of the business; the investment; equity in the business.

For Proprietorship or Partnership:
CAPITAL: Owner's original investment plus any profit reinvested in the business.
For Corporation:
CAPITAL STOCK: Value assigned to the original issue of stock by the directors of the corporation. If the stock sold for more than the assigned value, the excess will show as....
SURPLUS PAID IN: The difference between assigned value and selling price of the original issue of stock. (The subsequent selling price of stock does not change assigned value.)
RETAINED EARNINGS: Profits reinvested in the business AFTER paying dividends.

BALANCE SHEET EQUATION:
ASSETS = LIABILITIES + NET WORTH

Figure 4.3 (Reprinted courtesy of Bank of America).

tion as long-term debt (the total debt minus that part of the debt which will be paid off in the next year).

6. *Net worth* is the difference between assets and liabilities.

Assets are a use of funds. Liabilities and owners' equity are sources of funds. Figure 4.4 again shows the accounts circle.

The total dollar amount of assets equals the dollar amount of liabilities plus equity.

$$\text{Assets} = \text{liabilities} + \text{equity}$$

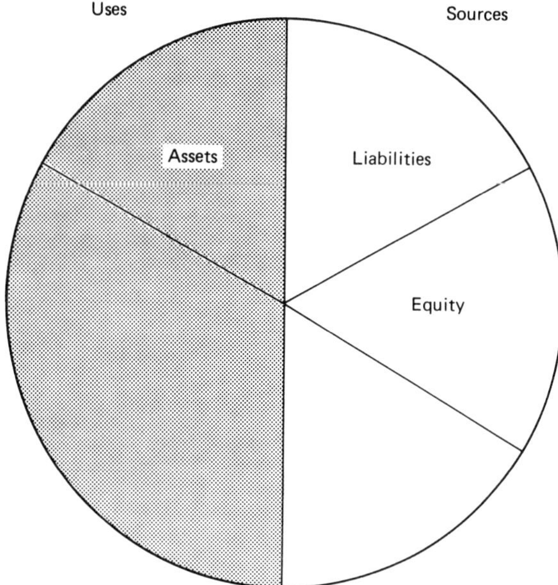

Figure 4.4 Circle of accounts.

Reconcilement (or Reconciliation) of Net Worth Statement

Currently the SBA may require a reconciliation of net worth statement in addition to the standard profit and loss statement and balance sheet. If yours is an existing business, you should have an accountant prepare the reconciliation statement (see Figure 4.5).

Net profit less taxes and withdrawals is retained in the equity of the business and is called *retained earnings* (see Figure 4.6).

Retained earnings equal net profit minus taxes minus withdrawals:

$$\text{Retained earnings} = \text{net profit} - \text{taxes} - \text{withdrawals}$$

Other Terms and Definitions

In preparing the loan analysis, you may run across some unfamiliar financial terms. Following is a list of terms and their definitions.

Cost of sales as a percentage of sales, or cost of sales percentage is derived by dividing cost of sales by sales. For example, if sales are $50,000 and cost of sales

Reconciliation of Net Worth	
Net worth at beginning of period	$____
Add:	
Net profit after taxes (or subtract loss)	$____
Other additions:	
Sales of assets.	
increase in money invested in business.	
sale of stock, etc.	$____
Less:	
Owners' or officers' withdrawals or dividends	$____
Net Worth as shown on balance sheet.	$____

Figure 4.5 Reconciliation of net worth.

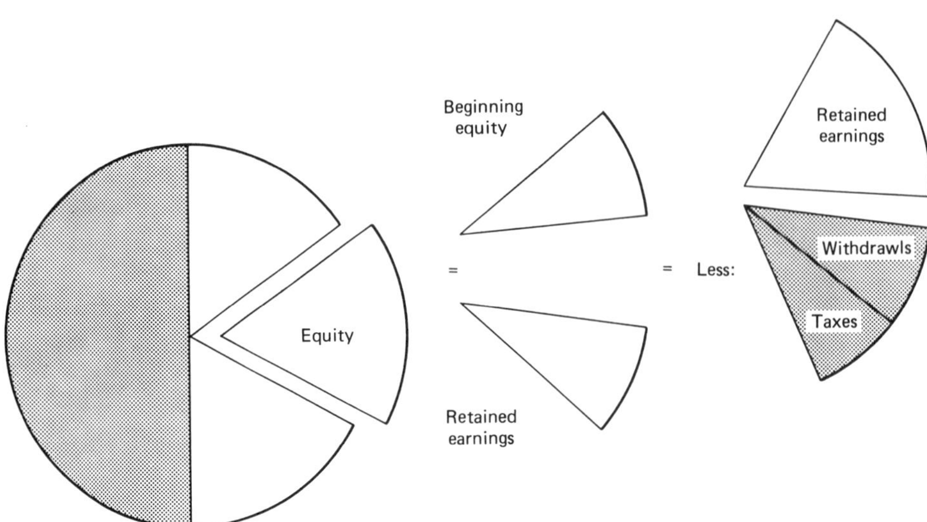

Figure 4.6 Retained earnings.

is $25,000, then the cost of sales percentage is $50,000 divided by $25,000, or 50%.

Cash margin is the amount of cash a business has left after it pays all expenses, principal loan payment, income tax, and owner's salary.

Cash flow represents how cash moves through the system. For example, a business has $1,000 cash sales and pays $500 for cost of sales, $400 for expenses, $50 for principal loan repayment, and $30 for owner's salary, leaving a $20 cash margin. This shows how the cash comes in and is paid out. The same business sells $1,000 on *credit;* that is, it has no *cash* sales but has to pay out all the cash expenses as described. Instead of having in the end a $20 cash margin, it has a $980 negative cash margin—the business has paid out $980 more than it took in. An example of the cash flow of cash sales versus credit sales is shown in Figure 4.7.

Variable expense is that expense which varies as sales do. If sales increase, variable expenses increase. One example of variable expense is a salesperson's commission.

Cash flow monthly is the amount of cash a business has at the end of each month from its operations—that is, the *cash margin* for that month.

	Cash Sales	Credit Sales
Sales	$1000	$-0-
Less		
Cost of sales	500	500
Gross profit	500	(500)*
Operating expense	400	400
Net profit	100	(900)
Less		
Principal loan repayment	50	50
Owner's salary	30	30
Cash margin	20	(980)

*( ) indicates negative number

Figure 4.7 Cash flow.

Cash flow cumulative is the total amount of cash the business has at any given time, or the "checking account balance" of the business.

Start-up costs are the costs of getting a business started or the cost of an expansion.

Working capital is the money that a business has to pay for expenses. For loan purposes, working capital is an estimate of operating capital for the loan period. For our purposes, working capital is generally synonymous with cash.

Deposits and prepayments are moneys that are put up to get into business, including such items as utility and phone deposits, rent deposits, buying association deposits, and one years life insurance.

Owner's salary or owner's draw is the amount of money drawn from the business's net profit, if it is a proprietorship or partnership, or charged as an operating expense (officer's salary) if the business is a corporation.

Principal loan repayment is the amount of loan repayment the business pays less the interest portion. Loan repayment includes principal and interest. The *interest* part of a loan payment is the amount the bank charges for the borrower's use of the money loaned. The *principal* portion of the loan payment is a direct reduction in the total amount the business owes. The business has to pay the loan repayment in cash; therefore, whenever cash calculations, such as cash flow analysis, are made, the principal loan repayment must be considered.

Seasonal sales adjustments are the adjustments made each month in preparing a monthly cash flow projection that reflect seasonal changes in sales.

Financial comparative is past financial data organized side by side and year by year to show changes, if any, in the statements. For instance, to do profit and loss comparatives for a given period (e.g., three years), all three profit and loss statements would be placed side by side, matching each expense—with sales, rent, and so on—in sequential order.

Projected financial data are the financial statements—profit and loss, balance sheet, and cash flow—that indicate how the figures will look in the future. The financial data are "projected" into the future.

Depreciation is the calculation of how much value your assets will lose each year through wear and tear and age. The loss in value of equipment, real estate (building only), and leasehold improvements is considered as an expense of the business. There are several methods of calculating depreciation—straight line (SL), double-declining balance, sum of the years digits, and others. In this book we use SL depreciation, which is calculated by taking the purchase price of an item, subtracting how much it will be worth at the end of the depreciation period (called *salvage value*), then dividing by the number of years of the depreciation period. For example, Hero Manufacturing buys a forklift for $20,000 and estimates it will last five years. At the end of that five-year period, the truck will be worth $4,000—its salvage value. The calculations to ascertain yearly depreciation on an SL basis are shown in Figure 4.8.

Calculation Example—Depreciation. Use the data on your company to complete your depreciation schedule, using forms like the following:

Purchase price	$20,000
Less: Salvage value	− 4,000
	$16,000
Depreciation is $3,200 per annum (16,000/5).	

Figure 4.8 Determining yearly depreciation on an SL basis.

Depreciation Schedule

Life (years)	Original Cost	Salvage Value	Depreciable Value
5 Equipment	______	______	______(*A*)
10 Leasehold improvements	______	______	______(*B*)
7 Furniture	______	______	______(*C*)

Divide depreciable value by life:

	Depreciable Value	÷	Life (years)	=	Depreciation per Year
Equipment	______(*A*)		5		______
Leasehold improvements	______(*B*)		10		______
Furniture	______(*C*)		7		______
Total annual depreciation					______(*D*)

Your annual depreciation *D* is important when your are projecting expense and preparing a pro forma balance sheet, which are discussed later in this book.

FINANCIAL CALCULATION STEPS

If you have a poor background in finance and the foregoing discussion was not enough to give you an understanding of the basic financial statements—the income statement and the balance sheet—we suggest that you take a look at a basic financial text. A good, quick source of this information is the SBA pamphlet called *A Handbook of Small Business Finance* (Small Business Management Series No. 15). This is available at any government publications store or from the SBA.

The Steps

Figure 4.9 shows the seven steps for preparing the financial calculation section of a loan proposal. These calculations are the heart of a loan proposal. From this information all else flows. These calculations show how the business will operate in the next year and sometimes in subsequent years. They show what the sales will be, what the cash flow will be, and how the loan will be repaid.

Since this section is fundamental to loan approval, go through it very carefully. If you have any questions about the material, consult the SBA or other sources on finance.

The seven steps for doing financial calculations are as follows:

1. Calculate operating expense.
2. Calculate the cost of sales percentage and other variable costs.
3. Determine other cash costs (loan principal repayment, tax, etc.).
4. Calculate annual cash break-even sales, and summarize historical cash flow.
5. Prepare the monthly income statement.
6. Prepare the monthly cash flow.
7. Prepare the pro forma balance sheet and ratios.

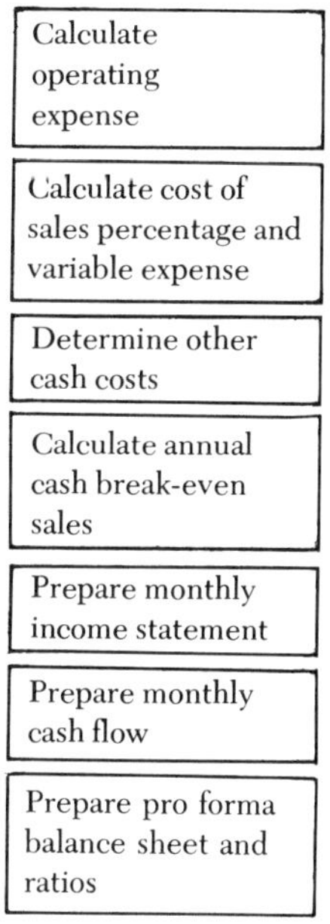

Calculate operating expense
Calculate cost of sales percentage and variable expense
Determine other cash costs
Calculate annual cash break-even sales
Prepare monthly income statement
Prepare monthly cash flow
Prepare pro forma balance sheet and ratios

Figure 4.9 Financial calculations.

CALCULATING OPERATING EXPENSE

The steps involved in calculating the operating expense of a business are:

1. Spread historical expenses from the last three years and from the current statement (for existing businesses only).
2. Predict the expected expense by using historical data (for existing businesses only).
3. Use industry percentages from your research data or personal expectations to predict projected expenses.
4. Calculate the depreciation schedule.
5. Determine the interest and principal payments for the proposed loan.

It is easier to find the expected operating expenses if you have a financial history of an existing business. If your business is new or a start-up, all the expense figures you use will have to be from your own research.

Spreading Historical Expenses

"Spreading" historical expenses is very simple. First take your last three years' and the current (not more than two months old) income statements. It is best to use Schedule C from your business income tax. Place the statements one on top of the other with the current statement on the bottom and the three-year-old statement on the top.

Take a six-column analysis sheet. In the left column write down the names of the expenses from your income statements (income tax form Schedule C). Across the top of the remaining five columns write the dates of the statements you have. For example, "12/31/80, 12 months, income tax" for the last three years' statements and "7/30/83, 7 months, P&L" for the current (or interim) statement. A sample sheet for Yourcompany is illustrated in Figure 4.10.

	12/31/80 12 Months Income Tax	12/31/81 12 Months Income Tax	12/31/82 12 Months Income Tax	7/30/83 7 Months P&L
Operating expense				
Salaries	50,000	73,000	85,000	58,480
Payroll tax	5,500	8,250	9,350	6,433
Rent	6,000	7,000	9,000	5,263
Office supplies	1,000	1,200	1,400	702
Bad debt	- 0 -	400	500	263
Advertising	1,000	4,000	5,000	3,216
Depreciation	4,000	5,000	6,000	3,909
Utilities	1,200	1,300	1,300	760
Phone	1,800	2,000	2,100	1,228
Accounting and legal	1,200	1,400	1,800	1,053
Auto and travel	500	1,000	1,900	1,170
Miscellaneous	150	200	250	117
Interest	- 0 -	1,500	1,750	1,023
Total operating expense	72,350	105,250	125,350	83,217

Figure 4.10 Analysis sheet for spreading historical expenses for Yourcompany.

Once the headings are written and all the expenses are listed, you simply go through each statement and write in appropriate dollar amounts for each expense and the total expenses. Be careful to leave room for other expense items that may not be in the first statement. Businesses usually add, delete, and incorporate expenses over a period of years. For instance, one year you may have one expense called "utilities" and one called "telephone," but the next year they both may be combined under the single account title "utilities." If you have changed accountants in the past three years, how your expenses are listed this year may differ from how they were in previous years.

So far, we've used only four columns. The column next to the interim statement should be used to "annualize" the interim statement. The last column is for the projecting the next year's expenses, which is discussed later.

Annualizing the interim current statement and its operating expenses is done by taking the shorter-than-one-year statement and changing it into an annual expense statement. In the examples for Yourcompany, the interim statement is for seven months (7/30/83). To compare these expenses with the expenses for the previous years, you must change the seven-month expenses into annual expenses.

It is very simple to annualize the interim (seven-month) expenses into annual expenses. First, you find out how many times the number of months in the interim statement will go into 12 months. Second, you multiply each expense by the number you find. For instance, seven months will divide into 12 months 1.71 times. You then multiply each expense in the seven-month statement by 1.71. In Figure 4.10, salaries for seven months totaled $58,480. If you multiply that figure by 1.71, you get $100,000.

Multiplying each interim expense by 1.71 will provide new annual figures for all the expense items. These should be put in the column next to the interim statement column and headed "7/30/83, 12 months, Annualized." This is shown in Figure 4.11.

Remember, if you have an interim statement for any number of months fewer than 12, the same procedure is used. Divide the number of months in the interim statement by 12, then multiply all the expenses for the interim period by the result of the first calculation.

	______(A) 12 Months Income Tax	______(B) 12 Months Income Tax	______(C) 12 Months Income Tax	______(D) ___(E) Months P&L	______(D) 12 Months Annualized
Sales	______	______	______	______	______
Cost of sales	______	______	______	______	______
Gross profit	______	______	______	______	______
Operating Expense					
Accounting and legal	______	______	______	______	______
Advertising	______	______	______	______	______
Auto and travel	______	______	______	______	______
Bad debt	______	______	______	______	______
Depreciation	______	______	______	______	______
Entertainment	______	______	______	______	______
Equipment lease	______	______	______	______	______
Interest	______	______	______	______	______
Insurance	______	______	______	______	______
License and tax	______	______	______	______	______
Office supplies	______	______	______	______	______
Payroll	______	______	______	______	______
Payroll tax	______	______	______	______	______
Postage	______	______	______	______	______
Promotion	______	______	______	______	______
Rent	______	______	______	______	______
Repairs and maintenance	______	______	______	______	______
Supplies	______	______	______	______	______
Utilities and phone	______	______	______	______	______
Total operating expense	______	______	______	______	______
Net profit	______	______	______	______	______

Figure 4.11 Income statement comparative.

When you have completed spreading the last three years' expenses, interim expenses, and annualized interim expenses, you are ready to predict the next year's expenses.

Figure 4.11 shows a comparative income statement spread with all the major catagories of expense. Write in the proper data for each column. You should use three full years of historical statements. If your last three years' income tax statements are 1981, 1980, and 1979, the dates would be written on the column heads in chronological order, 1979 for the *A* space on Figure 4.11, 1980 for the *B* space, and 1981 for the *C* space. The most recent financial statement should be not more than two months old. Space *D* is for the date of the statement and the annualized statement, and space *E* is for the number of months that interim statement covers.

Calculation Example—Annualization. To determine your annualized expenses, first find the number of months of the interim statement (*E* in Figure 4.11) and divide into 12 months. For instance, if the interim statement is for six months, the multiplication factor is 2 (12 months divided by 6 months). If the number of months in the interim statement is seven, the multiplication factor is 1.7143 (12 divided by 7).

Twelve months divided by the number of months in the interim statement (*E*) equals the multiplication factor (*F*). Take the annual expense items in the interim statement from Figure 4.11 and multiply by the multiplication factor *F*.

	Interim Statement Expense	×	Multiplication Factor	=	Annualized Expense
Operating expense					
Accounting and legal	______		______		______
Advertising	______		______		______
Auto and travel	______		______		______
Bad debt	______		______		______
Depreciation	______		______		______
Entertainment	______		______		______
Equipment lease	______		______		______
Interest	______		______		______
Insurance	______		______		______
License and tax	______		______		______
Office supplies	______		______		______
Payroll	______		______		______
Payroll tax	______		______		______
Postage	______		______		______
Promotion	______		______		______
Rent	______		______		______
Repairs and maintenance	______		______		______
Supplies	______		______		______
Utilities and phone	______		______		______
Total operating expense					______

Your answers from this example would be put in the last, annualized column of Figure 4.11.

Predicting Projected Expenses from Historical Expenses

If your business is an existing business like Yourcompany (see Figure 4.12), predicting future expenses is relatively easy. From annualization, you already know what the expected expense for the year will be if there is no change. This, along with statements of the last three years, constitutes a very good basis for predicting future expenses.

There are two ways you can use this historical data to predict future expenses. The easiest technique is the "eyeball" method; that is, you take a look at the historical trends and predict what the future expenses will be by making a *good guess*. The second method is to calculate projected expenses by doing a trend analysis of historical data.

For SBA purposes, the eyeball technique is just as good as the financial trend analysis. Figure 4.13 shows how the owner of Yourcompany eyeballed his historical data and predicted expenses. As you can see, the projected figures are close to the annualized figures—some are larger, some a little smaller. It is best to try to make your projected figures as close as possible to the last annual or annualized experience. Most projected expenses are higher than historical expenses because the trend has been for prices to go up. After you have projected these expenses based on past

	12/31/80 12 Months Income Tax	12/31/81 12 Months Income Tax	12/31/82 12 Months Income Tax	7/30/83 7 Months P&L	7/30/83 12 Months Annualize
Operating expense					
Salaries	50,000	73,000	85,000	58,480	100,000
Payroll tax	5,500	8,250	9,350	6,433	11,000
Rent	6,000	7,000	9,000	5,263	9,000
Office supplies	1,000	1,200	1,400	702	1,200
Bad debt	- 0 -	400	500	263	450
Advertising	1,000	4,000	5,000	3,216	5,500
Depreciation	4,000	5,000	6,000	3,909	6,000
Utilities	1,200	1,300	1,300	760	1,500
Phone	1,800	2,000	2,100	1,228	2,100
Accounting and legal	1,200	1,400	1,800	1,053	1,800
Auto and travel	500	1,000	1,900	1,170	2,000
Miscellaneous	150	200	250	117	200
Interest	- 0 -	1,500	1,750	1,023	1,750
Total operating expenses	72,350	105,250	125,350	83,217	142,300

Figure 4.12 Annualization for Yourcompany.

data, it is a good idea to review them carefully to see if they are reasonable. For instance, will rent remain the same? Are salaries likely to increase or decrease?

For depreciation and interest, projected expense will be affected by the most recent experience. Interest must be calculated based on the amount the business plans to borrow, and depreciation will be affected by the amount of equipment and the dollar amount of improvements the business will pay for from the loan proceeds. The projected expenses will include *present* depreciation plus *new* depreciation.

Because you have not yet calculated the interest and principal payments for the SBA loan or the new depreciation from fixed assets purchased with SBA funds, use your present interest and depreciation figures for now.

	12/31/80 12 Months Income Tax	12/31/81 12 Months Income Tax	12/31/82 12 Months Income Tax	7/30/83 7 Months P&L	7/30/83 12 Months Annualized	Projected 12 Months 1st Year
Operating expense:						
Salaries	50,000	73,000	85,000	58,480	100,000	100,000
Payroll tax	5,500	8,250	9,350	6,433	11,000	11,000
Rent	6,000	7,000	9,000	5,263	9,000	9,000
Office supplies	1,000	1,200	1,400	702	1,200	1,300
Bad debt	- 0 -	400	500	263	450	400
Advertising	1,000	4,000	5,000	3,216	5,500	6,000
Depreciation	4,000	5,000	6,000	3,909	6,000	6,000
Utilities	1,200	1,300	1,300	760	1,500	1,400
Phone	1,800	2,000	2,100	1,228	2,100	2,100
Accounting and legal	1,200	1,400	1,800	1,053	1,800	1,800
Auto and travel	500	1,000	1,900	1,170	2,000	2,100
Miscellaneous	150	200	250	117	200	200
Interest	- 0 -	1,500	1,750	1,023	1,750	1,750
Total operating expenses	72,350	105,250	125,350	83,217	142,300	143,050

Figure 4.13 Predicted expenses for Yourcompany.

Using Industry Information to Predict Projected Expenses

If yours is a new or start-up business, you will probably have very little idea how much your expenses will be for the first projected year of operation. In this case, you will have to depend on the industry studies such as NCR's *Expenses in Retailing*, discussed in Chapter 3. These statistics show expenses given as a percentage of sales. If you know what your sales will be, you can calculate the expenses.

If you have experience in this particular field, you may be able to predict expenses fairly well. If you don't know what all or some of the expenses will be, you can calculate expenses from industry studies. Some expenses—such as rent, depreciation, and interest—are already known in most cases. Rent is known because the business is going to move into certain premises. Depreciation is calculated on the equipment and improvements one expects to buy. Interest (discussed later in this chapter) is calculated according to how much you plan to borrow.

If you have a good idea of what sales will be, you can predict expenses by using industry data like those shown in Figure 4.14, from Accounting Corporation of America's (ACA) *Barometer of Small Business*, which shows expenses as a percentage of sales.

	Group 3 *(Nationally)* Annual Gross Volume \$100,000–\$200,000 (%)		All Groups *(Nationally)* Average (%)	
Description of Ratio Classification	This Year	Last Year	This Year	Last Year
Sales	100.00	100.00	100.00	100.00
Cost of sales	61.96	61.27	62.59	61.67
Gross profit	38.04	38.73	37.41	38.33
Controllable expenses				
Outside labor	.10	.10	.10	.10
Operating supplies	.72	.76	.80	.83
Gross wages†	14.28	13.65	12.48	11.98
Repairs and maintenance	.36	.36	.37	.37
Advertising	1.84	1.74	1.27	1.27
Car and delivery	.41	.40	.43	.42
Bad debts	.01	.01	.02	.02
Administrative and legal	.39	.38	.42	.41
Miscellaneous expense	.42	.45	.46	.49
Total controllable expenses	18.53	17.85	16.35	15.89
Fixed expenses				
Rent*	2.55	2.55	2.70	2.69
Utilities	1.16	1.16	1.30	1.30
Insurance	.58	.58	.61	.60
Taxes and licenses	.92	.92	.89	.90
Interest	.10	.10	.12	.12
Depreciation	1.05	1.05	1.08	1.08
Total fixed expenses	6.36	6.36	6.70	6.69
Total expenses	24.89	24.21	23.05	22.58
Net profit	13.15	14.52	14.36	15.75

†Does not include proprietor's wages.
*Ajusted to reflect calculates of forward premises.

Figure 4.14 Barometer of Small Business percentage table.

Item	% of Sales	Amount
Sales	100.0	$100,000
Cost of sales	61.96	61,960
Net profit	38.04	38,040
Operating expense		
Outside labor	0.10 (.001 × 100,000=)	100
Operating supplies	0.72 (.0072 × 100.00=)	720
Gross wages	14.28 (etc.)	14,280
Repairs and maintenance	0.36	360
Advertising	1.84	1,840
Car and delivery	0.41	10
Bad debts	0.01	10
Administrative and legal	0.39	390
Miscellaneous	0.42	420
Rent	2.55	2,550
Utilities	1.16	1,160
Insurance	0.58	580
Tax and license	0.92	920
Interest	0.10	100
Depreciation	1.05	1,050
Total expense	24.89	24,890
Net profit	13.15	13,150

Figure 4.15 Expenses as a percentage of sales and in dollars.

For example, if sales were expected to be $100,000 per year, the calculation based on percentages illustrated in Figure 4.14 would look like those in Figure 4.15.

Since you don't know what your projected sales will be yet, it is a little difficult at this time to calculate all your expenses as shown in the illustrations. The best idea is to list dollar amounts for the expenses you do know, such as rent, and list only the percentages for those expenses that you do not know.

Using Figure 4.14, you can construct a combination dollar expense and percentage expense schedule. Assume that you know rent will be $6,000 per year, salaries will be $40,000, payroll tax will be $4,400, and insurance will be $1,300 per year. You have not calculated interest or depreciation, so leave these items blank.

Item	Percentage	Expenses Expected
Outside labor	0.10	
Operating supplies	0.72	
Gross wages		$40,000
Repairs and maintenance	0.36	
Advertising	1.84	
Car and delivery	0.41	
Bad debts	0.01	
Administrative and legal	0.39	
Miscellaneous	0.42	
Rent		6,000
Utilities	1.16	
Insurance		1,300
Tax and license		4,400
Interest	N/A	N/A
Depreciation	N/A	N/A
Total expense	5.41	$51,700

Figure 4.16 Expense schedule for Starter Company.

	Industry Percentage	Expected Expenses
Operating expense:		
Accounting and legal	______	______
Advertising	______	______
Auto and travel	______	______
Bad debt	______	______
Depreciation	______	______
Entertainment	______	______
Equipment lease	______	______
Interest	______	______
Insurance	______	______
License and tax	______	______
Office supplies	______	______
Payroll	______	______
Payroll tax*	______	______*
Postage	______	______
Promotion	______	______
Rent	______	______
Repairs and maintenance	______	______
Supplies	______	______
Utilities and phone	______	______
Total operating expense	______	______

*Payroll tax is approximately 15% of payroll for state and federal obligations.

Figure 4.17 New business expenses.

	______(*D*) 12 Months Annualized	12 Months Projected
Cost of sales	______	______
Sales	______	______
Gross profit	______	______
Operating expense:		
Accounting and legal	______	______
Advertising	______	______
Auto and travel	______	______
Bad debt	______	______
Depreciation	______	______
Entertainment	______	______
Equipment lease	______	______
Interest	______	______
Insurance	______	______
License and tax	______	______
Office supplies	______	______
Payroll	______	______
Payroll tax	______	______
Postage	______	______
Promotion	______	______
Rent	______	______
Repairs and maintenance	______	______
Supplies	______	______
Utilities and phone	______	______
Total expense	______	______
Net Profit	______	______

Figure 4.18 Income statement projection.

Calculation Example—New Company Expense. Before you can do any calculation, you must get statistical information for your industry. If you are in a retail or service business, this information is available from NCR's *Expenses in Retailing*. If your company is in wholesale or manufacturing, the information may come from an industry association, manufacturers of your raw materials, or from Dun and Bradstreet's *Cost of Doing Business*.

Figure 4.16 shows a combination percentage and dollar expense schedule for Starter Company using the expenses listed in Figure 4.16.

Later, when you find out what your sales should be, you can convert all the percentages into expenses by multiplying as illustrated previously.

Using Figure 4.17, copy down the expenses you know you will have such as interest, depreciation, salaries (payroll), payroll tax (use 15% of payroll as your figure), and rent. Then write down the percentage you find in industry publications or from other sources.

Established companies must prepare their projections based on their actual performance. These companies would prepare an annualized 12-month statement (explained earlier) and use it to prepare a 12-month projection. An example of this form is Figure 4.18.

CALCULATING COST OF SALES AND VARIABLE COSTS

Determining the cost of sales and variable costs of a business is relatively easy. There are only two basic ways to determine cost of sales and variable costs. An existing business can use historical experience. For a new or start-up business, cost of sales percentages and variable expense percentages can generally be found in industry studies or by calling suppliers.

Fixed and Variable Costs

Fixed costs are expenses such as rent, depreciation, interest, utilities, supplies, professional services, and so on, which remain at about the same dollar amount no matter what sales volume exists. If you are paying a fixed amount of rent (not rent as a percentage of gross), you may sell millions of dollars worth of merchandise or you may sell nothing at all, but the rent you pay remains the same. Most of the operating expenses that were discussed earlier in this chapter can be considered *fixed* expenses.

Cost of sales will increase in dollar amount when sales increase and decrease in dollar amount when sales decrease. If you sell an item for $1 and it cost you 50 cents, then the more items you sell, the more costs you will have. The less you sell, the lower your costs. If you sell $1,000 worth of items, it costs you $500. If you sell $100 worth, it costs you only $50. Cost of sales is therefore a *variable cost*.

There are other variable costs as well. Commission is one variable cost with which everyone is familiar. If a salesperson sells your merchandise, he or she receives a certain percentage of those sales as a commission. The more he or she sells, the more he or she makes as commission. Other variable costs include franchise costs, percentage leases (a certain percentage of sales is for rent), and advertising costs based on a percentage of gross sales.

One of the most common percentages in finance is cost of sales as a percentage of gross sales, generally called the *cost of sales percentage*. When someone tells you that a cost of sales is 50%, that means that for every dollar of sales, 50 cents is the cost of that sale.

Although most accountants show percentages along with their income statements, you might find it necessary to determine your own cost of sales percentage for your business. Use this formula:

$$\frac{\text{Cost of sales in dollars}}{\text{gross sales in dollars}} = \text{cost of sales percentage}$$

If a company has $300,000 in sales for one year and $120,000 in cost of sales, its cost of sales percentage would be 40% ($120,000 ÷ $300,000).

Cost of Sales and Variable Expenses for Existing Businesses

The quickest way to find what next year's cost of sales is to use the cost of sales percentage for past years.

Example. Yourcompany has the following sales, cost of sales, and cost of sales percentage for the past three years and the current year:

Year	Sales	Cost of Sales	Cost of Sales Percentage
1980	$420,000	$264,600	63% or 0.63
1981	490,000	318,500	65% or 0.65
1982	600,000	369,000	61.5% or 0.615
1983	380,117	235,673	62% or 0.62

Can you predict what Yourcompany's cost of sales percentage will be next year? You can approach this in two ways: You can determine the average, or you can use a weighted average.

To get the average cost of sales percentage, you add the cost of sales percentage for all four years, then divide by 4 using this formula:

$$\frac{\text{Total cost of sales percentage for all years}}{\text{number of years}} = \text{average cost of sales percentage}$$

$$\text{Total cost of sales} = 63\% + 65\% + 61.5\% + 62\% = 251.5\%$$

$$\frac{251.5\%}{\text{four years}} = 62.875\% \text{ average cost of sales over the periods}$$

If you were to predict the cost of sales percentage for the next year, you could use 62.875%.

You might also weigh the different periods and eyeball the answer, mentally giving each year a certain weight. The cost of sales percentages have varied between 61.5% and 65%. The most recent experience is 62% and 61.5%. If you eyeball the percentages and say that next year should be around 62% because that has been the most recent experience, this is justifiable.

Finding Cost of Sales and Variable Expenses for a New Business

With a new business, cost of sales and other variable costs must be gathered from industry information, just as expenses were gathered.

NCR's *Expenses in Retailing*, Bank of America's *Small Business Reporter*, Robert Morris's *Annual Statement Studies*, and trade association material give you exact percentages for cost of sales and other costs.

Calculation Example—Cost of Sales. If you have an existing business, you can predict the future cost of sales by using historical data.

Date	Cost of Sales ÷	Sales	= Cost of Sales Percentage
______	______	______	______
______	______	______	______
______	______	______	______
______	______	______	______
______	______	______	______
______	______	______	______
Total cost of sales percentage			______(*A*)

Divide cost of sales percentage *A* by the number of periods to find the average cost of sales percentage *B*.

DETERMINING OTHER CASH COSTS

In addition to expenses, other cash costs come out of the net profit of a company. These cash costs include owner's draw (if the company is a sole proprietorship or partnership), income tax, principal loan repayment, and other items.

Owner's Draw

If the company is a sole proprietorship (one owner, not a corporation) or a partnership, the earnings of the business that go to the owner(s) must come out of net profit. It is *not* an expense of the business, even though it is a cash item.

On an SBA loan application, owner's draw should be included as a cash flow item. The banker believes that the person who is submitting the loan should show enough of a draw to pay for his or her normal living expenses.

How much draw will a banker consider reasonable? Usually, an amount similar to what the applicant received last year. For instance, if the applicant made $20,000 last year, the banker does not like to see a draw of $40,000 for the projected year. On the other hand, the banker would not think a $20,000 salary earner could make do with $10,000. In short, your draw should be at least enough to pay the living expenses at your current standard of living.

Expected Income Tax

Income tax, for both the state and the federal governments, has to be paid before you make an owner's draw or before the bank can be paid. This is why the lender is greatly concerned about your expected income tax. Income tax is a *cash* cost.

Income tax is generally considered to be a percentage of net profit. Therefore, to determine what your *taxes* will be in the projected year, you must determine what your *net profit* will be.

We want to determine the minimum it will take to break even after the cash costs are paid (cost of sales, expenses, owner's draw, principal loan repayment, and taxes). For cash break-even, you must find what your *minimum* net profit will be.

If net profit is at a minimum to cover costs, that means that it *equals* the amount required to pay owner's draw, principal loan repayment, and taxes. Since we don't know yet what the tax percentage is, we can disregard the tax component of net profit and use the following formula:

Minimum net profit = owner's draw + principal loan repayment − depreciation

Put another way:

Net profit + depreciation = owner's draw + principal loan repayment

Figure 4.19 shows the tax percentages we use. Like most devices that make calculations convenient, it is not totally accurate. Taxes vary from state to state and from year to year, but for our purposes, Figure 4.19 should suffice. One column shows the range of net profit, the second column shows the income tax percentage we usually use. For instance, if owner's draw plus principal loan repayment minus depreciation equals \$1–\$15,000, the income tax percentage is 10%.

Example. What is the income tax for ABC Company if it has the following costs: owner's draw, \$25,000; principal loan repayment, \$14,000; and capital equipment purchases, \$11,000? Depreciation is \$15,000 per year. Net profit is calculated by the following formula:

Owner's draw + principal loan repayment + other cost (equipment) − depreciation = net profit

\$25,000 + \$14,000 + \$11,000 − \$15,000 = \$35,000

If the net profit is \$35,000 for XYZ Company, looking at Figure 4.19, we see that the income tax percentage is 30%. The income tax is therefore \$10,500 (\$35,000 × 0.30).

Calculation Example—Taxes. Determine your net profit by adding owner's draw plus principal loan repayment minus depreciation:

		Dollar Amount
	Owner's draw	______
Plus:	Principal loan repayment	______
Less:	Depreciation	______
Equals:	Estimated net profit	______(A)

Look at the tax table shown in Figure 4.19 to find your estimated income tax percentage. Find where the amount of your estimated net profit appears, and use the corresponding percentage to find your estimated income tax percentage *B*.

If principal loan repayment + owner's salary + other cash costs − depreciation equals:	The income tax percentage equals:
\$1 to 15,000	10%
15,000 to 30,000	20
30,000 to 50,000	30
50,000 to 99,000	40
100,000 plus	45

Figure 4.19 Income tax percentage chart.

Investment Tax Credit. The IRS allows you to write directly off your taxes an amount equal to up to 10% of any new investments made in equipment, furniture, or improvements.

From time to time, there are tax credits larger than 10%. In 1981 a special energy tax credit of up to 20% was allowed for certain energy-producing or energy-efficient improvements and machinery. Generally, however, the investment tax credit is from 6.67–10% of the purchase price of the asset. Assets with a depreciable life of from three to five years have a 6.7% tax credit and a 10% credit for more than five years. These percentages are subject to change, and you should consult the local IRS office before you do your calculations. Generally equipment is depreciated over five to seven years, and furniture and improvements are depreciated over seven years.

For instance, if X Company's net profit before taxes is $10,000, its tax is 10%, or $1,000. Assume that X Company purchased a $5,000 piece of equipment that year, and it is depreciating it for four years. Its tax credit would be $333.50 ($5,000 equipment cost times 0.0667 income tax credit for an asset with a four-year life). The tax X Company has to pay is $1,000 tax before the tax credit minus $333.50, or $666.50.

Calculation Example—Investment Tax Credit. Before you complete this calculation, go ahead in the book, to the next section in this chapter, and first prepare your cash break-even sales. To get the income tax credit, you must know the *dollar amount* of the taxes you owe. Once you know the dollar amount of the taxes projected to be due in the first year, determine the dollar amount of the investment tax credit and the taxes owed as follows:

	Cost				Investment Credit
3–5 years equipment	______	×	0.0667	=	__________
7 years plus leasehold improvements, fixtures, and furniture	______	×	0.1000	=	__________
Total investment credit					__________(*A*)

The dollar amount of taxes before credit minus total investment tax credit *A* equals taxes payable *B*.

DETERMINING CASH BREAK-EVEN SALES, HISTORY, AND ANNUAL CASH FLOW

The projected year's sales show the lender how you will repay the debt. If you cannot demonstrate the ability to repay, you cannot qualify for the loan. If your sales projections are too optimistic, the lender will discount them.

The best plan for determining your projected sales is to calculate the *minimum sales* needed to pay all the cash costs of the business. You must determine the amount of sales it will take to pay for cost of sales, expenses, owner's draw, principal loan repayment, and income tax. The minimum sales amount needed to pay all the cash costs is the *cash break-even sales*, and there is a formula for determining them.

Once cash break-even sales are determined, you still must add a safety margin. Furthermore, the whole cash flow must be put in a special format, and the new annual projection should be compared to historical data.

Cash Break-Even Sales

Cash break-even analysis is important for two reasons: to determine how many sales it will take to pay all cash costs and to determine if it is even possible to go into business. If the break-even sales are too high or too difficult to achieve, you will have to reconsider some of your expenses.

Traditional sales break-even analysis uses charts and various formulas. Since you want to determine the *cash* break-even, one particular formula is perhaps the easiest.

First, why do you want to know cash break-even, and what are the components? Cash break-even is, literally, the amount of cash you are going to need to pay not only your expenses and cost of sales, but also your taxes, your owner's salary, and the principal portion of the loan. The best way of generating sufficient cash is through sales. So how much in sales are you going to need? The components of break-even analysis are:

Cost of sales percentage.
Depreciation.
Variable operating expenses.
Total fixed operating expenses including interest.
Total principal loan repayment.
Total owner's salary.
Estimated income tax requirement.

By now you should have a good idea what your expenses and cost of sales percentage are. You also know what the principal loan repayment for the year should be. The proper income tax percentage can be derived by consulting Figure 4.19.

The formula for calculating cash break-even sales is seen in Figure 4.20. To calculate the cash break-even sales, follow these steps:

1. Add owner's salary (the money you will draw from the business) to the principal loan repayment for the year plus other costs, and subtract the amount of depreciation for the year.
2. The number thus arrived at is divided by 1 minus the income tax percentage from the income tax percentage chart (Figure 4.19).
3. Take the resulting figure and add to it the total fixed operating expense.
4. Take the new number arrived at and divide it by 1 minus the cost of sales percentage plus the variable cost percentage.

The resulting figure is the exact cash break-even sales required for the year.

Note. In many cases your company probably won't have variable operating expenses, so for variable cost percentage substitute the number 0.

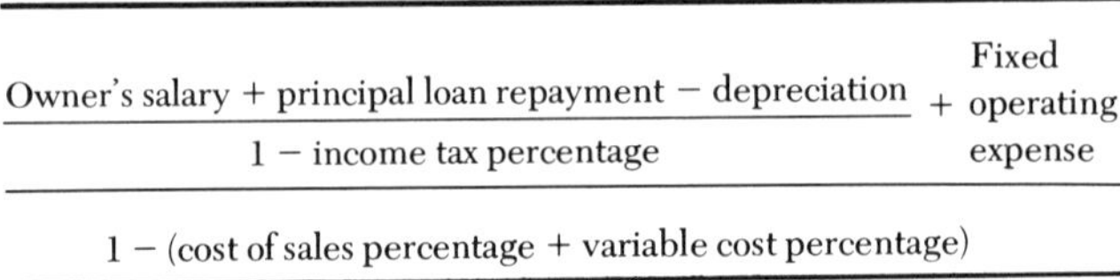

Figure 4.20 Cash break-even sales formula.

Yourcompany has the following cash expenses and percentages for the year:

Fixed operating expense	$147,350
Income tax percentage*	30% of net profit
Cost of sales	6[illegible]% of sales
Owner's salary	$24,000
Principal loan repayment+	24,460
Depreciation	10,300

Calculations:

$$\frac{\dfrac{\$24,000 + \$24,460 - \$10,300 + \$147,350}{1 - 0.3}}{1 - .63} = \frac{38,160 + 147,350}{0.37} = \$545,579.15$$

or $545,579 rounded

*The income tax percentage of 30% (or 0.30) is arrived at by adding owner's salary ($24,000) and principal loan repayment ($24,460) and subtracting depreciation ($38,160) to arrive at $10,300 total and then using the income tax percentage chart (Figure 4.19).

+Loan repayments on $200,000 for 6 years @ 10% interest.

Figure 4.21 Calculating cash break-even sales for Yourcompany.

If your company is a start-up and you have determined operating expense as a percentage of sales from industry studies, use these percentages as a variable cost. You would use the expenses that you know—rent, salaries, and so on—as the total operating expenses and the expenses as a percentage of sales total as a variable cost.

Example 1. Figure 4.21 shows how the cash break-even sales for Yourcompany is calculated when fixed operating expense, variable costs, cost of sales, owner's draw, principal loan repayment, and depreciation are known. The cash break-even sales is $545,579.

Figure 4.22 takes the $545,579 as the cash break-even sales figure and works backward to prove that the calculation is accurate. This is the first-year cash flow summary.

Example 2. Starter Company is a start-up company. You know only some of the operating expenses in dollars; the rest are given as percentages of sales that were

Sales	$545,579
Cost of sales (48%)	343,715
Gross profit	201,864
Less:	
Fixed operating expenses	147,350
Net profit	54,514
Add:	
Depreciation	10,300
Less:	
Owner's salary	(24,000)
Income tax (30% of net profit)	(16,354)
Principal loan repayment	(24,460)
Cash margin	$ - 0 -

Figure 4.22 First-year cash flow summary for Yourcompany.

found from industry averages. Use the expenses and percentages from earlier in this chapter. Figure 4.23 shows the figures involved.

The cash break-even sales figure for Starter Company is $337,895. To prove it, we show the first-year cash flow summary in Figure 4.24.

The cash break-even formula that we have been using is to the best of our knowledge the only cash break-even formula in all business literature that takes into consideration all the cash outlays—including income tax—in determining cash break-even sales. This formula was developed by Rick Hayes and later perfected by Jeff Malzahn. It is always accurate, and it will always come out to the exact dollar. We call the formula the Hayes–Malzahn Cash Break-Even Formula.

Starter Company had the following cash costs and percentages for the first year:

Total known fixed costs*	$99,825
Variable expenses—industry average**	5.41%
Cost of sales percentage	61.96%
Owner's draw	$20,000
Principal loan repayment	17,387
Depreciation	28,000
Income tax %+	10% of net profit

Calculations:

$$\frac{\dfrac{\$20,000 + \$17,387 - \$28,000}{1 - 0.10} + 99,825}{1 - (0.6196 + 0.0541)} = \$337,894.58 \quad \text{annual cash break-even sales}$$

*Total known fixed costs include: (Figure 4.15, and Examples in Interest and Depreciation Sections of this chapter):

Gross wages	$40,000
Rent	6,000
Insurance	1,300
Tax and license	4,400
Interest	20,125
Depreciation	28,000
	$99,825

**Variable expenses—industrial averages include the following expenses as a percentage of sales found in the *Barometer of Small Business* (Figure 4.14):

Outside labor	0.10%
Operating supplies	0.72
Repairs and maintenance	0.36
Advertising	1.84
Car and delivery	0.41
Bad debts	0.01
Administration and legal	0.39
Miscellaneous	0.42
Utilities	1.16
	5.41%

+Calculated by adding owner's draw ($20,000) and principal loan repayment ($17,387) minus depreciation ($28,000), which equals $9,387, and looking at the income tax table (Figure 4.19).

Figure 4.23 Calculating expenses and percentages.

Sales		$337,895
Cost of sales (61.96%)		209,360
Gross profit		$128,535
Operating expense:		
Known expenses	$99,825	
Percentage expenses (5.41%)	18,280	
		$118,105
Net Profit		10,430
Add: Depreciation	$28,000	
Total cash inflow		$ 38,430
Less:		
Owner's draw	$20,000	
Principal loan repayment	17,387	
Income tax*	1,043	$ 38,430
Cash margin (inflow minus outflow)		$ -0-

*Income tax is 10% of net profit according to the tax table, Figure 4.19.

Figure 4.24 First-year cash flow summary for Starter Company.

Calculation Example—Cash Break-Even. First fill in the components of cash break-even sales:

Total fixed operating expense	______(A)
Depreciation	______(B)
Owner's draw or dividends	______(C)
Principal loan annual payment	______(D)
Cost of sales percentage	______(E)
Income tax percentage	______(F)
Commissions (in %)	______(G)
Variable operating expense (in %)	______(H)

Note. Commissions and variable operating expense are relevant only if yours is a new business or you have commission sales. Variable operating expense is for the operating expenses for which you have no dollar amounts but for which you know the equivalent in percentages (such as those found in NCR's Expenses in Retailing. See Figure 4.15).

Remember that when you use percentages in calculations, they must be written in their decimal form. Ten percent is written 0.1, and 3.33% is written 0.0333.

Next take these items and substitute them in the cash break-even formulas according to the following steps:

1. Owner's draw or dividends C plus principal loan payment D minus depreciation B equals profit before tax I.
2. Profit before tax I divided by [1 minus income tax percentage (F)] equals cash break-even net profit J.
3. Cash break-even net profit J plus total dollar operating expense A equals cash break-even gross profit K.
4. Cash break-even gross profit K divided by {1 minus [cost of sales percentage E + variable costs (G + H)]} equals cash break-even sales L.

Add a Cash Margin by Increasing Break-Even Sales

We would like to add one more thing to the discussion of break-even analysis. Most lenders want to have sales projected slightly higher than break-even so that there is a positive cash margin in the end. It is advisable that you add $10,000 or more to the break-even sales to guarantee a small cash margin.

For instance, if cash break-even sales was $337,895 as in the example above, the projection should be increased to at least $350,000.

Format for First-Year Annual Projected Cash Flow

One of the requirements of your loan proposal is that there be an annual profit and loss statement, one that is converted to a cash flow, for the first projected year.

The format is as follows for annual financial statements:

Sales
Less: Cost of sales
Gross profit
Less: Total operating expense
Net profit
Add: Depreciation
Total cash inflow
Less: Owner's draw
    Income tax
    Principal loan repayment
    Other cash payments
Total cash outflow
Cash margin

Your annual sales are placed first, then the annual cost of sales. Subtracting cost of sales from sales gives you the gross profit. Total operating expense is listed, then subtracted from gross profit to give the first year's net profit. This is the *income statement* or *profit and loss statement* for the first projected year.

Next you convert the income statement to a cash flow statement. Add depreciation to net profit to arrive at *total cash inflow*. Total cash inflow is the total amount of each available from operations to pay cash costs that are not considered expenses or cost of sales. The cash costs are usually owner's draw, income tax, and principal loan repayment. The amounts for these items are written down, then totaled to get *total cash outflow*. Total cash outflow is the cash costs you must pay besides operating expenses and cost of sales.

Total cash inflow minus total cash outflow gives us the *cash margin*. The cash margin is the amount of cash available to put back into the business at the end of the year.

Next, list sales, cost of sales, gross profit, total operating expense, and net profit as a percentage of sales. This is called a *common-sized percentage*.

Example. The following is a format and percentage "common-sized" for an annual projection for Starter Company:

Sales	$350,000
Less: Cost of sales	216,860
Gross profit	$133,140
Less: Total operating expense	118,760

Net profit	$ 14,380
Add: Depreciation	$ 28,000
Total cash inflow	$ 42,380
Less: Owner's draw	$ 20,000
Income tax	7,438
Principal loan repayment	17,387
Total cash outflow	$ 38,825
Cash margin	$ 3,555

Common-Sized Percentages

Sales	100.00%	(sales/sales)
Cost of sales	61.96%	(cost of sales/sales)
Gross profit	38.04%	(gross profit/sales)
Total operating expense	33.93%	(operating expense/sales)
Net profit	4.11%	(net profit/sales)

Calculation Example—Format. Take your information from the previous examples and place it in this format:

Sales	$________	L + additional margin
Cost of sales	________	$E \times$ sales
Gross profit	________	Sales − cost of sales
Operating expense		
Fixed	________	A
Variable	________	$G \times$ sales
Net profit	________	Gross profit − fixed and variable operating expenses
Add: Depreciation	________	B
Total cash inflow	________	Net profit + B
Less: Owners' draw	________	C
Income tax	________	($F \times$ net profit) − investment tax credit
Principal loan repayment	________	D
Total cash outflow	________	Owners' draw + income tax + principal loan repayment
Cash margin	$________	Total cash inflow − total cash outflow

SUMMARY

To prepare a financial analysis requires a basic understanding of accounting, especially of the income statement and balance sheet.

The actual preparation work requires that you follow these steps:

1. For an existing business, the first step is to spread (put items and years side by side) historical financial statements and annualize the current income state-

ment. New businesses should determine their expected operating expenses by using industry percentage data and expectations. The first items of expense to be calculated for the projected year are interest and depreciation.

2. Calculate or research the cost of sales and variable expenses.
3. Determine nonexpense costs such as owner's draw, principal loan repayment, and income tax less investment tax credit.
4. Using all the expense, cost of sales, and nonexpense costs, determine the cash break-even sales for the company.
5. Put this information in the appropriate format.

Chapter Five

Financial Calculations: Monthly Projections

In addition to an annual projection, SBA loans require a monthly projected income statement, a monthly projected cash flow, and a pro forma balance sheet.

To prepare these schedules, you need no new information. You use as your basis the data you already have: the annual projected cash flow, the use of funds statement, the present balance sheet, and some industry information.

PREPARING A MONTHLY INCOME STATEMENT

Preparing the monthly income statement requires three steps:

1. Use industry seasonal adjustments and sales to determine monthly income.
2. Use cost of sales percentage times income to determine monthly cost of sales.
3. Divide annual operating expense into monthly amounts.

Seasonal Adjustments for Monthly Sales

Monthly expected sales for a new business may be calculated by dividing annual sales by 12 months, then adjusting each month for growth. For instance, if sales for Starter Company will be $350,000 per year, dividing by 12 gives you average sales of $29,167 per month. If you want to adjust for growth, you simply multiply the average monthly sales by 0.8 for the first two months of the projected year, 0.9 for the next two, and so on, as illustrated in Figure 5.1.

By multiplying the average monthly sales by these factors, you get a gradual increase in monthly sales, which appears to be more realistic than $29,167 for each month.

Most businesses have seasonal fluctuations. Retailers usually experience their greatest volume of sales in December. Because of these seasonal fluctuations, it is best to use a monthly sales index (see Figure 5.3, from ACA's *Barometer of Small Business*, or the Department of Commerce's *Survey of Current Business*. The procedure for determining seasonally adjusted monthly sales with this index is simple:

1. Take the total dollar amount of sales, and divide by the total index number.
2. Multiply the resulting factor by each month's index number.

$$\frac{\text{Total annual sales } \$120{,}000}{12 \text{ months}} = \$10{,}000 \text{ Average monthly sales}$$

Months	Percentage Factors	×	Average Month	=	Monthly Sales
1st and 2nd	0.8		29,167		23,333
3rd and 4th	0.9		29,167		26,250
5th through 8th	1.0		29,167		29,167
9th and 10th	1.1		29,167		32,083
11th and 12th	1.2		29,167		35,000

23,333 + 23,333 + 26,250 + 26,250 + 29,167 + 29,167 + 29,167 + 29,167 + 32,083 + 32,083 + 35,000 + 35,000 = 350,000 total annual sales.

Figure 5.1 Monthly sales for Starter Company adjusted for growth.

Monthly index-adjusted sales can be calculated as shown in Figure 5.2, using the sales index in Figure 5.3 and $350,000 as the total annual sales.

Because of rounding errors, the monthly index-adjusted sales sometimes will not add up to your total annual break-even sales. In that case, add (or subtract) equally from each month to make it accurate.

If the business is a new one, like Starter Company, or is an existing company that must increase sales over the previous year, a combination of both the index seasonal adjustment and the percentage adjustment is called for. Figure 5.4 illustrates the combination of methods for Starter Company, assuming $350,000 total annual sales.

These numbers, too, are liable *not to add up* to the break-even cash sales total. In this case, each month should be adjusted so that it adds up to the break-even cash sales total ($350,000 in the example). See the Sales-Adjusted column in Figure 5.4. The correct sales ($350,000) is subtracted from the unadjusted amount ($353,495).

$$\frac{\text{Total Cash Break-Even Sales}}{\text{Total Index for Year}} = \text{Index-Adjusted Sales Factor}$$

$$\frac{350{,}000}{1312} = 266.768$$

Month	Index #	×	Index-Adjusted Sales Factor	Monthly Sales
January	103		266.768	$ 27,477
February	101		266.768	26,944
March	104		266.768	27,744
April	104		266.768	27,744
May	105		266.768	28,011
June	105		266.768	28,011
July	105		266.768	28,011
August	105		266.768	28,011
September	106		266.768	28,277
October	107		266.768	28,544
November	110		266.768	29,344
December	157		266.768	41,882
Total sales				$350,000

Figure 5.2 Calculation of monthly sales.

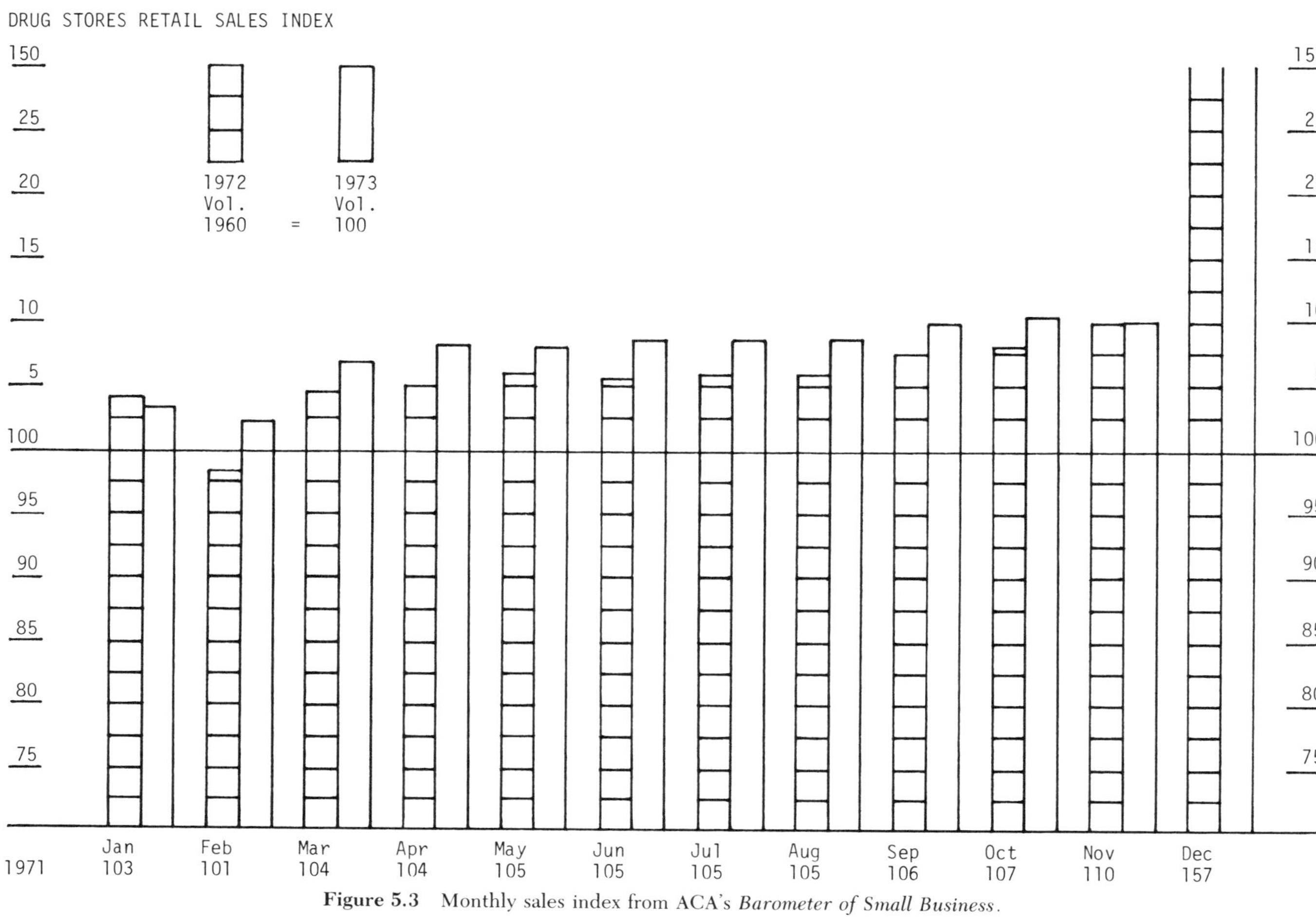

Figure 5.3 Monthly sales index from ACA's *Barometer of Small Business*.

Month	Index #	×	Index-Adjusted Sales Factor	Percentage Factor	Monthly Sales	Sales Adjusted
January	103		266.768	0.8	$ 21,982	$ 21,691
February	101		266.768	0.8	21,555	21,264
March	104		266.768	0.9	24,970	24,678
April	104		266.768	0.9	24,970	24,678
May	105		266.768	1.0	28,011	27,720
June	105		266.768	1.0	28,011	27,720
July	105		266.768	1.0	28,011	27,720
August	105		266.768	1.0	28,011	27,720
September	106		266.768	1.1	31,105	30,814
October	107		266.768	1.1	31,398	31,107
November	110		266.768	1.2	35,213	34,922
December	157		266.768	1.2	50,258	49,966
Total					$353,495	$350,000

Figure 5.4 Combination of index seasonal adjustment and percentage adjustment for Starter Company.

The difference ($3,495) is then divided by 12 ($3,495 ÷ 12 = $291), and the resulting amount is subtracted from each month. The adjusted monthly sales then add up correctly (to $350,000).

Calculation Example—Seasonal Sales Adjustment. Take the annual sales (*A*) calculated in the Chapter 4, then:

1. Use monthly sales figures from an index such as the *Survey of Current Business* or from industry data.
2. Add up the monthly sales index to get total index sales for the year *B*.
3. Divide total annual sales *A* by total index sales *B*, which equals the sales equivalent factor *C*.
4. Multiply the index number for each month by the sales equivalent factor *C* to arrive at a monthly sales figure for your own projections.

Month	Monthly Index	×	Sales Equivalent Factor	=	Monthly Sales
January	______		______		______
February	______		______		______
March	______		______		______
April	______		______		______
May	______		______		______
June	______		______		______
July	______		______		______
August	______		______		______
September	______		______		______
October	______		______		______
November	______		______		______
December	______		______		______
Total	______				______

5. Add the monthly sales to see if the total equals your annual sales *A*. There may be rounding errors so the total may not add correctly. If the monthly sales

don't total to the right number, subtract amounts from each month's sales until the individual months add up to annual sales. The annual sales figure and the total of the monthly sales shouldn't be more than $15 off. If they are off by more than $15, you have probably made some multiplication errors. Go back and multiply each month's figures again.

Using Cost of Sales Percentages to Calculate Monthly Cost of Sales

A monthly cost of sales is calculated by multiplying each seasonally adjusted monthly sales amount by the cost of sales percentage. This makes the calculations simple because only the sales have to be adjusted for seasonal fluctuations, not the cost of sales.

Example. Using the sales figures for Starter Company shown in Figure 5.4, if the cost of sales percentage for Starter Company was the industry average of 61.96%, the January monthly sales of $21,691 would have a cost of sales of $13,440 (21,691 × 0.6196).

Calculation Example—Cost of Sales. Multiply each monthly sales figure by the cost of sales percentage (in decimal equivalent).

1. Find the cost of sales percentage *A* in decimal equivalent by dividing total annual sales by the total annual cost of sales.
2. Multiply each monthly sales figure (from the previous example) by the cost of sales percentage (in decimal form):

Month	Monthly Sales	×	Cost of Sales Percentage	=	Monthly Cost of Sales
January	______		______		______
February	______		______		______
March	______		______		______
April	______		______		______
May	______		______		______
June	______		______		______
July	______		______		______
August	______		______		______
September	______		______		______
October	______		______		______
November	______		______		______
December	______		______		______
Total	______		______		______

Calculation Example—Monthly Operating Expense. Divide total operating expense *A* by 12 to get monthly operating expense *B*.

Determining Monthly Operating Expense

Monthly operating expense can be determined once you know the annual operating expense. Assume that the operating expenses are fixed and do not vary with sales.

No matter what the sales are for the month, operating expense will be the same as it was in previous months. Therefore, calculate the monthly operating expense by dividing the annual operating expense by 12 months. Starter Company's annual operating expenses are turned into monthly operating expenses as follows:

$$\frac{\text{Annual operating expense}}{\text{12 months}} = \text{average monthly expense}$$

$$\frac{\$118{,}760}{12} =$$ The figure \$9,896.67 is rounded to 9,897 for the first eight months and \$9,896 for last four months.

Completing the Monthly Projected Income Statement Format

Figure 5.5 shows a sample format for the projected income statement and the projected cash flow. This is the SBA format. The first part of the illustration is the *forecast for profit (loss)*, or the *projected monthly income statement*. The first line is for the sales for each month, and monthly projected seasonally adjusted sales are put on the first line. For Starter Company, the first month's sales would be \$21,691; the second month's \$21,264, and so on, ending with the last month's sales of \$49,966. These sales figures are shown in Figure 5.4.

The second line of the format calls for the projected monthly cost of sales. These are arrived at by multiplying the monthly sales by the cost of sales percentage. In the case of Starter Company, this is 61.96%. So cost of sales for the first month would be \$13,440 (\$21,691 January sales × 0.6196 cost of sales); the second month's cost of sales would be \$13,175 (\$21,264 February sales × 0.6196); and the last month's (December's) cost of sales would be \$30,959 (\$49,966 sales × 0.6196).

The next line shows the gross profit, which is determined by subtracting the cost of sales (line 2) from sales (line 1). For example, gross profit for January would be \$8,251 (\$21,691 sales minus \$13,440 cost of sales).

Figure 5.6 shows how these first three steps are carried out in the Starter Company example.

If you check the calculations that went into Figure 5.6, you find that the cost of sales figures, when rounded, actually come to \$216,858 for the total year. Since 61.96% of the total sales for the year (\$350,000) is \$216,860, there is a rounding error of 2. To correct this, you must go back and subtract \$1 from each of the figures you rounded upward until two are so reduced. The cost of sales will then total \$216,860 for the year.

Annual operating expenses are converted into monthly figures by dividing by 12. On rare occasions you may choose to have some expense vary as a percentage of sales. In that case each month's variable expense would be a percentage of that month's sales, as with the cost of sales. For instance, if you had a variable sales commission expense of 10%, the commission expense for the first month would be 10% of first month's sales, and so on.

Net profit or loss is equal to the gross profit minus the operating expense. Figure 5.6 demonstrates how net profit is recorded. Note in the example that the net profit figures for the first four months (January through April) are enclosed in parentheses. This means that these months' figures represent a net loss.

PREPARING THE MONTHLY CASH FLOW

Figure 5.5 shows the format for both the projected monthly income statement and the projected monthly cash flow.

Forecast of Profit (Loss)

		Start-up or Prior to Loan	1st Month	2nd Month	3rd Month	4th Month	5th Month	6th Month	7th Month	8th Month	9th Month	10th Month	11th Month	12th Month	Total Year
1.	Total sales (net)														
2.	Cost of sales*														
3.	Gross profit (line 1 minus line 2)														
4.	Expenses (operating)														
5.	Salaries (other than owner)														
6.	Payroll taxes														
7.	Rent														
8.	Utilities (including phone)														
9.	Insurance														
10.	Professional services (i.e., accounting)														
11.	Taxes and licenses														
12.	Advertising														
13.	Supplies (for business)														
14.	Office supplies (forms, postage, etc.)														
15.	Interest (on loans, contracts, etc.)														
16.	Depreciation														
17.	Travel (including operating costs of vehicle)														
18.	Entertainment														
19.	Dues and subscriptions														
20.	Other														
21.															
22.	Total expenses (add lines 5 through 21)														
23.	Profit before taxes (line 3 minus 22)														

Figure 5.5 Monthly projection form available from the SBA.

Forecast of Cash Flow

24.	Income (cash received)	______
25.	Cash sales	______
26.	Collection of accounts receivable	______
27.	Other	______
28.	Total income (add lines 25, 26, and 27)	______
29.	Disbursements (cash paid out)	______
30.	Owner's draw	______
31.	Loan repayments (principal only)	______
32.	Cost of sales (line 2)	______
33.	Total expenses (minus line 16)	______
34.	Capital expenditures (equipment, buildings vehicles leasehold improvements)	______
35.	Reserve for taxes	______
36.	Other	______
37.	Total disbursements (add lines 30 through 36)	______
38.	Cash flow monthly (line 28 minus 37)	______
39.	Cash flow cumulative (line 38 plus line 39 of previous month)	

*Line 2—Cost of sales: *Retail*—beginning inventory purchases minus ending inventory; *Manufacturing*—cost of material, labor manufacturing.

Figure 5.5 (*Continued*)

	Jan.	Feb.	Mar.	Apr.	May	June	July	Aug.	Sept.	Oct.	Nov.	Dec.	Total Year
Sales	$21,691	21,264	24,678	24,678	27,720	27,720	27,720	27,720	30,814	31,107	34,922	49,966	350,000
Cost of sales	$13,440	13,175	15,290	15,290	17,175	17,175	17,175	17,175	19,092	19,274	21,638	30,959	216,860
Gross profit	$ 8,251	8,089	9,387	9,387	10,545	10,545	10,545	10,545	10,545	11,833	13,284	19,007	133,140
Operating expense	$ 9,842	9,842	9,842	9,842	9,842	9,842	9,842	9,842	9,842	9,842	9,842	9,843	118,105
Net profit (loss)	$(1,591)	(1,753)	(455)	(455)	703	703	703	703	703	1,991	3,442	9,165	15,035

Figure 5.6 Starter Company: projected monthly income statement, one year.

Cash flow, as the name suggests, concerns *cash* income and expenditures of the business. The projected income statement does not take into consideration that you may not collect all the sales that you make. For instance, you can sell $20,000 worth of goods in one month and give 30 days' credit. That means that you do not collect any of the first month's $20,000 until 30 days later, or the next month. Your sales for the first month are $20,000, but *cash* income (which represents collection of your receivables) is *zero*. Just as receivables are not immediately collected, accounts payable are not immediately paid.

Another characteristic of cash flow that is different from income statement projections is in the payment of cash costs that are not expenses. Income tax, the principal portion of the SBA or other loan repayment, owner's draw, and capital expenditures on equipment are not expenses. But they do represent out-of-pocket cash costs. Depreciation, by contrast, *is* an expense, but it is *not* an out-of-pocket cash cost.

Cash flow projections, therefore, take the projected income statements and adjust for collections, payable period, depreciation, and cash costs such as income tax, principal loan repayment, owner's draw, and so on.

The steps in preparing monthly cash flow projections are:

1. Adjust monthly sales for the collection period.
2. Treat loan proceeds and equity as a cash inflow item.
3. Adjust cost of sales for the payable period, if any.
4. Use total monthly operating expense less depreciation.
5. Divide annual principal loan repayment, owner's draw, and income tax into monthly amounts.
6. Record all use of funds except working capital.
7. Calculate cash flow monthly and cash flow cumulative and complete the format.

Calculation Example—Monthly Projected Income Statement. Copy Figure 5.5 and complete it for your company.

1. Write in all the totals in the thirteenth column. Write in total sales and cost of sales. Subtract cost of sales from sales to yield gross profit. Subtract operating expense from gross profit to yield net profit before taxes.
2. Substitute in the monthly sales, cost of sales and monthly operating expense calculated above.
3. Subtract cost of sales from sales to get gross sales, and then subtract operating expense from gross profit to arrive at net profit.

Monthly Cash Income (Collection of Receivables)

In the cash flow projection, *income* is represented by cash sales and/or the collection of receivables. Cash sales and collection of receivables are not the same. You can sell $20,000 worth of goods one month on 30-day terms and have no cash income for that month. That $20,000 in sales is not cash income until it is paid 30 days later. Figure 5.7 illustrates the difference.

The best way to determine the receivable collection period is to use historical data (if available). One can find the receivable period from historical data by means of the average collection period ratio. The ratio looks like this:

Step 1. $\dfrac{\text{Net sales (from P\&L)}}{\text{days in the accounting period}} = \text{average sales per day}$

Step 2. $\dfrac{\text{Receivables (from balance sheet)}}{\text{average sales per day}} = \text{average collection period in days}$

Example. Yourcompany has $288,000 in sales for the first seven months of the year and has on its balance sheet receivables of $115,164. What is the average collection period in days?

Step 1. $\dfrac{\$288{,}000 \text{ (net sales)}}{210 \text{ (30 days} \times \text{7 months)}} = \$1371 \text{ average sales per day}$

Step 2. $\dfrac{\$115{,}164 \text{ (receivables)}}{\$1371 \text{ (average sales per day)}} = \text{84-day average collection period}$

If the business is a new venture and no historical data is available, there is information on receivable collection periods in the Robert Morris *Financial Statement Studies* and other similar publications.

On the monthly cash flow projections format, there are entries for both cash sales and collection of receivables. A company has a combination of cash sales and receivables if not all the merchandise is sold on credit. List your cash sales for the month and your credit sales *collections* for the same month separately.

Now that you know your collection period, how do you use it in the projections? Arriving at the numbers for the projections requires three pieces of data and five calculation steps. This procedure is shown in Figure 5.8.

Data Needed

1. The collection period in days (calculated as explained above).
2. The dollar amount of each month's sales.
3. The number of the month for which you are calculating sales (January is the first month in the projection, February is the second month, etc.).

	Sold on 30-Day Terms	Cash Sales
Sales	$ 20,000	$20,000
Cash income	- 0 -	20,000
Cost of sales	19,000	10,000
Gross profit (cash)	(10,000)	10,000
Operating expense (cash)	8,000	8,000
Net profit (cash)	(18,000)	2,000

Figure 5.7 Difference between cash sales and collection of receivables.

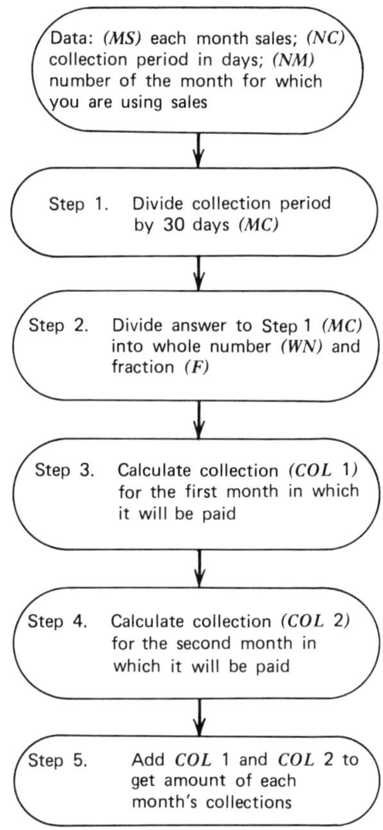

Figure 5.8 Arriving at the numbers for projections.

Calculation Steps

1. Divide the collection period in days *DC* by 30 days to arrive at the collection period in months *MC*. This number will usually be a whole number and a fraction. For instance, the day collection period illustrated for Yourcompany would be 2.8 months (84 ÷ 30 = 2.8).
2. The result from Step 1 (*MC*) should be divided into a whole number *WN* and a fraction *F*. For instance, an 84-day collection period is 2.8 months. In this step, divide the number 2.8 into a whole number, 2, and a fraction, 0.8.
3. Calculate collections that will be *paid* for the first month. Multiply the monthly sales figure *MS* by 1 minus the fraction *F* found in Step 2. For instance, if the first month's credit sales were $40,000, the amount that would first be received is $8,000. First month's sales of $40,000 are multipled by 0.2 (1 − 0.8).

   You know how much credit sales will be first collected by *MS* × (1 − 0.8). You do not know in which month they will be received. If the $40,000 in sales was for the first month of the projection, January, and $8,000 of that will be collected some time later, which month will that be? If it takes 2.8 months to collect all of the $40,000 sold in January, then the money would not start coming in until 2.8 months later, or the last part of March. Use the following system for the calculation. Take the number of the original month of sale *NM*, and add the whole number *WN* found in Step 2. The original month is 1 in the case of the first month of the projection. The example being used is $40,000 sales in month 1, January, with a 2.8-month collection period. The first payment will be in month 1 plus 2 (whole number from Step 2), that is, the third month, March.

4. Calculate the collection for the second month *COL* 2 in which the collections will be made. Take the amount of collections for the first month *COL* 1, found in Step 3, and subtract it from the monthly sales *MS*. For instance, collections in March from the $40,000 January sales in a 2.8-month collection period are $8,000. To find out what the next month's (April's) collections will be, subtract March collections of $8,000 from $40,000.

   The balance of the collections would be received the month after the one in which the collections *started*. If the collections started in March, as in the example, they will be finished in April. If the company collects $8,000 of the $40,000 in March, it should collect the balance of $32,000 in April.

5. The last step requires adding the collections for each month (*COL* 1 and *COL* 2) to get the total. For instance, $32,000 of January sales is collected in April. Some of February's sales, however, will also be collected in April because of the collection period. If there were $35,000 in sales in February, $7,000 [sales $35,000 × (1 − fraction 8.8)] would be collected in April (number of month, 2, plus whole number 2 = number of month disbursed: the fourth month, April).

Note. It is possible that your company might have a 30-, 60-, or 90-day collection period. If this is the case, all the collections will be made in one month. For a 30-day receivable period, all of January's sales will be collected in February, 30 days later. If the collection period is 60 days, all of January's sales will be collected in March. For 90 days, sales would be collected in April.

Example. Starter Company has the monthly adjusted sales shown in Figure 5.4, $21,691, for the first month (January), $21,264 for the second month (February), and $24,678 for the third month (March). All sales are on credit. The collection period in Starter Company's industry is 45 days. What are the collections for January through May?

The first step is to convert the days of the collection period DC into months. This is done by the following formula:

$$\frac{DC}{30 \text{ days}} = \frac{45}{30} = 1.5\text{-month collection period } MC$$

Divide the monthly collection period into the equivalent whole number *WN*, 1, and fraction *F*, 0.5.

The third step is to multiply the January sales *MS 1* by the fraction *F*. This is calculated as follows:

$$MS\ 1 \times F = \$21{,}691 \times 0.5 = \$10{,}846 \text{ first-month collection } COL\ 1$$

This amount (*COL* 1) would be collected in the second half of February. We know that it will be collected in the second month by adding the number of the month *NM* calculated—January, the first month—to the whole number *WN* found in Step 2.

$$NM + WN = 1 + 1 = 2 \text{ number of month collected, or February}$$

The fourth step is to find the amount of dollars collected for the second month period (*COL* 2). Subtract February's collection (*COL* 1) from January's total sales (*MS* 1). Collections in February were found to be $10,846 in Step 3. The balance of the collections, $10,845, occurs in March. This calculation is as follows:

$$MS\ 1 - COL\ 1 = \$21{,}691 - \$10{,}846 = \$10{,}845 \text{ collections for March } (COL\ 2)$$

Item Number	Jan.	Feb.	March	April	May
Sales	$21,691	$21,264	$24,678	$24,678	$27,720
Collections					
From January		10,846	10,842		
From February			10,632	10,632	
From March				12,339	12,339
Total collections					
Each month		10,846	21,474	22,971	Incomplete

Figure 5.9 Sales and collections for Starter Company.

For Step 5, add the collections for each month together. However, you have only one collection figure for each month so far. Let us put this in a table:

	January	February	March	April
Sales	$21,691	$21,264	$24,678	$24,678
Collections				
January sales	-0-	$10,846	$10,845	

For each month's collections, you repeat Steps 3, 4, and 5 and add the results to the calculations for the previous month. February sales of $21,264 would show as $10,632 collected in March and $10,632 in April. March's sales of $24,678 would have $12,339 appear in April and $12,339 in May.

Figure 5.9 shows how each of the first three months' collection figures are presented for the projections. Note that collections for all but the first two months have received amounts from two months' sales. The month of January has *no* collections because the company is new and the first month of the operation's sales are not collected until February. In March money is collected from both January and February sales. In April collections are from February and March sales, and so on. Note that collections are different from sales in *every* month.

Calculation Example—Cash Collections. First, find your collection period. The collection period is the time it takes you to collect on sales. If you are a new company you may use the industry ratios such as Robert Morris's *Annual Statement Studies* or Dun and Bradstreet's "Key Business Ratios." Find the average collection period *E* for your industry.

If you have an existing business, you may determine your average collection period by actual experience, using the following steps:

1. Divide annual credit sales *A* by the number of days in the accounting period *B* (30 days = one month, 90 days = one quarter, and 360 days = one year). This calculation will give you average sales per day *C*.
2. Divide the accounts receivable figure *D* on your balance sheet by average sales per day *C*. This equals the average collection period *E* in days.

Then, calculate your collections for the projected period by using these steps:

1. Use the form like the following to copy down your monthly sales from the previous example and calculate your monthly collections:

	Month 1	Month 2	Month 3	Month 4	Month 5	Month 6
Sales	______	______	______	______	______	______
Collections						
First part	______	______	______	______	______	______
Second part	______	______	______	______	______	______
Total collections	______	______	______	______	______	______

	Month 7	Month 8	Month 9	Month 10	Month 11	Month 12	Year
Sales	______	______	______	______	______	______	______
Collections							
First part	______	______	______	______	______	______	______
Second part	______	______	______	______	______	______	______
Total collections	______	______	______	______	______	______	______

2. Change the average collection period *E* from the previous calculations into a monthly equivalent by dividing by 30 days. This equals the collection period in months *F*.
3. Separate the collection period in months *F* into a whole number *G* and a fraction *H*.
4. Multiply the first month's sales *I* by 1 minus the fraction *H*. This equals the first part of the collections *J* − 1. This is the number that would be put in the table on the first-part collections in the column of the first month that collections will be paid. The first month in which it will be paid is determined by adding the whole number *G* to the month in which the sales are made. For example, a 75-day collection period is 2.5 months. The whole number is 2. To determine in which month the first month's sales are actually collected, you would add the whole number 2 to month 1; the first part of the collections will be in month 3. Using the same collection period, first-part collections for the *fifth* month would be paid in the *seventh* month (whole number 2 plus month 5).
5. Subtract the first-part collections *J* − 1 from first month's sales *I* to determine the second part of the collections *J* − 2, which will be in the month following the first-part collections.
6. Repeat Steps 4 and 5 for every month's sales. At the end of the year, you will have some amount of sales that has not been collected yet. These represent your accounts receivable at the end of the year and will go on your pro forma balance sheet.

Calculation Example—Collection Projection. The collection period is 72 days, or 2.4 months. Sales are as indicated in Figure 5.10.

Equity (Owner's Cash) and Loan Proceeds as Cash Inflow

The cash flow projection tells how much cash flows into the business each month and how much is spent. The collections on accounts receivable, just discussed, are one source of cash inflow. Other sources of cash inflow are loans and the owner's cash injection.

Because SBA or other loan proceeds are a source of cash, they are recorded in

	Month 1	Month 2	Month 3	Month 4	Month 5	Month 6	
Sales	$10,000	$12,000	$14,000	$16,000	$18,000	$20,000	
Collections							
First part*	—0—	—0—	4,000	4,800	5,600	6,400	
Second part**	—0—	—0—	—0—	6,000	7,200	8,400	
Total collections	—0—	—0—	$4,000	$10,800	$12,800	$14,800	
	Month 7	**Month 8**	**Month 9**	**Month 10**	**Month 11**	**Month 12**	**Year†**
Sales	$22,000	$24,000	$26,000	$20,000	$20,000	$28,000	$230,000
Collections							
First part	7,200	8,000	8,800	9,600	10,400	8,000	72,800
Second part	9,600	10,800	12,000	13,200	14,400	15,600	97,200
Total collections	$16,800	$18,800	$20,800	$22,800	$24,800	$23,600	$170,000

*First-part collections are determined by multiplying the sales by the fraction (0.4) in the monthly collection period (2.4 months).

**The second-part collections are determined by subtracting first-part collections from monthly sales. (First month: $10,000 × 0.4 = $4,000 for the first part, and $10,000 − $4,000 = $8,000 for the second part.)

†Although sales are $230,000 for the year, collections are only $170,000. The balance of $100,000 represents accounts receivable at year-end.

Figure 5.10 Monthly collections calculation.

the projected cash flow as cash inflow. Usually the loan will be disbursed (paid out) in the first month. The projection will reflect this by having loan proceeds as an entry in the first-month column.

If the business is a new one, like Starter Company, the initial funds for the business will come not only from a loan, but also from the owner's cash injection. For a new business, the SBA usually requires at least a 20% cash injection by the owner.

Collections, loan proceeds, and owner's cash injection represent cash inflow and are put at the top of the projected cash flow statement.

Cost of Sales and Cash Flow

Cost of sales is the amount each business pays for the goods it sells. Most businesses pay for these goods on credit terms. A shoe retailer might order shoes to be delivered in January, but he does not have to pay for these goods until one month later because he ordered the shoes on 30-day credit.

Every industry has a different period for which credit is extended. For instance, a grocery store usually pays cash for produce, pays for milk in 10 days, and pays for the standard grocery items monthly.

Because the cost of sales might be on credit, the expense used each month in an income or projected income statement may not involve any cash outlay until the next month or later. When you are preparing a cash flow projection, you must consider this.

Example. Starter Company buys all its merchandise on credit for 30 days, and at the end of the 30 days it pays its suppliers. From Figure 5.6, Starter will have $13,440 in cost of sales for January, $13,175 for February, $15,291 for March, and so on. What is its cash outlay for merchandise for these months?

Since Starter has 30 days to pay for the merchandise it sold in January, it does not have to pay any money until February. February cost of sales is not paid until March, March cost of sales is not paid until April, and so on.

The following is a summary of the first five months' cost of sales and payment of accounts payable:

	January	February	March	April	May
Cost of sales	$13,440	$13,175	$15,291	$15,291	$17,175
Payment of cash	—0—	13,440	13,175	15,291	15,291

If your company has a mixed payable period because it handles several different products with different credit terms (e.g., a supermarket), you may use an average period for payment. For instance, if 20% of your products are paid for in cash, 30% in 15 days, and 50% in 30 days, you might work out a weighted average as follows:

Percentage of Products Sold	× Terms in Days	= Weighted Adjustment
20	-0-	-0-
30	15	450
50	30	1500
100		1950

$$\frac{\text{Total adjustment}}{\text{total percentages}} = \frac{1950}{100} = 19.5\text{-day average}$$

The average payable period would be 19.5 days, or 20 days when rounded to the nearest day. One-third of the cost of sales is paid for in the first month, and two-thirds are paid for in the second month. The goods that you use the first 10 days (one-third of a month) will be paid for by the end of the month, 20 days later. The merchandise you sell in the last 20 days (two-thirds of a month) will not be paid for until the first of the next month.

Calculation Example—Cost of Sales Paid.

1. What are the average payable terms in days *A* for your suppliers (to be paid in 10 days, 30 days, etc.)? If you have several suppliers who have different credit terms, use the following form to calculate the average receivable period:

Percentage of Products Purchased	× Terms in Days	= Weighted Average
______________	________	________
______________	________	________
______________	________	________
______________	________	________

Total percentages ______________ (*B*) Total average______________ (*C*)

$$\frac{\text{Total weighted average } (C)}{\text{total percentages } (B)} = \text{average daily terms } (A)$$

At this point the procedures for determining accounts payable paid are exactly the same as those for accounts receivable paid, discussed above.

2. Use a form like the following to determine your monthly cost of sales that is paid on credit. Labor expenses are not paid on credit, nor is factory overhead, so if these elements are part of your cost of sales, they should be separated out and considered as cash payments.

Monthly Payable Paid Calculation

	Month 1	Month 2	Month 3	Month 4	Month 5	Month 6
Cost of sales						
Payables	______	______	______	______	______	______
Labor, overhead	______	______	______	______	______	______
Total cost of sales	______	______	______	______	______	______
Payable payments						
First part	______	______	______	______	______	______
Second part	______	______	______	______	______	______
Labor, overhead	______	______	______	______	______	______
Total cost of sales paid	______	______	______	______	______	______

	Month 7	Month 8	Month 9	Month 10	Month 11	Month 12	Year
Cost of sales							
Payables	______	______	______	______	______	______	___
Labor, overhead	______	______	______	______	______	______	___
Total cost of sales	______	______	______	______	______	______	___
Payable payments							
First part	______	______	______	______	______	______	___
Second part	______	______	______	______	______	______	___
Labor, overhead	______	______	______	______	______	______	___
Total cost of sales paid	______	______	______	______	______	______	___

3. Change average payable period A into a monthly equivalent by dividing by 30. This equals the payable period in months D.
4. Separate payable period in months D into a whole number E and a fraction F.
5. Multiply the first month's cost of sales G by 1 minus the fraction F. This equals the first part of the payables paid $H - 1$. You would place this number in the table on the first-part row in the column of the first month in which it will be paid. The first month in which it will be paid is determined by adding the whole number E to the month in which the sales are made. For example, a 75-day payable period is 2.5 months. The whole number is 2. For first-month payables, you would add the whole number 2 to month 1. The first part of the payables will be in month 3. Using the same payable period, first-part payables for the *fifth* month would be paid in the *seventh* month (whole number 2 plus month 5).
6. Subtract the first-part payables paid $H - 1$ from the first month's payables I to determine the second part of the collections $H - 2$, which will be placed in the month following the first-part payables paid.
7. Repeat Steps 5 and 6 for every month's payables. At the end of the year, you will have some amount of payables that has not been paid yet. This represents your accounts payable at the end of the year and will go on your pro forma balance sheet.

Calculation Example—Cost of Sales and Accounts Payable Projection. The payable period is 45 days, or 1.5 months. Labor and overhead expenses are paid each month when incurred and are considered cash payments. The monthly payables paid calculation is shown in Figure 5.11.

	Month 1	Month 2	Month 3	Month 4	Month 5	Month 6
Cost of sales						
Payables	$5,000	$ 6,000	$ 7,000	$ 8,000	$ 9,000	$10,000
Labor, overhead	4,000	4,000	5,000	5,000	6,000	6,000
Total cost of sales	$9,000	$10,000	$12,000	$13,000	$15,000	$16,000
Payable payments						
First part[a]	—0—	$ 2,500	$ 3,000	$ 3,500	$ 4,000	$ 4,500
Second part[b]	—0—	—0—	2,500	3,000	3,500	4,000
Labor, overhead	$4,000	4,000	5,000	5,000	6,000	6,000
Total cost of sales paid	$4,000	$ 6,500	$10,500	$11,500	$13,500	$14,500

	Month 7	Month 8	Month 9	Month 10	Month 11	Month 12	Year†
Cost of sales							
Payables	$11,000	$12,000	$13,000	$10,000	$10,000	$14,000	$115,000
Labor, overhead	7,000	7,000	8,000	8,000	8,000	9,000	77,000
Total cost of sales	$18,000	$19,000	$21,000	$18,000	$18,000	$23,000	$192,000
Payable payments							
First part*	$ 5,000	$ 5,500	$ 6,000	$ 6,500	$ 5,000	$ 5,000	$ 50,500
Second part**	4,500	5,000	5,500	6,000	6,500	5,000	45,500
Labor, overhead	7,000	7,000	8,000	8,000	8,000	9,000	77,000
Total cost of sales paid	$16,500	$17,500	$19,500	$20,500	$19,500	$19,000	$173,000

*First-part payables paid are determined by multiplying payables by the fraction (0.5) in the average payable period (1.5 months).

**Second-part collections are determined by subtracting first-part collections from monthly payables (first month: $5,000 × 0.5 = $2,500 for the first part, and $5,000 − $2,500 = $2,500 for the second part).

†Although cost of sales payables are $115,000 for the year, only $96,000 is paid. The balance of $19,000 represents accounts payable at year-end.

Figure 5.11 Monthly payables paid calculation.

Calculating Monthly Operating Expense for the Cash Flow Projections

The operating expense is an out-of-pocket cash expense only if you *exclude* depreciation. Depreciation is not a cash expense, so when preparing the monthly cash flow, use operating expense minus depreciation. Use the same operating expense calculated for the monthly projected income statement, shown in Figure 5.6, except that in the cash flow depreciation is excluded.

Example. Total operating expense for each month from January to August in the income statement projections (Figure 5.6) is $9,842. This total operating expense includes depreciation of $2,333 per month. To figure the operating expense for each of these months for the projected monthly cash flow, subtract depreciation from each month ($9,842 − $2,333 = $7,509).

Calculation Example—Monthly Operating Expense. Take total annual operating expense *A*, calculated previously, subtract from that total annual depreciation *B*, and then divide it by 12 months to get the average monthly operating expense *C*.

Other Cash Costs in the Cash Flow Projection

Other costs that usually appear on a projected cash flow statement are income tax payments, principal loan repayment, and owner's draw and could include asset increases other than those from the use of funds statement.

To get monthly projected cash flow, take the annual costs for income tax, principal loan repayment, and owner's draw, and divide by 12.

Example. In the case of Starter Company, the income tax is $1,504 for the year (10% of the $15,035 profit); principal loan repayment on a year loan is $17,387; and owner's draw is $20,000. Dividing each total by 12 would give the following:

Item	Total Year	Monthly	Explanation*
Income tax	$ 1,504	$ 125	First 8 months
		126	Last 4 months
Principal loan repayment	17,387	1,449	First 11 months
		1,448	Last month
Owner's draw	20,000	1,667	First 8 months
		1,666	Last 4 months

Note. Some totals are not evenly divided by 12; therefore, round and then compensate by a higher or lower number in some months so that the total will come out even.

Calculation Example—Other Cash Costs. Take the annual income tax *A*, principal loan repayment *B*, and owner's draw *C*, and divide by 12 months to get the average monthly cost of income tax *D*, principal loan repayment *E*, and owner's draw *F*.

Use of Loan Proceeds (Use of Funds) in Projected Cash Flow

Usually SBA loan proceeds will be spent in the first year, and this is reflected in the cash flow projections. Use of funds for the purchase of assets or repayment of debt show up as a cash cost. Since these costs are not an expense, they are shown in the projected *cash flow* but not in the projected income statement.

When loan proceeds—plus owner's cash injection in the case of a new business—are spent, they are usually labeled in the monthly cash flow as capital expenditures.

To keep the cash flow projection accurate, the loan proceeds should be shown as being spent in the months in which these expenditures are likely to occur. For instance, if $20,000 of the loan proceeds is to be used to pay off a debt, the $20,000 would be shown as spent in the very first month of the cash flow projection. However, money to purchase inventory or to pay for construction would be disbursed over the projected first year.

In some cases it might be difficult to determine *when* the money is to be disbursed; therefore, most lenders approve the convention of showing the entire amount of the use of funds in the first month.

Note. All the loan proceeds *except* working capital are shown as disbursed in the projected cash flow. Working capital is cash that the business has after it pays for equipment, debt, fixtures, deposits, and so on. Working capital should *not* be shown as a cash disbursement. The working capital balance is reflected in the cash flow cumulative total.

Example. Starter Company has requested a $175,000 SBA loan, and the owners are putting up an additional $75,000. The use of funds is as follows:

Furniture	$ 8,000
Equipment	155,000
Improvements	10,000
Inventory	57,000
Working capital	20,000
Total funds required	$250,000

Inventory and deposits will be paid immediately (January of the projected year). Equipment will be paid for in the third month (March), when it is delivered. Improvements will be disbursed in January ($5,000) and February ($5,000). Disbursements of Starter's funds under the heading of capital expenditures is recorded in the projected monthly cash flow statement, shown in Figure 5.12.

Calculation Example—Use of Funds, Capital Disbursements. Copy the following table, and use it to restate your use of funds, calculated earlier:

Furniture and fixtures	________(*A*)
Equipment	________(*B*)
Improvements and building	________(*C*)
Inventory	________(*D*)
Other	________(*E*)
Working capital	________(*F*)
Total funds required	________

The expenditure of these funds should be grouped into one row on the projected cash flow, shown in the month that they are likely to be spent. Note that if you don't know in which month the funds will be spent, the convention is to show the funds disbursed in the first month. Working capital is never shown under capital disbursements.

	Month 1	Month 2	Month 3	Month 4	Month 5	Month 6
Capital disbursements	______	______	______	______	______	______

	Month 7	Month 8	Month 9	Month 10	Month 11	Month 12	Year
Capital disbursements	______	______	______	______	______	______	___

Calculating Cash Flow Monthly and Cash Flow Cumulative, and Completing the Cash Flow Format

Cash flow monthly is the amount of money that is left over each month after costs have been paid out of income. For instance, if a company collects $100,000 in one month and pays outs $45,000 in cost of sales, $15,000 in expenses (not including depreciation), and $20,000 in tax reserves, principal loan repayment, and other costs, the cash flow for the month will be $20,000. For example:

Collections	$100,000
Total cash inflow	$100,000
Disbursements	
Cost of sales	46,000
Expenses (less depreciation)	15,000
Other costs	20,000
Total cash outflow	$ 80,000
Cash flow monthly (inflow-outflow)	$ 20,000

	Jan	Feb	March	April	May	June	July	Aug	Sept	Oct	Nov	Dec	Total Year
Cash inflow													
Collections		10,846	21,474	22,971	24,678	26,199	27,720	27,720	27,720	27,720	29,267	30,961	277,276
Loan proceeds	175,000												175,000
Owners cash injection	75,000												75,000
Total Cash Inflow	$250,000	10,846	21,474	22,971	24,678	26,199	27,720	27,720	27,720	27,720	29,267	30,961	527,276
Disbursements													
Cost of Sales		13,440	13,175	15,291	15,291	17,175	17,175	17,175	17,175	19,092	19,274	21,638	185,901
Operating Expenses (Less: Depreciation)	7,509	7,509	7,509	7,509	7,509	7,509	7,509	7,509	7,509	7,508	7,508	7,508	90,105
Income Tax	125	125	125	125	125	125	125	125	126	126	126	126	1,504
Principal Loan repayment	1,449	1,449	1,449	1,449	1,449	1,449	1,449	1,449	1,449	1,449	1,449	1,448	17,387
Owner's draw	1,667	1,667	1,667	1,667	1,667	1,667	1,667	1,667	1,666	1,666	1,666	1,666	20,000
Capital disbursements	50,000	5,000	155,000	-0-	-0-	-0-	-0-	-0-	-0-	-0-	-0-	-0-	210,000
Total Disbursements	$ 60,750	29,190	178,925	26,041	26,041	27,925	27,925	27,925	27,925	29,841	30,023	32,386	524,897
Cash flow monthly	$189,250	(18,344)	(157,451)	(3,070)	(1,363)	(1,726)	(205)	(205)	(205)	(2,121)	(756)	(1,425)	
Cash flow cumulative	$189,250	170,906	13,455	10,385	9,022	7,296	7,091	6,886	6,681	4,560	3,804	2,379	

Figure 5.12 Starter Company: projected cash flow monthly, one year.

Cash flow cumulative is the amount of cash the business has from month to month, that is, the amount of cash accumulated over the months. It is the running total of cash the company has "in the bank," much like the checking account balance of a company. For instance, if a company starts out with $1,000 in its banking account and the first month it has a monthly net cash flow of $2,000, its cash flow cumulative becomes $3,000. If the next month the company made $3,000 in net cash inflow, the cash flow cumulative figure would be $6,000.

Figure 5.13 shows the first five months' cash flow monthly and cash flow cumulative for Starter Company.

Looking at Figure 5.12, you can see that in the first month the cash flow cumulative and the cash flow monthly are the same number. This is because Starter is a new company and all its money that will be invested in the business (SBA proceeds and owner's cash) comes in the first month. Starter does not have a previous balance in its checking account. If Starter were an existing company like Yourcompany, the projection would show a beginning cash balance equal to the amount of cash it had in the bank at the *beginning* of the projected month.

Notice also that all the months except January have a negative cash flow monthly. This is because expenditures in those months exceed collections income. These negative cash flow months do not cause the company difficulty because Starter will have enough in its cash flow cumulative account to compensate. Notice that the negative February cash flow monthly of $18,344 reduces the cumulative balance of cash from $189,250 to $170,906. The negative cash flow of $157,451 in March further reduces the cash flow cumulative to $13,455, and so on.

The format of the monthly cash flow is completed when the projection is carried out across the full 12-month period. Figure 5.12 shows the projected cash flow monthly for Starter Company for the first projected year.

In Figure 5.12 notice that the collections for the first month are zero because the sales for that month are not collected until February. Even though total sales will be $350,000, total receipts (collections of receivables) will be only $277,276 for the year. Cost of sales represents payment of accounts payable, and since these are due in 30 days, the cost of sales for each month is not paid until the following month.

Calculation Example—Cash Flow Monthly and Cumulative. Use a form like the following to calculate cash flow monthly and cash flow cumulative on your projection.

	Jan.	Feb.	Mar.	Apr.	May
Collections		10,846	21,474	22,971	24,678
SBA proceeds	175,000				
Owner's cash	75,000				
Total cash inflow	250,000	10,846	21,474	22,971	24,678
Disbursements					
Cost of sales	-0-	13,440	13,175	15,291	15,291
Operating expense (Less Depreciation)	7,509	7,509	7,509	7,509	7,509
Owner's draw	1,667	1,667	1,667	1,667	1,667
Income tax	125	125	125	125	125
Principal loan repayment	1,449	1,449	1,449	1,449	1,449
Capital expenditures	50,000	5,000	155,000	-0-	-0-
Total disbursements	60,750	29,190	178,925	26,041	27,925
Cash flow monthly	189,250	(18,344)	(157,451)	(1,363)	(1,726)
Cash flow Cumulative	189,250	170,906	13,455	9,022	7,296

Figure 5.13 Starter Company: cash flow projection, first five months.

To keep it simple, we'll just use four entries: cash inflow, cash outflow, cash flow monthly, and cash flow cumulative. Cash inflow for the month includes collections, loans, and owner's equity injections. Cash outflow includes accounts payable paid, other cost of sales that doesn't create accounts payable (labor etc.), operating expense less depreciation, principal loan repayment, owner's draw, taxes, and capital disbursements.

Cash Flow Monthly and Cumulative

	Month 1	Month 2	Month 3	Month 4	Month 5	Month 6
Cash inflow	______	______	______	______	______	______
Cash outflow	______	______	______	______	______	______
Cash flow monthly	______	______	______	______	______	______
Cash flow cumulative	______	______	______	______	______	______

	Month 7	Month 8	Month 9	Month 10	Month 11	Month 12	Year
Cash inflow	______	______	______	______	______	______	___
Cash outflow	______	______	______	______	______	______	___
Cash flow monthly	______	______	______	______	______	______	___
Cash flow cumulative	______	______	______	______	______	______	___

1. Add collections, loans, and equity injection for each month, and place the total in the spaces for cash inflow.
2. Add payables paid, cost of sales that are cash (labor etc.), operating expense less depreciation, principal loan repayment, taxes, capital disbursements, and owner's draw for each month, and put that total in the spaces for cash outflow.
3. Subtract cash outflow from cash inflow. This gives you the cash flow monthly for each month. Put the figure in the appropriate spaces.
4. The first month's cash flow cumulative is the same as the first month's cash flow monthly if the business is a new one, because whatever is left after the first month stays in the checking account; it accumulates. If your business is an established one, however, cash flow cumulative for the first month equals cash flow monthly for the first projected month *plus* the money you have in the bank when the projected month starts.
5. Cash flow cumulative in month 2 equals cash flow cumulative for month 1 plus cash flow monthly for month 2. Cash flow cumulative is like a checking account: The cash you have at the end of the month equals the cash you started with (balance at the end of the previous month) plus the cash you made or minus the cash you lost during that month.

PREPARING THE PRO FORMA BALANCE SHEET AND RATIOS

Pro Forma Balance Sheet

When the loan is disbursed to Yourcompany, and the money is spent according to the use of funds statement, Yourcompany has a new balance sheet. A balance sheet at the time of disbursement of the loan is usually called a *pro forma balance sheet*.

Figure 5.14 shows how a new business and an existing business differ in their approach to preparing a pro forma balance sheet.

New Business	Existing Business
Use of funds = assets	Previous assets + use of funds = assets
Loan amount = liabilities	Previous liabilities + loan amount = liabilities
Owner's cash injection = equity	Previous equity = equity

Figure 5.14 Pro forma balance sheet.

In a *new business* the use of funds is the same as the assets, the loan amount is the same as the liabilities, and the owner's cash injection is the same as the equity.

In an *existing business* the assets on the pro forma balance sheet are a combination of the previous assets from the most current financial statement and the use of funds. For an existing business the liabilities on a pro forma balance sheet are a combination of previous liabilities and the new loan. In an existing business the pro forma balance sheet equity is *equal* to the owner's equity on the previous balance sheet. Looking at Figure 5.15, you can see that Starter Company, a new business that borrows

Use of Loan Funds		Pro Forma Balance Sheet	
		Current assets:	
Working capital	$ 40,000	Cash	$ 40,000
Inventory	37,000	Inventory	37,000
		Total current assets:	$ 77,000
		Fixed assets:	
Equipment	155,000	Equipment	155,000
Improvements	10,000	Improvements	10,000
Furniture	8,000	Furniture	8,000
		Total fixed assets:	173,000
Total funds required	250,000	Total assets	$250,000
Funds to come from loan (first year)		Current liabilities:	
Loan repayment*	17,387	Current portion debt:	17,387
Repayment after first Year*	157,613	Long-term liabilities Long-term debt	157,613
Total loan	$175,000	Total liabilities	$175,000
Owner's equity injection**	$ 75,000	Equity	$ 75,000
Total funds	$250,000	Total liability and equity	$250,000

*The principal portion of the first year's payments on the debt is equivalent to the current portion of a long-term debt. Interest payments are considered expense items, and do not show up on the balance sheet.

**Owner's equity injection is the cash the owner puts into the business.

Figure 5.15 Comparison of use of funds and balance sheet items.

$175,000 from a bank and puts up $75,000 in cash, will prepare a pro forma balance sheet.

In Figure 5.15 use of funds items become balance sheet items, as the following illustrates:

Use of Funds		Balance Sheet
Working capital	becomes	Cash (asset)
Inventory	stays	Inventory (asset)
Equipment	stays	Equipment (asset)
Improvements	stays	Improvements (asset)
Office furniture	stays	Furniture (asset)
Total funds required	becomes	Total assets
First-year principal loan repayment	becomes	Note payable—current portion (liability)
Balance of the loan (total loan minus first-year principal)	becomes	Note payable—long term (liability)
Owner's cash injection	becomes	Owner's equity

Existing businesses have a balance sheet already because they have assets, liabilities, and a net worth (equity). To prepare a pro forma balance sheet requires the use of funds plus the current balance sheet. As illustrated in Figure 5.16, the current balance sheet is put next to the use of funds. With the loan proceeds, an existing company buys new assets and sometimes pay off debt. In most cases the loan proceeds will be used to furnish the company with cash (working capital) and to purchase equipment, fixtures, and so on. To prepare a pro forma balance sheet, the company takes its existing balance sheet and adds the *new assets* it purchases with the loan proceeds to the existing assets. It adds the *new loan* to existing liabilities. Present equity will be the same as their equity on their present balance sheet.

Figure 5.16 shows how Yourcompany, an existing company, prepares its pro forma balance sheet.

Notice that the use of funds is added to the assets on the current balance sheet. Working capital is added to the existing cash, and the cash on the pro forma balance becomes $55,000. The business now has $70,000 in inventory. With the loan proceeds, the company will buy $60,000 more in inventory, so the pro forma balance sheet shows $130,000 in inventory. Similarly, the business will buy $35,000 in equipment to add to its present $190,000 in equipment.

Each month the existing business will make loan payments. These loan payments are made of up interest (an expense) and principal (the amount the loan is reduced by). The first year's principal loan repayment, therefore, represents the amount of the loan that will be paid in that year. This is called the *current portion* of the loan. The principal loan repayment in the example is $24,460, so the current portion of the debt, which is now part of the company's current liabilities, is $24,460.

Since the company is borrowing $200,000 and $24,460 will be paid the first year, the amount that is due after one year (the long-term portion of the debt) is $175,540 ($200,000 − $24,460).

Note that the equity, or net worth, which was $224,364 on the previous balance sheet, will *remain* $224,364 on the pro forma balance sheet. Since the business owner(s) did not put any new money into the business, their equity in the business remains the same.

Current Balance Sheet		Use of Funds		Pro Forma Balance Sheet	
Current assets:					
Cash	$ 10,000	Working capital	$ 45,000	$ 55,000	Cash
Accounts receivable	115,164			115,164	Accounts receivable
Inventory	70,000	Inventory	60,000	130,000	Inventory
Deposits	1,750	Prepayments	1,450	3,200	Deposits
Total current assets	$ 196,914			$ 303,364	Total current
Fixed assets:					
Equipment	$ 190,000	Equipment	35,000	$ 225,000	Equipment
Office furniture	24,000	Furniture	5,000	29,000	Furniture
Improvements	26,000	Improvements	10,000	36,000	Improvements
Less: Accumulated depreciation	(83,000)	Loan less		(83,000)	Depreciation
Total fixed assets	$ 157,000	debt repayment	$156,450	$ 207,000	Fixed assets
Total assets	$ 353,914			$ 510,364	Total assets
Current liabilities:					
Trade payable	$ 86,000			$ 86,000	Trade payable
Current portion—				24,460*	Current—SBA
debt	6,350*	Pay off current		$ 110,460	Total current
Total current Liabilities	$ 92,350	and long-term debt	$ 43,550		
Long-term liabilities:					
Long-term debt	37,200*			$ 175,540*	Long term—SBA
Total long-term				$ 175,540	Total long term
liabilities	$ 37,200	Debt payment		$ 286,000	Total liabilities
Total liabilities	$ 129,550	portion of loan	$ 43,550*		
Equity	$ 224,364			$ 224,364	Equity
Total liabilities				$ 510,364	Total
and equity	$ 353,914				

*Part of the loan proceeds are used to reduce present debt.

Figure 5.16 Yourcompany: pro forma and comparative balance sheet.

Some of the money Yourcompany borrowed is used to pay off a present loan of $43,550 ($6,350 current portion, plus $37,200 long-term portion). The present debt of the company will be paid off in full, and the new debt of $200,000 will be substituted ($24,460 current portion and $175,540 long term). The new debt *replaces* the old debt; it is *not added to* the old debt. If an existing company does not borrow money to pay off debt, then current debt from the current balance sheet is *added to* the loan amount.

Calculation Example—Pro Forma Balance Sheet.

1. List your use of funds on a form like the following:

Furniture and fixtures	__________
Equipment	__________
Improvements and building	__________

Inventory	__________
Other	__________
Working capital	__________
Total funds required	__________

2. Follow this form to prepare your pro forma balance sheet:

Current assets		Current liabilities	
Cash	________	Accounts payable	________
Accounts receivable	________	Current portion SBA debt	________
Inventory	________	Current portion other debt	________
Deposits	________	Total current liabilities	________
Total current assets	________		
Fixed assets		Long-term liabilities	
Equipment	________	Officer loans	________
Furniture and fixtures	________	Long-term portion SBA	________
Improvements	________	Long-term portion other	________
Less: Depreciation	________	Total long-term liabilities	________
Total fixed assets	________	Total liabilities	________
Other assets	________	Owner's equity	________
		Retained earnings	________
		Total owner's equity	________
Total assets	________	Total liabilities and equity	________

3. If yours is a new business, transfer the use of funds items to the balance sheet form. The names for the balance sheet items are the same as the names for the use of funds items except for working capital, which becomes cash on the balance sheet. A new business will probably not have accounts receivable, accumulated depreciation, accounts payable, other debt, and retained earnings on the pro forma balance sheet.
4. If yours is an existing business, you must take your current balance sheet and add the use of funds to it. For instance, cash from the present balance sheet is added to working capital from the loan proceeds, value of present equipment is added to equipment to be purchased with the loan proceeds, and so on. Accounts receivable, accumulated depreciation, accounts payable, other debt, present equity, and retained earnings are simply carried over from your current balance sheet.
5. Add up all items to make sure that the total for assets equals the total for liabilities and equity.

Ratios

Along with your other financial statements, projections, and pro forma, the lender generally likes to see the calculations of two ratios: the debt-to-worth ratio and the current ratio. Both ratios are calculated from balance sheet items. The ratios go right after the pro forma balance sheet. Both the present ratios from the current balance sheet are used in the loan proposal. The ratios are as follows:

Debt-to-worth ratio = total debt ÷ net worth

Current ratio = current assets ÷ current liabilities

Using the figures from Yourcompany's current balance sheet (Figure 5.16), total debt is \$129,550 (total liabilities), net worth is \$224,364, current assets are \$196,914, and current liabilities are \$92,350.

Debt-to-worth = \$129,550 ÷ \$224,364 = 0.57

Current ratio = \$196,914 ÷ \$92,350 = 2.13

When the company borrows more money and adds to its assets and liabilities, these ratios change. From the pro forma balance sheet in Figure 5.16, debt is \$286,000, net worth is \$224,364, current assets are \$303,364, and current liabilities are \$110,460.

Debt-to-worth ratio = \$286,000 ÷ \$224,364 = 1.27

Current ratio = \$303,364 ÷ \$110,460 = 2.74

Calculation Example—Ratios.

1. To calculate the ratios you need total debt *A*, net worth *B*, current assets *C*, and current liabilities *D*.
2. To determine your debt-to-worth ratio, divide total debt *A* by net worth *B*.
3. To arrive at the current ratio, divide current assets *C* by current liabilities *D*.

Note. If yours is an existing business, calculate ratios for both the present company balance sheet and the pro forma balance sheet. For a new business, only pro forma balance sheet ratios can be calculated.

Preparing the Pro Forma Balance Sheet and Ratios

What do these ratios mean? The *debt-to-worth ratio* shows a lender how highly "leveraged" your business is—that is, how much debt you have in relation to your equity in the business. If this number gets higher, it indicates to the bank that the business has much more of other people's money than owner's money. For instance, the debt-to-worth ratio of 0.57 means that the owner owes *less* than he or she has invested, which is to a lender excellent. When the owner takes out the loan, the ratio changes to 1.27, that is, the owner now owes 1.27 times *more* than he or she has invested. Small debt-to-worth ratios are all right, but you can see that if the ratio approached 10 to 15, the lender would be concerned because the owner would not have much to lose if the business goes under.

The *current ratio* indicates whether a business can use current assets (those that can be liquidated within one year) to pay off current liabilities (those due within one year). The higher this number, the better, because a high number assures the bank that for the next year the company can cover its existing debt. If the number is less than 1, it means that the company cannot cover its short-term debt out of its current assets.

Chapter Six

Proposal Write-Up

The market analysis you have prepared is the justification for your sales. The financial schedules you have prepared are the justification for your loan.

In this chapter all the data, calculations, schedules, and write-ups you have prepared are assembled in a proposal format. There are three basic steps:

1. Footnote the financial statements.
2. Prepare the loan summary and market analysis write-up.
3. Fill out the government loan forms, and organize the exhibits.

FOOTNOTE FINANCIAL STATEMENTS

When you prepared the financial projections and proposed use of funds, you knew where the data came from. But the banker does not. Footnotes justify the numbers used in your financial analysis. A lender considers a financial projection without footnotes to be pure fiction. Footnotes answer the following questions:

Where did you get the information for the projections or use of funds?

How do the projected figures differ from historical or industry data?

For categories of costs such as salaries, depreciation, cost of sales, and so on, what are the individual items in that category? For instance, $20,000 in salaries could include one person, two persons, three persons, or more. Each person is a component of the salary cost.

Is there any special information about the projected numbers or use of funds that the banker should know?

As you can see in Figure 6.1, the following are always footnoted:

1. Use of funds statement.
2. Annual comparative and projected financial statements.
3. Operating expense schedule (if separate from annual comparative and projected financial statement).
4. Projected monthly income statement.
5. Projected monthly cash flow statement.
6. Pro forma and comparative balance sheet and ratios.

Statement	Always Footnote	Also Footnote
Use of funds statement	Equipment; debt repayment leasehold improvements; land and building, deposits, and prepayments, owner's cash injection	Working capital if amount is over 25% of total loan request
Annual	Sales; cost of sales; total operating expense; principal loan repayment; income tax	Extraordinary cash flow items
Operating expense	Salaries, payroll tax; rent, depreciation, interest	All expenses that are large or fluctuate over history
Monthly income statement	Sales, cost of sales; total operating expense	None
Monthly cash flow statement	Collections; loan proceeds and equity; operating expense; principal loan repayment; income tax; capital disbursements	Cost of sales if a payable period is used or any extraordinary cash cost
Pro forma balance sheet	Modifications made in historical figures; unusual ratio results	None

Figure 6.1 Footnoting financial statements.

Some items in these schedules are always footnoted as a matter of course because lenders are particularly interested in these figures. Sales, for example, are footnoted in any schedule in which they appear because sales determine your company's ability to repay the lender. Many people tend to overestimate sales and base their sales projection on speculation. Therefore, the lender is interested in your explanation for projected and historical sales.

Use of Funds Statement

The use of funds statement tells the lender what you will purchase with the loan proceeds and what kind of collateral the banker will have. If you intend to borrow money for equipment, leasehold improvements, or whatever, all these items should be based on written estimates of cost. If you ask for $20,000 for equipment, you should have a written estimate for $20,000 from a supplier in the exhibit section of your loan proposal. A footnote for these items would read, "See written estimates, Exhibit II." Or you could list the separate costs of each item and add a reference to the written estimates. For instance: "Equipment includes one printing press at $16,000, one automated test line at $5,400, and one computer system at $42,000. See written estimate, Exhibit II."

Debt repayment from loan proceeds requires a special footnote. The lender wants to know what debt you are repaying, how much you are paying on the debt now, what the interest rate is, and who holds the note. He or she might also want to know why you feel you must pay off this debt with your loan. A sample footnote for debt repayment might be: "Debt repayment is for $55,000 note owed Gold Bank, 20 Tops Drive, Jewel, Minnesota. The interest rate is 14.0% payable in four years at $1,502.96

per month. Present balance is $43,550. Better cash flow calls for a substitution of the lower interest loan requested."

Working capital should be footnoted whenever it amounts to more than 25% of the total loan amount. The lender gets nervous when working capital exceeds 25% of the funds. Therefore, you must footnote working capital to explain why so much is required. Reasons might be that the company has a long receivable period, which requires large amounts of working capital, or that the business is growing rapidly.

If you are starting a new business and part of the capitalization is your own cash injection, footnote your source of funds. Most businesspeople get the money to start a business from a number of sources: personal loans, savings, stocks, mortgages on residences, cash value of their life insurance policies, and so on. The lender would like to know from what sources the cash injection is coming to determine if you have overextended yourself financially.

Example. Starter Company has the following use of funds statement that requires the illustrated footnotes:

Use of Funds		
Equipment	$155,000 (1)	
Leasehold improvements	10,000 (2)	
Office furniture	8,000 (2)	
Working capital	40,000	
Inventory	37,000	
Total funds required		$250,000
Less: Owner's cash injection		75,000 (3)
Total SBA loan required		$175,000

Footnotes:

(1) Equipment includes the following items and costs. For written estimates, see Exhibit I.

Two Ford half-ton pickups	$25,000
Clark forklift	27,000
Shipping and packaging equipment	63,000
ZigZag Systems computer	40,000

(2) For leasehold improvements and office furniture estimates, see Exhibit I.
(3) Owner's cash injection will be from:

Cash in Gold Bank (savings account No. 234.23-789)	$18,000
Second trust deed on residence	50,000
Cash value of life insurance	7,000

Calculation Example—Use of Funds. The following form can be used as a model for your own loan proposal; you can use it word for word, copying all the information you've researched and calculated onto it. You can ignore uses of funds items that you do not use for your own business and delete them from the final presentation. For example, if you are not buying equipment with the loan proceeds, you need not include it on your form.

Use of Funds Format

Equipment and auto	________(1)
Furniture and fixtures	________(1)
Improvements and building	________(1)
Land	________(1)
Inventory	________
Goodwill	________(2)
Advertising and brochures	________(3)
Deposits	________(4)
Other	________(5)
Working capital	________
Total funds required	________
Less: Owner's cash injection	________(6)
Total loan requested	________

Footnotes:

(1) Equipment, furniture, improvements, and land include the following items and costs. For written estimates, see Exhibit I.

Item	Amount ($)

(2) Goodwill is calculated according to the purchase agreement shown in Exhibit I.

(3) Advertising and brochures costs are required to ____________________ __________. The costs are as follows:

Item	Amount ($)

(4) Deposits are: lease deposit $______, utility deposits $______, license fees $______ and (add any other deposits you may have).

(5) Include an explanation for any other item you are required to pay for, referring the lender to Exhibit I for written estimates.

(6) Owners' cash injection comes from the following sources:

Institution (Bank)	Account Number	Amount ($)

(This is not required if you have an existing business.)

Annual Comparative and Projected Financial Statements

For the annual comparative and projected financial statements, you must always footnote:

Sales
Cost of sales
Total operating expense
Principal loan repayment
Income tax

Sales, cost of sales, and operating expense footnotes must explain the projected figures and indicate the historical trends. A footnote might read, "Sales increased 12% from 1978 to 1979 and 14% from 1979 to 1989."

If your company cannot produce the sales, you cannot repay the lender. If your company is an existing one and does not have to increase sales by much to repay the loan, footnoting can be very modest, only suggesting historical growth patterns and trends. If the business is a new one or the company has to expand present sales by a substantial amount (more than 25%) to make cash break-even sales, footnotes to sales must be extensive. A sample loan proposal appears in Appendix II.

If your company is new, summarize the market analysis in about half a page under the sales footnote and refer the lender to the full market analysis elsewhere in your loan proposal.

For an established business, summarize historical sales growth in the sales footnote. This is illustrated in Figure 6.2.

Sales	$350,000 (1)
Cost of sales	216,860 (2)
Gross profit	133,140
Operating expense	118,105 (3)
Net profit	15,035
Add:	
Depreciation	28,000
cash inflow	43,035
Less:	
Principal loan repayment	17,387 (4)
Income tax	1,504 (5)
Owner's draw	20,000
Cash outflow	38,891
Cash margin	4,144

Footnotes:

(1) *Sales* are based on a conservative estimate of the home electronics market for New City. The 21,500 residents of the city have an average family income of $47,200. The National Home Electronics Association suggests this is the right type of market for sales of electronics that range in price from $100 to several thousand dollars. The average sales nationally of a store this size is $500,000. See the Market Analysis that follows for more details.

(2) *Cost of sales* is 61.96%, the same as the national average for home electronics stores.

(3) *Total operating expense* is spelled out item-by-item in the following schedule and notes.

(4) *Principal loan repayment* is for $175,000, 11.5%, SBA-guaranteed loan amortized over 7 years. Principal and interest payments are $37,512 per annum, $3,126 per month.

(5) *Income tax* is 10% of net profit to pay state and federal income tax.

Figure 6.2 Starter Company: projected annual financial statement, first year.

Principal loan repayment is footnoted to indicate the amount of the loan and the terms. For instance, "Principal loan repayment is on the $175,000, six-year, 11.5% SBA loan requested." If principal loan repayment includes principal from more than one loan, this should be explained. For instance, "Principal loan repayment includes $20,386 for $175,000, six-year, 11.5% SBA loan and $6,345 for $200,000, 20-year, 10% mortgage loan."

Income tax footnotes should indicate the tax percentage used in the calculations. For instance, "Income tax represents 20% of net income for state and federal income taxes."

Figure 6.2 shows how a sample annual projected financial statement from Starter Company, a start-up business, is footnoted.

Operating Expense Schedule

When you footnote operating expenses, always make a notation of:

Salaries
Payroll tax
Rent or leases
Depreciation
Interest

Also footnote any expense item that is unusual or that has fluctuated greatly over the past few years (e.g., from $1,000 to $7,000 to $3,000).

Salaries footnotes show how many people the expense includes and at what pay. For instance, a footnote could read, "Salaries include $14,000 per annum for one full-time employee and $8,000 per year for each of two part-time employees."

Payroll tax expense will vary over time as a percentage of total payroll. Now in most states it will be about 13% or more of salaries.

When footnoting rent or leases (e.g., duplicating equipment), the lease contracts should be referred to and explained briefly. For instance, the footnote could read, "Rent is presently $1,500 per month for 1,000 square foot area. Lease is triple net and has a cost of living clause. See Exhibit II."

The depreciation footnote uses a schedule of depreciation that includes the assets being depreciated, their original cost, the depreciation method used, the life of the asset, its salvage value, and the amount of depreciation for each year. For instance, the footnote might read:

Depreciation for Starter Company is calculated according to the following schedule:

Cost	Item	Method	Salvage	Life (years)	Annual Depreciation
$ 25,000	Automobile	SL	$ 7,000	3	$ 6,000
130,000	Equipment	SL	30,000	5	20,000
8,000	Furniture	SL	1,000	7	1,000
10,000	Leasehold improvements	SL	–0–	10	1,000
Total					$28,000

Interest is footnoted to restate the loan amount and terms. For instance, the footnote for Starter Company would be; "Interest is for $175,000, seven-year, 11.5% SBA loan. Principal and interest payments are $37,512."

Projected Monthly Income Statement

The projected monthly income statement would have footnotes for the following items:

Sales
Cost of sales
Total operating expense

The footnotes for these items are exactly like those on the annual projections just discussed. You may choose to use the same footnote for both schedules.

There are usually no other items footnoted on the projected monthly income statement.

Projected Monthly Cash Flow

The projected monthly cash flow has footnotes for the following items:

Collections (for companies with accounts receivable) and sales (for other companies)
Loan proceeds and equity injection
Operating expense
Principal loan repayment
Income tax
Capital disbursements

Operating expense, principal loan repayment, and income tax are footnoted exactly as they appear in the annual projections.

Collections is the money you collect on your sales. Because the amount of money you collect is the main source of cash inflow, the lender is extremely interested in collections. Collections should be footnoted indicating the collection period and any past history. For instance, collections could be footnoted, "Collections are for a 52-day period in accordance with recent data. Collection periods in previous years were: 1980, 60 days; 1981, 57 days; 1982 (last year), 52 days."

Capital disbursements are expenditures for fixed assets, deposits, other assets, inventory, and liability repayment. Capital disbursements include every item of the use of funds statement *except* working capital. Footnotes for capital disbursements should include a list of the items and the amounts spent. For instance, the footnote could read:

Capital disbursements include the following items and amounts:

Equipment	$ 54,000
Deposits	3,000
Debt repayments	9,000
Inventory	23,000
Liquor license	20,000

Example. Figure 6.3 shows the comparative and projected annual financial statements and monthly income and cash flow schedules with corresponding footnotes for Yourcompany. The comparative and projected financial statements include income statements from the last three years, a current statement, an annualized current statement, and a projected annual income statement and annual cash flow.

	12 Month 12/31/81 Income Tax	12 Month 12/31/82 Income Tax	7/30/83 7 Months P&L	7/30/83 12 Months Annualized	Projected 12 Months
Sales	490,000	600,000	380,117	651,629	650,000 (1)
Cost of sales	318,500	369,000	235,673	404,010	403,000 (2)
Gross profit	171,500	231,000	144,444	247,619	247,000
Operation expenses:					
Salaries	73,000	85,000	58,480	100,000	85,000 (A)
Payroll tax	8,250	9,350	6,433	11,000	9,350 (B)
Rent	7,000	9,000	5,263	9,000	9,000 (C)
Office supplies	1,200	1,400	702	1,200	1,200
Bad debt	400	500	263	450	450
Advertising	4,000	5,000	3,216	5,500	4,400
Depreciation	5,000	6,000	3,909	6,000	10,300 (D)
Utilities	1,300	1,300	760	1,500	1,500
Phone	2,000	2,100	1,228	2,100	2,100
Accounting and legal	1,400	1,800	1,053	1,800	1,800
Auto and travel	1,000	1,900	1,170	2,000	2,000
Miscellaneous	200	250	117	200	250
Interest	1,500	1,750	1,023	1,750	20,000 (E)
Total operating expenses	105,250	125,350	83,217	142,300	147,350 (3)
Net profit	66,250	105,650	61,227	105,319	99,650
Add: Depreciation	5,000	6,000	3,909	6,000	10,300 (D)
Cash inflow	71,250	111,650	65,136	111,319	109,950
Less: Principal loan repayment	2,000	2,100	1,225	2,100	24,460 (E)
Income tax	29,813	50,243	27,552	47,394	44,843 (4)
Owners' draw	18,000	19,000	13,417	23,000	24,000 (5)
Cash outflow	49,813	71,343	42,194	72,494	93,303
Cash margin	21,437	34,307	22,942	38,825	16,647
Common-sized:					
Sales	100.00	100.00	100.00		100.00
Cost of sales	65.00	61.50	62.00		62.00
Gross profit	35.00	38.5	38.00		38.00
Operating expense	21.47	20.89	21.89		22.67
Net profit	13.53	17.61	16.11		15.33

Comments Re Projected Items

Note: All projections, except where otherwise noted, are based on historical experience of Yourcompany.

(1) *Sales* are projected at the same figure as the 7/30/83 annualization. This represents a very conservative projection of sales because the company has in the past shown a history of annually increasing sales. The following schedule of sales demonstrates this:

Year	Dollar Sales	Percentage Increase Over Previous Year
1981	$490,000	16.67%
1982	600,000	22.45
1983 (annual)	651,621	8.6
Projected	650,000	No increase

(2) *Cost of sales* are projected at 62% of sales in line with the most recent experience (7/30/83). Historical cost of sales have varied from 61.5% (1982) to 65% (1981).

(3) *Total operating expense* is explained in the following footnotes 3-A to 3-E.

Figure 6.3 Yourcompany: comparative and projected financials.

(3-A) *Salaries* will decline from historical levels after the proposed purchase of the automated system requested with the SBA loan. In the projected year, salaries will include:

Personnel	Annual Salary
Engineer	$ 35,000
2 Shipping Clerks	30,000 ($16,000 and $14,000)
Secretary	10,000
Part-time help	10,000

One shipping clerk and a part-time bookkeeper have been eliminated from the previous year.

(3-B) *Payroll tax* is 11 percent of salaries.

(3-C) *Rent* is $750 per month as per the lease, Exhibit II. Rent is scheduled to increase in 1985 and after.

(3-D) *Depreciation* is according to this schedule:

Method	Item	Cost	Life	Salvage	Depreciation
SL	Slapinator	$15,000	10 yrs.	$4,000	$ 1,100
SL	Assembly line equipment	20,000	10 yrs.	3,000	1,700
SL	Shelving and improvements	10,000	8 yrs.	2,000	1,000
SL	Furniture	5,000	8 yrs.	1,000	500
—	Present equipment	—	—	—	6,000
Total					$10,300

(3-E) *Interest* and *Principal* are for $200,000 SBA, 10%, 6-year loan. Interest appears as an expense, principal appears as a cash cost. Monthly payments are $3705; annual payments are $44,460 for both principal and interest.

(4) *Income tax* is calculated at 45% of net profit for payment of both state and federal income tax.

(5) *Owners' draw* represents $22,000 for John Your and $2000 for 20% partner Tath Tacki (see SBA Form 4).

(6) *Collections* of accounts receivable are based on the historical experience of 84 days. Monthly inflow is represented by the following schedule. In the schedule the heading "M—2" means that the collections indicated come from the month two previous to the present month. "M—3" means that the receipts are from a month three months previous to the present month. Part of December 1983 Sales are collected in February of 1984 (indicated by "M—2") and the balance is collected in March of 1984 (called "M—3").

	Dec. 83	Jan. 84	Feb.	March
From M—2 (× 0.2)	13,806	14,352	21,671	8,125
From M—3 (× 0.8)	48,724	55,224	57,408	86,684
Total month	62,530	69,576	79,079	94,809
	April	**May**	**June**	**July**
From M—2 (× 0.2)	6,773	8,125	8,398	9,204
From M—3 (× 0.8)	32,500	27,092	32,500	33,592
Total month	39,273	35,217	40,898	42,796
	Aug.	**Sept.**	**Oct.**	**Nov.**
From M—2 (× 0.2)	10,296	8,125	8,944	12,181
From M—3 (× 0.8)	36,816	41,184	32,500	35,776
Total month	47,112	49,309	41,444	47,957

Figure 6.3 (*Continued*)

(7) *Capital Disbursements* include the following items:

Inventory	$60,000*
Prepayments	1,450*
Equipment	35,00 (paid in February 1984)
Improvements	10,000 (paid in January 1984)
Furniture	5,000*
Debt repayment	43,550*

*Indicates that items are to be disbursed in the first month, December 1983.

Figure 6.3 (***Continued***)

	12 Month _/_/_ Income Tax	12 Month _/_/_ Income Tax	_Month _/_/_ P&L	12 Month _/_/_ P&L	Projected 12 Month	
Sales	____	____	____	____	____	(1)
Cost of sales	____	____	____	____	____	(2)
Gross profit	____	____	____	____	____	
Operating expenses						
Administration	____	____	____	____	____	
Advertising	____	____	____	____	____	
Automobile	____	____	____	____	____	
Bank service	____	____	____	____	____	
Cash short	____	____	____	____	____	
Depreciation	____	____	____	____	____	(3A)
Entertainment	____	____	____	____	____	
Insurance	____	____	____	____	____	
Interest	____	____	____	____	____	(3B)
Legal and accounting	____	____	____	____	____	
Licenses and tax	____	____	____	____	____	
Losses	____	____	____	____	____	
Laundry	____	____	____	____	____	
Miscellaneous	____	____	____	____	____	
Office Supplies	____	____	____	____	____	
Officer's Salary	____	____	____	____	____	
Outside Service	____	____	____	____	____	
Postage	____	____	____	____	____	
Payroll	____	____	____	____	____	(3C)
Payroll tax	____	____	____	____	____	(3D)
Rent	____	____	____	____	____	(3E)
Repairs and Maintenance	____	____	____	____	____	
Supplies	____	____	____	____	____	
Travel	____	____	____	____	____	
Utilities and phone	____	____	____	____	____	
Total Operating Expense	____	____	____	____	____	(3)
Net Income	$____	____	____	____	____	
Add: Depreciation	____	____	____	____	____	
Total cash inflow	____	____	____	____	____	
Less: Income tax	____	____	____	____	____	(4)
Principal repayment	____	____	____	____	____	(3B)
Owner's draw	____	____	____	____	____	
Total cash outflow	____	____	____	____	____	
Cash margin	$____	____	____	____	____	

Figure 6.4 Comparative and projected financial statements.

Calculation Example—Financial Statement Projection and Footnotes. The form shown in Figure 6.4 can be used as a model for your loan proposal, but delete any item that does not apply to your business.

Fill in all the headings with the appropriate date. You should have annual statements for at least two years if your business is an existing one. The last financial statement you have is probably an interim statement for less than a whole year. This statement is then annualized to give the figures on an annualized basis as calculated in Chapter 5. If your business is new, you will have only the projected-year column to fill out.

Fill in all other blanks with information from the financial statements you have and the financial calculations you did for the projection.

When you have filled in the comparative and projected financial statement form, the next step is to do monthly projections using a format like that shown in Figure 6.5.

Footnotes on Projected Items. Use the following format for your footnotes to the projections. In some cases you may decide to use this exact wording, but adding other information to footnotes is a good idea.

(1) *Sales* are based on expected income for the first year of operations. See Market Analysis, which follows, for details. Monthly sales and collections on the monthly projections are seasonally adjusted according to the *Survey of Current Business*'s retail sales index for 19__________ (see Exhibit II).

(2) *Cost of sales* is based on __________% of sales as represented in the *RMA Annual Statement Studies 1980*. (For existing businesses, this would read, "Cost of Sales is based on __________%, the average cost of sales for the company from financial statements for years 19__________, 19__________, and 19__________.")

(3) *Operating expenses* are based on historical and industry averages. Operating expenses are explained in more detail in the following footnotes.

(3A) Depreciation is based on the following table:

Value	Item	Life (years)	Salvage	Method	Annual Depreciation
\$____	Automobile and truck	5	\$____	SL	\$__________
____	Equipment	5	____	SL	__________
____	Furniture and fixtures	7	____	SL	__________
____	Improvements	10	____	SL	__________
	Total depreciation				\$__________

(3B) *Interest* is for \$____ SBA direct loan for ____years at ____% per annum. *Principal loan repayment* represents \$____ the first year.

(3C) *Payroll* is for _____employees as follows:

Employee Position	Monthly Salary	Annual Salary
________________	\$__________	\$__________
________________	__________	__________
________________	__________	__________
________________	__________	__________
Totals	\$__________	\$__________

	Month 1	Month 2	Month 3	Month 4	Month 5	Month 6
Monthly projected income statement						
Sales (1)	$____	$____	$____	$____	$____	$____
Cost of sales (2)	____	____	____	____	____	____
Gross profit	____	____	____	____	____	____
Expenses (3)	____	____	____	____	____	____
Net profit	$____	$____	$____	$____	$____	$____
Monthly projected cash flow						
Collections (5)	$____	$____	$____	$____	$____	$____
Equity	____					
Loan proceeds	____					
Cash inflow	$____	$____	$____	$____	$____	$____
Cost of sales	$____	$____	$____	$____	$____	$____
Operating expense (less depreciation)	____	____	____	____	____	____
Income tax (4)	____	____	____	____	____	____
Principal loan repayment	____	____	____	____	____	____
Owner's draw	____	____	____	____	____	____
Capital disbursements (6)	____					
Cash outflow	$____	$____	$____	$____	$____	$____
Cash flow monthly	$____	$____	$____	$____	$____	$____
Cash flow cumulative	$____	$____	$____	$____	$____	$____

	Month 7	Month 8	Month 9	Month 10	Month 11	Month 12	Total
Monthly projected income statement							
Sales	$____	$____	$____	$____	$____	$____	$____
Cost of sales	____	____	____	____	____	____	____
Gross profit	____	____	____	____	____	____	____
Expense	____	____	____	____	____	____	____
Net profit	$____	$____	$____	$____	$____	$____	$____
Monthly cash flow							
Collections	$____	$____	$____	$____	$____	$____	$____
Equity							____
Loans							____
Cash inflow	$____	$____	$____	$____	$____	$____	$____
Cost of sales	$____	$____	$____	$____	$____	$____	$____
Operating expense	____	____	____	____	____	____	____
Income tax	____	____	____	____	____	____	____
Principal loan repayment	____	____	____	____	____	____	____
Owner's draw	____	____	____	____	____	____	____
Asset P							____
Cash out	$____	$____	$____	$____	$____	$____	$____
Cash flow monthly	$____	$____	$____	$____	$____	$____	$____
Cash flow cumulative	$____	$____	$____	$____	$____	$____	$____

Figure 6.5 Monthly projections.

(3D) *Payroll tax* and *benefits* are projected at ______ of salaries for state, federal, and local authorities.

(3E) *Rent* for the premises is expected to be $______ per month. The proposed lease is shown in Exhibit II.

Note. Total operating expense in the projected monthly cash flow is less depreciation, a noncash expense.

(4) *Income tax* is based on ______% of net profit. Investment tax credit is not taken into consideration.

(5) *Collections* of accounts receivable are based on historical experience ("industry average" if the business is new). Collections are based on an average collection period of ______days for credit sales. Cash sales are recorded in the month in which they occur. Cash sales represent ______% of total sales.

(6) *Capital disbursements* are based on use of funds. See first page of proposal and Exhibit II.

Calculation Example—Personal Financial Statement and Footnotes. All financial lenders require personal financial statements on borrowers. Usually they require a personal financial statement with a detailed explanation for each person who owns 20% or more of the company.

Lenders also require a résumé on each person who owns 20% or more and on all major personnel in the company. An example for this is given later in this chapter.

Get together all your notes payable (debts you owe but haven't yet paid off, including your mortgage note). Copy Figure 6.6, the personal financial statement, and fill in the information requested,

______________(person's name) Personal Financial Statement

Assets		Liabilities and Worth	
	$______	Credit cards	$______
Deposits in escrow	______(1)	Notes payable	______(5)
Automobiles	______(2)	Mortgages	______(4)
Notes receivable	______(3)	Total liabilities	$______
Real estate	______(4)		
Personal property	______	Net Worth	______
Total assets	$______	Total liabilities minus net worth	$______

Footnotes:

(1) Deposits in escrow as part of purchase agreement.

(2) Automobiles include: year/make/model ______________

(3) Borrower ______________ is owed the following amounts by these persons:

Debtor and Address	Amount Owed	Terms
______	______	______
______	______	______
______	______	______

(4) Real estate owned includes:

Property Address	Market Value	Amount owed	Mortgage Holder
______	______	______	______
______	______	______	______

(5) Notes payable include the following:

Note Holder	Amount	How Secured
______	______	______
______	______	______

Figure 6.6 Personal financial statement.

Pro Forma and Comparative Balance Sheet

The pro forma balance sheet generally does not have any footnotes. The comparative and pro forma balance sheets would be footnoted only if changes in historical data have to be made before the balance sheet is accurate (e.g., if loans payable are shown as $20,000 but are in fact $25,000).

When calculating the debt-to-worth ratio or other ratios, if you find that your ratios do not correspond to industry averages, explain the differences in a footnote.

Calculation Example—Pro Forma Balance Sheet. Figure 6.7 is a pro forma balance sheet form. Copy it, and fill in the At Disbursement column according to the instructions in Chapter 5.

The Year-end year 1 column can be filled in only after you've prepared the monthly cash flow for the year. The year-end balance sheet will be different than the at disbursement balance sheet because during the year the company has had financial transactions that alter the balance sheet. For instance, the amount of cash is going to be different, and so are the amount of debt you owe and your (owner's) equity in the business.

To prepare the year-end statement, you need the following items from your other calculations:

1. The last cumulative cash flow amount in column 12 of the monthly cash flow projection represents the amount of cash you have in your checking account

	At Disbursement		Year-end Year 1	
Assets				
Cash	$______		$______	
Inventory	______		______	
Deposits	______		______	
Total current assets		______		______
Automobile	______		______	
Equipment	______		______	
Furniture and fixtures	______		______	
Improvements and buildings	______		______	
Less: Depreciation	______		______	
Land	______		______	
Total fixed assets		______		______
Goodwill	______		______	
Research and development	______		______	
Total other assets		______		______
Total assets		$______		$______
Liabilities and net worth				
Accounts payable	$______		$______	
SBA loan payable—current	______		______	
Notes payable—other	______		______	
Total current liabilities		______		______
SBA loan payable—long term	______		______	
Other notes payable—long term		______		______
Owner's capital	______		______	
Retained earnings	______		______	
Owner's equity		______		______
Total liabilities and owner's equity		$______		$______

Figure 6.7 Pro forma balance sheet.

at the end of the first year. Therefore, this figure becomes the cash item in the year-end balance sheet.

2. Accounts receivable is the amount of sales that went uncollected at the end of the year. Accounts receivable represents the difference between the sales you made in the projected year and the amount you collected. For a new business, the amount of accounts receivable at the end of the year is determined as follows:

   Total annual sales − total collections = year-end accounts receivable

Note. Total annual sales are from the projected income statement. Total collections are from the monthly projected cash flow.

If yours is an existing business, you know you collected last year's accounts receivable during the first part of this year. Total collections at the end of this year equal the receivables from last year plus the amounts collected this year. For existing businesses, accounts receivable at year-end would equal total annual sales minus total collections.

Total annual sales − total collections = year-end accounts receivable

3. Inventory, deposits, auto, equipment, furniture and fixtures, improvements, and other assets are generally the same amount for both at disbursement and year-end. Carry the same numbers across the columns for these items.
4. Accumulated depreciation increases each year. Add the depreciation at disbursement (zero dollars if you are a new business) to the annual depreciation expense from your projected annual income statement, and place the new number in the space for depreciation.
5. Accounts payable differs each year. Accounts payable are the amounts for materials you have not paid at year-end. This figure is the difference between the material cost of sales on the annual income statement and the accounts payable paid total from the monthly cash flow projection.

   Material cost of sales − accounts payable paid = accounts payable

   Place this figure in the Year-end column blank opposite accounts payable.
6. Notes payable including both SBA and other notes payable will be less in the Year-end column than in the At Disbursement column. During the year a business makes monthly payments on its loan. Part of that payment is interest, an expense, and part of the payment is principal, which reduces the amount owed. The current portion of a loan is the amount you will pay to reduce your debt in the upcoming year. The amount of principal loan repayment the company will pay in the *next* year equals the current portion of the notes payable.

   The long-term debt is calculated by taking the long-term portion of notes payable at the beginning of the period (at disbursement) and subtracting (1) the principal loan repayment made during the year (from monthly cash flow projections) and (2) the current portion notes payable from the Year-end column.
7. Owner's capital for the Year-end column should be the same dollar amount as owner's equity in the At Disbursement column. Total owner's equity at the beginning of the period (at disbursement) becomes owner's capital at the end of the period. The increase or decrease in owner's equity from the beginning of the period to the end is retained earnings.
8. Retained earnings is the most important part of the balance sheet at year-end

because the calculation of this determines if the rest of your projections are correct. Retained earnings is calculated by a simple formula:

Net profit (from annual income statement) − income tax and owner's draw (for proprietorship or partnership) or dividends (for corporation) = retained earnings

Place retained earnings in the year-end blank.

9. Now add up all your liabilities and equity. Does the total equal the total assets at year-end? It should. If total assets do not equal total liabilities plus total owner's equity, you've made a mistake in the monthly income statement, monthly cash flow, or the balance sheet you just prepared. You have to do your calculations and schedules again. But don't be discouraged; this happens frequently. The "assets equals liabilities plus equity" balance in the balance sheet is your check on the accuracy of your calculations. The greatest cause of imbalance is inaccuracy in the monthly cash flow projections (whence you get your cash, accounts receivable, and accounts payable figures). Check for errors in arithmetic.

PREPARING THE LOAN SUMMARY AND MARKET ANALYSIS

The loan summary includes all the projections and schedules, a use of funds statement, a statement as to the loan amount and repayment, an ownership section, a summary of personal data, and a collateral summary. The market analysis is separate from the loan summary and follows it.

The loan summary is divided into nine sections:

Application.
Purpose and use of funds.
Ownership.
Repayment.
Owners' personal data (résumé and personal financial statement).
Collateral summary.
Pro forma balance sheet.
Business history.
Market analysis.

Application

The application section opens the loan summary. This section gives the owners' name, business name, business address, and business telephone. It also shows the amount of the loan applied for, percentage rate, period of time, amount of monthly payments, and type of program applied for. The application section has standard wording that changes little from loan to loan. The following describes the application section and then gives an example of a completed section.

Application Wording. (Amount of loan) partially secured term loan payable over (number of years) years in (number of months in the period) monthly installments of (amount of monthly loan repayment) including interest at (interest percentage) percent per annum. A (% of loan guarantee) loan guarantee is requested under the special criteria of the (government agency such as SBA) (name of loan program). Completed sample.

John Your, President
Yourcompany
2010 Twenty Penny Lane
Chevy, Minn. 50000
(800) 873-6678

Application: $200,000 partially secured term loan payable over six (6) years in 72 monthly installments of $3,705, including interest at 10% per annum. A 90% loan guarantee is requested under the special criteria of the SBA 7a program.

Purpose and Use of Funds

A sample statement usually just titled "Purpose" would be:

To enable John Your to expand a computer distributship called Yourcompany located at the above address.

If the company is a new one, the purpose might be stated:

To enable Starter Company to purchase equipment, furniture, make improvements, and start a retail home electronics store.

After a brief statement of the purpose, the use of funds is presented. A sample would be:

Purpose: To enable John Your to expand operations of a wholesale-retail computer sales company located at the above address. Funds from the loan will be used as follows:

Equipment	$155,000 (1)
.	.
.	.
.	.

See the example in the footnote explanation earlier in this chapter.

Ownership

The ownership section states who owns what percentage of the company. In the case of a sole proprietorship this section can be eliminated since there is just one owner. In a partnership or a corporation the ownership details should be listed. The section might look as follows:

Ownership: Your Company is a partnership with the following owners:

Shareholder and Address	Percentage Ownership/Office
John Your 85 Ole Fifty-Five Trail Chevy, Minn.	50%—President
Tath Tacki 1222 Fromp Chevy, Minn.	30%—Vice President
Ed Syrup 7211 Last Street Chevy, Minn.	20%—Treasurer

Repayment

The repayment section contains the annual comparative and projected financial statements, the projected monthly income statement, the projected monthly cash flow, operating expense, and other financial schedules and footnotes.

The financial schedule presentation is usually prefaced by a paragraph similar to the following:

Repayment: The ability to repay the proposed loan is demonstrated in the following annual comparative and projected financial statements, monthly projected income statement, monthly projected cash flow, and accompanying footnotes.

After this statement, end the typewritten page and present the financial schedules, followed by the footnotes. Look at the sample loan proposal in Appendix II.

Personal Data

The personal data section of the loan proposal includes the résumé and personal financial statement of the owners of major officers owning 20% or more of the stock. Also include résumés of all important personnel in the business, such as managers, comptrollers, and so on. Personal financial data are required only if the person owns 20% or more of the company.

The résumé is a *brief* summary of important points. Lengthy résumés should be reserved for an exhibit to the loan proposal. The following is a sample of a résumé.

PERSONAL DATA	John Your 85 Ole Fifty-Five Chevy, Minnesota (411) 333-3333
BORN:	September 14, 1948, in Torrance, California
MARITAL STATUS:	Married with one child, age seven
EDUCATION:	Notre Dame University—B.A., Psychology, 1967
EXPERIENCE:	1977 to Present—President, Yourcompany 1972 to 1977—Comptroller, Software Development Company, Thompson, Wisconsin 1969 to 1972—Auditor, Arthur Anderson, CPA's, 200 Englewood Avenue, Denver, Colorado

After the résumé, you should include the personal financial statement of those who own more than 20% of the company. The personal financial statement should be current, accurate, and footnoted. You can submit a personal financial statement on SBA Form 413.

The following is an example of a personal financial statement for John Your of Yourcompany. Since the company is a partnership, a personal financial statement is required for all who own 20% or more.

The following is a personal financial statement for John Your, dated 7/30/83:

Assets		Liabilities and Net Worth	
Cash (1)	$ 6,000	Charge cards	$ 2,000
Cash value of life insurance	3,000	Note on automobile	7,000
Stock (2)	4,000		

Assets		Liabilities and Net Worth	
Real Estate	150,000	Real estate mortgage (3)	60,000
Automobile 1965 MB 280SL	15,000	Total liabilities	$ 69,000
		Net worth	$109,000
Total assets	$178,000	Total liabilities and net worth	$178,000

Footnotes for Personal Financial Statement

(1) Cash represents $4,000 in savings and $2,000 in checking (account Nos. 14-628 and 384-16) at Gold Bank, Jewel, Minnesota.

(2) Stock represents 100 shares of S-T-S Development Company, market price $40 per share.

(3) Real estate is residence located at 85 Ole Fifty-Five, Chevy, Minnesota, purchased in 1974 for $80,000, original mortgage balance $68,000. Present mortgage balance held by Supercal Savings and Loan is $60,000.

Collateral Summary

The collateral summary summarizes the collateral that the bank is offered for the loan. This would include all the fixed assets and inventory that your company buys with the loan proceeds as well as a security interest in the home(s) of the owner(s) of the company. Sometimes accounts receivable are offered for collateral as well.

The summary of collateral lists all the property offered. An example for Yourcompany might be as follows:

Collateral: The following is a summary of property offered as collateral by Yourcompany and its owners for the proposed loan:

Business assets		
Equipment	$225,000	
Leasehold improvements	36,000	
Office furniture	29,000	
Inventory	130,000	
Total business assets		$420,000
Personal assets		
Net worth of Your, Taki, and Syrup Real Estate (market value minus balance owed)		130,000
Total collateral pledged		$550,000
Plus: Life insurance on applicants for benefit of bank		$200,000

Note that the summary of collateral comes directly from the pro forma balance sheet for the business assets portion and from the personal financial statement for the personal assets portion. Business assets include only fixed assets, accounts receivable, and inventory. Personal assets include only the net worth in real property.

In an existing business the collateral would include *present* assets as well as the assets *purchased from the proceeds* of the loan.

See the sample loan proposal, Appendix II, for an illustration of the summary of collateral for a new business. A new business will have as collateral only those items purchased with the loan proceeds and the owner's cash injection.

Pro Forma Balance Sheet

The pro forma balance sheet section includes the pro forma balance sheet and footnotes, if any, preceded by the following words:

Pro forma balance sheet: The following is a comparative and pro forma balance sheet. The pro forma balance sheet is at the time of loan disbursement.

After this sentence, the comparative (if the business is now in existence) and pro forma balance sheets appear. See the sample loan proposal, Appendix II.

Business History

The business history is a statement of when the business was started, what kind of sales and product history it has, some of the major customers it now has, how it is managed, and what it plans to do in the future. In short, the business history section tells the lender everything that you think he or she should know about the business that has not been covered elsewhere in the loan summary.

Market Analysis

After the loan summary you should include your market study. In the case of existing businesses the market study need not be lengthy. But if the enterprise is a new one, the market study should be more detailed.

Example—Loan Summary Preparation. Figure 6.8 shows you the wording and information required for the proposal summary written in a fill-in-the-blank style. You may use as many of the examples as are appropriate to your business. This format is intended as a guide only; let your best judgment rule the final written presentation.

On your own form, do not write the words that appear in capital letters preceding the blanks, and do not include those parentheses following the blanks. These are for your information only.

BORROWER ______________________(name of owner or president)
COMPANY ______________________(company name)
ADDRESS ______________________(company address)
CITY ______________________
Phone: ______________________(business phone)
Home: ______________________(owner's/president's home phone)

Application: LOAN AMOUNT $__________ partially secured term loan payable in NUMBER OF MONTHS __________ monthly installments of MONTHLY PAYMENT $__________ including interest at ANNUAL INTEREST RATE ____ % per annum. An SBA-guaranteed loan is requested.

Purpose: To enable BORROWER __________ to purchase necessary equipment and fixtures and inventory to operate ("to start," if a new company) COMPANY ____ __________.

Use of funds: The money required and uses of funds are as follows:

Figure 6.8 Proposal summary.

(Insert use of funds statement and footnotes that you prepared in the first part of this chapter.)

Ownership: COMPANY ______________ is a ______________ (proprietorship, corporation, etc.) with the following owners:

Owner and Address	Percentage Ownership/Office
______________	______________
______________	
______________	
______________	______________
______________	
______________	

Repayment: The following comparative and projected financial statements and footnotes demonstrate COMPANY's ______________ ability to repay the proposed loan from cash flow.

(Insert comparative and projected financial statements, monthly income statement, monthly cash flow projections, and footnotes [Comments re: Projections])

Personal data: The following is a personal financial statement of BORROWER ______________ as of ______________.

(Insert personal financial statement and notes prepared in first part of chapter.)

Résumé: The following is BORROWER'S ______________ recent resume:

HOME ADDRESS ______________
HOME CITY ______________
HOME PHONE ______________
BORN ______________
MARITAL STATUS ______________

EDUCATION ______________
____
____

EXPERIENCE:
19— to present: ______________
____

19___ to 19___: ______________
____

(Continue until you have included all your most significant employment experience. Concentrate on management and other functions that would give you good experience for your present business.)

Pro forma: The following pro forma and comparative balance sheets show COMPANY ______ at disbursement and at the end of the first projected year.

(Insert pro forma balance sheet from the first part of of chapter here.)

History: The following is a history of COMPANY ______________. The company was started in ______________. The major products of the company are ______________. (Briefly relate the history of your company, listing everything you think the lender might find important in considering the loan.)

Figure 6.8 (***Continued***)

PREPARING GOVERNMENT LOAN FORMS

Government forms usually give specific directions on how to complete them. If you read the forms and if you have done your homework, the forms should be fairly easy to complete.

The three important things to remember when filling out government application forms are:

1. Read the instructions very carefully.
2. Fill everything out completely. If there is a blank space or question that does not apply to you, write NA (not applicable) in the space.
3. If you don't understand something or it doesn't make sense, don't ignore it; call the agency for more information.

There are generally at least four loan forms for SBA loans.

Application form (SBA Forms 4 and 4A), which may have several schedules.

Personal history form used by agency investigators to check your credit and criminal records (SBA Form 912).

Owners' personal financial statement form (SBA Form 413).

Preparation compensation form (SBA Form 159) if the loan proposal is prepared by someone other than the applicant.

Other forms may also be necessary to comply with government standards (minority hiring, environmental impact, etc.).

Application

Form 4 is the SBA application form. Figure 6.9 is an SBA Form 4 filled out for John Your of Yourcompany. These forms were revised in September of 1978. The form is one page printed on both sides in blue ink and features six sections, instructions for completing the sections, and a checklist of the other items that must accompany the loan proposal.

The first three sections ask for the names and addresses of the business and owners. Section I should contain the name of the owner or the president of the company.

Section II contains the name, address, telephone number, type of business, date started, number of employees, IRS employer's I.D. number, and the name of the bank where the business has a checking account. Type of business would be "retail liquor," "franchised fast food," "steel manufacturing," and so on. The IRS employer's I.D. number is the number assigned to your business to be used in connection with federal income tax withholding, Social Security payments, and the like. If your business is new, place the Social Security number of the owner in the space entitled "IRS Employer I.D. Number."

Section III asks for the name, address, percentage ownership, and annual compensation of every person who owns 20% or more of the company.

Section IV asks for the use of the funds for the loan. This is taken from the use of funds statement in the loan summary. This use of funds does *not* include uses of owners' cash injection required for a new business—it is for the use of SBA loan funds *only*. "Other" uses of loan proceeds include all items not specifically mentioned in the section. In the Yourcompany example, Exhibit A is attached showing inventory ($60,000), prepayments ($1,450), and furniture ($5,000).

SBA Form 4 Loan Number OMB # 100-R 0081

U.S. Small Business Administration

APPLICATION FOR LOAN

I. Applicant/Information About You

Name: John Your

Street Address: 85 Ole Fifty-Five Trail

City, State, Zip Code: Chevy, Minn.

Telephone: 411/333-3333

II. Information About Your Business

Name of Business: Yourcompany

Address of Business: 1010 Twentypenny Lane

City, State, Zip Code: Chevy, Minn.

County	Telephone
Watcha	411/222-2222
Type of Business	**Date Established**
Computer Wholesale	1977
Number of Employees	**IRS Employer I.D. Number**
Present: 3 After Approval: 4	000-00-0000

Bank Where Your Business Has An Account: Gold Bank

III. Information About Management:

List the name of all owners (having 20% or greater interest), officers, directors, and/or partners. Provide the percent of ownership and the annual compensation.

Name and Title / Address	% of Ownership / Annual Compensation
John Your, President	50
Address: 85 Ole Fifty-five Trail, Chevy, Minn.	$22,000
Tath Tacki	30
Address: 1222 Fromp, Chevy, Minn.	$ 2,000
Ed Syrup	20
Address: 7211 Last Street, Chevy, Minn.	-0-
Name and Title	% of Ownership
Address	Annual Compensation

IV. How You Plan to Use the Loan Money

Building	Amount for Building	Amount for Land
☐ New ☐ Purchase ☐ Renovate	$	$

Amount for New Equipment: $ 35,000	Amount for Notes Payable: $ 43,550
Amount for Working Capital: $ 45,000	Amount for Equipment Repair: $ None
Amount for Accounts Payable: $ None	Other (See Instructions): $ 66,450
Total Loan Requested ➡	$ 200,000
Term of Loan ➡	Years: Months:

V. Summary of Collateral

	Present Market Value	Present Mortage Balance	Cost Less Depreciation
A. Land and Building	36,000	$200,000/SBA	$32,000
B. Inventory	130,000	" "	130,000
C. Accounts Receivable	115,164	" "	115,164
D. Machinery and Equipment	225,000	" "	150,000
E. Furniture and Fixtures	29,000	" "	25,000
F. Other			
Total Collateral $	535,164		452,164

SBA Form 4 (9-78) Previous Editions Are Obsolete

VI. Assistance

255

List the names of attorneys, accountants, appraisers, agents, or other persons rendering assistance in preparation of this form.

Name and Occupation	Total Fees Paid
Address	Fees Due
Name and Occupation	Total Fees Paid
Address	Fees Due

INSTRUCTIONS FOR APPLICATION FORM

Sections I, II, III. Please provide the information requested. "You" refers to the proprietor, general partner or corporate officer signing this form.

Section IV. Use of the loan money; if your use of the loan fits one of the categories listed on the application form, please fill out this section. If you use "other" submit a list on a separate sheet of paper and label the list Exhibit A.

Section V. Summary of collateral: if your collateral consists of (A) Land and Building, (B) Inventory, and/or (C) Accounts Receivable, fill in the appropriate blanks. If you are using (D) Machinery and Equipment, (E) Furniture and Fixtures, and/or (F) Other, please provide an itemized list (labeled Exhibit B) that contains serial and identification numbers for all articles that had an original value greater than $500.

Section VI. Provide the information requested for all professional services used while preparing the application. You will be asked to complete another form **after loan closing** that will itemize compensation actually paid for services rendered in connection with this application.

Yes	No	CHECKLIST FOR APPLICATION PACKAGE
		All Exhibits must be signed and dated by person signing this form.
☒	☐	1. Have you submitted **SBA Form 912** (Personal History Statement) for each person e.g. owners, partners, major stock holders, etc.; the instructions are on **SBA Form 912**?
☒	☐	2. Have you filled out a personal balance sheet (**SBA Form 413** may be used for this purpose) for each stockholder (with **20%** or greater ownership), partner, officer, and owner. Label this Exhibit C.
☒	☐	3. Have you included the statements listed below: **1,2,3** for the last three years; **1,2,3,4** dated within **90 days** of filing the application; and statement 5? This is Exhibit D. (Management Assistance has **Aids** that help in the preparation of financial Statements.) 1. Balance Sheet 2. Profit and Loss Statement 3. Reconciliation of Net Worth 4. Aging of Accounts Receivable and Payable 5. Earnings projections for at least one year (If Profit and Loss Statement is not available, explain why and substitute Federal Income Tax Forms.)
☐	☐	4. Have you completed a list which contains the original date and amount, present balance owed, interest rate, monthly payment, maturity and security for each loan or debt that your business currently has? Please indicate whether the loan is current or delinquent. An asterisk (*) should be placed by any of these debts that will be paid off with the **SBA** loan. This should be labeled Exhibit E. *(over)*

Figure 6.9 SBA Form 4: application for loan.

Yes	No	
☒	☐	5. Have you provided a brief history of your company and a paragraph describing the expected benefits it will receive from the loan? If not, you must do so. Label it Exhibit F.
☒	☐	6. Have you provided a brief description of the educational, technical and business background for all the people listed in **Section III** under management? If not, you must do so. Please mark it Exhibit G.
☐	☒	7. Do you have any co-signers and/or guanrators for this loan? If so, please submit their names, addresses and personal balance sheets as Exhibit H.
☒	☐	8. Are you buying machinery or equipment with your loan money? If so, you must include a list of the equipment and the cost. This is Exhibit J.
☐	☒	9. Have you or any officers of your company ever been involved in bankruptcy or insolvency proceedings? If so, please provide the details as Exhibit K.
☐	☒	10. Are you or your business involved in any pending lawsuits? If yes, provide the details as Exhibit L.
☐	☒	11. Do you or your spouse or any member of your household, or anyone who owns, manages, or directs your business or their spouses or members of their households work for the **Small Business Administration,** Small Business Advisory Council, SCORE or ACE? If so, please provide the name and address of the person and the office where employed. Label this Exhibit M.
☐	☒	12. Does your business have any subsidiaries or affiliates? If yes, please provide their names and the relationship with your company along with a current balance sheet and operating statement for each. This should be Exhibit N.
☐	☒	13. Do you buy from, sell to, or use the services of any concern in which someone in your company has a significant financial interest? If yes, provide details on a separate sheet of paper labeled Exhibit P.
☐	☐	14. If your business is a franchise, have you included a copy of the franchise agreement? Please include it as Exhibit R.
☐	☒	15. If you or any principals or affiliates have ever requested government financing, list the name of the agency (including **SBA**), the amount requested or approved, date of request or approval, present balance, and status (i.e. current, delinquent). This should be Exhibit S.
		CONSTRUCTION LOANS ONLY
☐	☐	16. Have you included in a separate exhibit (Exhibit T) the estimated cost of the project and a statement of the source of any additional funds? If not, please do so.
☐	☐	17. Have you filed all the necessary compliance documents **(SBA Form Series 601)**? If not, loan officer will advise which forms are necessary.
☐	☐	18. Have you provided copies of preliminary construction plans and specifications? If not, include them as Exhibit U. Final plans will be required prior to disbursement.
		DIRECT LOANS ONLY
☐	☐	19. Have you included two bank declination letters with your application? These letters should include the name and telephone number of the persons contacted at the banks, the dates and terms of the loan, the reason for decline and whether or not the bank will participate with **SBA**. In towns with 200,000 people or less, one letter will be sufficient.

SBA Form 4 (9-78) Previous Editions Are Obsolete

AGREEMENTS AND CERTIFICATIONS

Agreement of Nonemployment of SBA Personnel: I/We agree that if **SBA** approves this loan application **I/We** will not, for at least two years, hire as an employee or consultant anyone that was employed by the **SBA** during the one year period prior to the disbursement of the loan.

Certification: I/We certify: (a) I/We have not paid anyone connected with the Federal Government for help in getting this loan. **I/We** also agree to report to the **SBA Office of Security and Investigations, 1441 L Street N.W., Washington, D.C., 20416** any Federal Government employee who offers, in return for any type of compensation, to help get this loan approved.
(b) All information in this application and the Exhibits is true and complete to the best of my/our knowledge and is submitted to **SBA** so **SBA** can decide whether to grant a loan or participate with a lending institution in a loan to me/us. **I/We** agree to pay for or reimburse **SBA** for the cost of any surveys, title or mortage examinations, appraisals etc., performed by non-**SBA** personnel provided **I/We** have given my/our consent.
(c) I/We give the assurance that we will comply with sections 112 and 113 of volume 13 of the Code of Federal Regulations. These Code sections prohibit discrimination on the grounds of race, color, sex, religion, martial status, handicap, age, or national origin by recipients of Federal financial assistance and require appropriate reports and access to books and records. These requirements are applicable to anyone who buys or takes control of the business. **I/We** realize that if **I/We** do not comply with these non-discrimination requirements **SBA** can, call, terminate, or accelerate repayment or my/our loan.

Authority to Collect Personal Information: This information is provided pursuant to Public Law 93-579 (Privacy Act of 1974). **Effects of Nondisclosure:** Omission of an item means your application might not receive full consideration.

I/We authorize disclosure of all information sumitted in connection with this application to the financial institution agreeing to participate in the loan.

As consideration for any Management and Technical Assistance that may be provided, **I/We** waive all claims against **SBA** and its consultants.

I/We understand that **I/We** need not pay anybody to deal with **SBA**. **I/We** have read and understand Form 394 which explains **SBA** policy on representatives and their fees.

For Guaranty Loans please provide an original and one copy (Photocopy is Acceptable) of the Application Form, and all Exhibits to the participating lender. For Direct Loans submit one original copy of application and Exhibits to **SBA**.

It is against SBA regulations to charge the applicant a percentage of the loan proceeds as a fee for preparing this application.

If you make a statement that you know to be false or if you over value a security in order to help obtain a loan under the provisions of the Small Business Act you can be fined up to $5,000 or be put in jail for up to two years, or both.

Signature of Preparer if Other Than Applicant

Print or Type Name of Preparer

Address of Preparer

If Applicant is a proprietor or general partner, sign below:

By: ______ 9/20/83 Date

If Applicant is a corporation, sign below:

Corporate Seal　　Date

By: ______
Signature of President

Attested by: ______
Signature of Corporate Secretary

Figure 6.9 *(Continued)*

If your business is an existing one, as in the sample loan proposal, Appendix II, the *cost less depreciation* should represent the book value of these assets. New assets to be purchased with the loan proceeds are added to this. The *present mortgage balance* blocks would either read "proposed SBA loan" or give the amount of the debt on building or equipment.

Section VI asks for names and addresses of any attorney, accountant, appraiser, loan packager, or other individual whom you have paid to prepare the loan or the loan documentation.

There are 19 checkpoints listed, starting on the front side and continuing on the back. They ask for other items such as financial statements, other SBA forms, legal problems, and so on. Read this checklist *carefully*, and answer all questions *completely*.

The form is signed on the back by the loan preparer if the loan was done by someone other than the applicant. Below that, the owner, general partner, or corporate president signs the document. If the company is a corporation, the corporate seal and signature of the corporate secretary are also required.

SBA Office of Security and Investigations

Figure 6.10 shows SBA Form 912 filled out for John Your of Yourcompany.

Each person who owns 20% or more of the applicant company must submit an SBA Form 912. For Yourcompany, this would mean submitting Form 912 for three people: Your, Tacki, and Syrup, who own 50%, 30%, and 20%, respectively.

Personal Financial Statement of Owner(s)

Most government loans require a personal financial statement from the applicant. The SBA requires a personal financial statement for everyone owning at least 20% of the company. This is standard procedure.

The personal financial statement information may be taken directly from the personal data section of the loan summary discussed earlier in this chapter. The form lists what the owner has in the way of assets, liabilities, and net worth.

Figure 6.11 is a completed SBA Form 413, the personal financial statement form. The form is self-explanatory. One note, though: The term *accounts payable* on the liability side of the front page means credit card debt. Notes payable to others could be money owed to individuals or financial institutions other than banks. Installment accounts are those debts paid each month that are not for house or automobile notes. This includes student loans.

Preparation Compensation Forms

Because government requirements are difficult to meet by yourself, it is frequently necessary to pay someone for help. This help could include the cost of an accountant to prepare a current financial statement, an attorney to look at a purchase agreement or lease, a business broker who charged you a fee for a particular business purchase, architects, planners, and others. If you have the loan proposal prepared by someone other than yourself, you must declare that fee.

SBA Form 159, illustrated in Figure 6.12, is a preparation compensation form. The form must be signed by both the applicant representing the business and the professional who assisted the business for a fee. If the fee amounts to more than $300, the professional must submit a detailed schedule of hours and activities with Form 159.

If the business received no paid help, the form is still submitted, but it is signed

Return Executed Copies 1, 2, and 3 to SBA

United States of America

SMALL BUSINESS ADMINISTRATION

STATEMENT OF PERSONAL HISTORY

Please Read Carefully - Print or Type

Each member of the small business concern requesting assistance or the development company must submit this form in TRIPLICATE for filing with the SBA application. This form must be filled out and submitted:

1. If a sole proprietorship, by the proprietor;
2. If a partnership, by each partner;
3. If a corporation or a development company, by each officer, director, and additionally, by each holder of 20% or more of the voting stock;
4. Any other person, including a hired manager, who has authority to speak for and commit the borrower in the management of the business.

Name and Address of Applicant (Firm Name)(Street, City, State and ZIP Code)

Yourcompany
1010 Twentypenny Lane
Chevy, Minn.

SBA District Office and City

Amount Applied for: $200,000

1. Personal Statement of: (State name in full, if no middle name, state (NMN), or if initial only, indicate initial). List all former names used, and dates each name was used. Use separate sheet if necessary.

First	Middle	Last
John	Lazarus	Your

2. Date of Birth: (Month, day and year) Sept. 14, 1948

3. Place of Birth: (City & State or Foreign Country) Torrance, California

U.S. Citizen? [X] yes [ ] no

If no, give alien registration number: #

4. Give the percentage of ownership or stock owned or to be owned in the small business concern or the Development Company. 50%

Social Security No. 513-69-6969

5. Present residence address

From	To	Address	City	State
1974	Present	85 Ole Fifty-five	Chevy,	Minn.

Immediate past residence address

From	To	Address	City	State
1970	19/4	G0 Carvette	Chevy,	Minn.

BE SURE TO ANSWER THE NEXT 3 QUESTIONS CORRECTLY BECAUSE THEY ARE IMPORTANT.

THE FACT THAT YOU HAVE AN ARREST OR CONVICTION RECORD WILL NOT NECESSARILY DISQUALIFY YOU. BUT AN INCORRECT ANSWER WILL PROBABLY CAUSE YOUR APPLICATION TO BE TURNED DOWN.

6. Are you presently under indictment, onparole or probation?

[ ] Yes [X] No If yes, furnish details in a separate exhibit. List name(s) under which held, if applicable.

7. Have you ever been charged with or arrested for any criminal offense other than a minor motor vehicle violation?

[ ] Yes [X] No If yes, furnish details in a separate exhibit. List name(s) under which charged, if applicable.

8. Have you ever been convicted of any criminal offense other than a minor motor vehicle violation?

[ ] Yes [X] No If yes, furnish details in a separate exhibit. List name(s) under which convicted, if applicable.

9. Name and address of participating bank

Gold Bank
Jewel, Minn.

The information on this form will be used in connection with an investigation of your character. Any information you wish to submit, that you feel will expedite this investigation should be set forth.

Whoever makes any statement knowing it to be false, for the purpose of obtaining for himself or for any applicant, any loan, or loan extension by renewal, deferment or otherwise, or for the purpose of obtaining, or influencing SBA toward, anything of value under the Small Business Act, as amended, shall be punished under Section 16(a) of that Act, by a fine of not more than $5000, or by imprisonment for not more than 2 years, or both.

Signature	Title	Date
John L. Your	president	9/20/83

It is against SBA's policy to provide assistance to persons not of good character and therefore consideration is given to the qualities and personality traits of a person, favorable and unfavorable, relating thereto, including behavior, integrity, candor and disposition toward criminal actions. It is also against SBA's policy to provide assistance not in the best interests of the United States, for example, if there is reason to believe that the effect of such assistance will be to encourage or support, directly or indirectly, activities inimical to the Security of the United States. Anyone concerned with the collection of this information, as to its voluntariness, disclosure or routine uses may contact the FOIA Office, 1441 "L" Street, N.W., and a copy of §9 "Agency Collection of Information" from SOP 40 04 will be provided.

SBA FORM 912 (5-78) SOP 50 10 1 EDITION OF 4-75 WILL BE USED UNTIL STOCK IS EXHAUSTED

1. SBA FILE COPY

Figure 6.10 SBA Form 419: statement of personal history.

Form Approved
OMB No. 100-R-0081

PERSONAL FINANCIAL STATEMENT As of Sept. 9 , 19 83 .	Return to: Small Business Administration	For SBA Use Only SBA Loan No.

Name and Address, Including ZIP Code (of person and spouse submitting Statement) John Your 85 Ole Fifty-Five Trail Chevy, Minn. SOCIAL SECURITY NO. 000-000-0000 Business (of person submitting Statement)	This statement is submitted in connection with S.B.A. loan requested or granted to the individual or firm, whose name appears below: Name and Address of Applicant or Borrower, Including ZIP Code

Please answer all questions using "No" or "None" where necessary

ASSETS		LIABILITIES	
Cash on Hand & In Banks	$ 2,000	Accounts Payable	$ 7,000
Savings Account in Banks	4,000	Notes Payable to Banks	
U. S. Government Bonds		(Describe below - Section 2)	
Accounts & Notes Receivable		Notes Payable to Others	
Life Insurance-Cash Surrender Value Only	3,000	(Describe below - Section 2)	
Other Stocks and Bonds	4,000	Installment Account (Auto)	7,000
(Describe - reverse side - Section 3)		Monthly Payments $	
Real Estate	150,000	Installment Accounts (Other)	
(Describe - reverse side - Section 4)		Monthly Payments $	
Automobile - Present Value	15,000	Loans on Life Insurance	
Other Personal Property		Mortgages on Real Estate	60,000
(Describe - reverse side - Section 5)		(Describe - reverse side - Section 4)	
Other Assets		Unpaid Taxes	
(Describe - reverse side - Section 6)		(Describe - reverse side - Section 7)	
		Other Liabilities	
		(Describe - reverse side - Section 8)	
		Total Liabilities	69,000
		Net Worth	109,000
Total	$ 178,000	Total	$ 178,000

Section 1. Source of Income (Describe below all items listed in this Section)		CONTINGENT LIABILITIES	
Salary	$ 22,000	As Endorser or Co-Maker	$ none
Net Investment Income	900	Legal Claims and Judgments	none
Real Estate Income		Provision for Federal Income Tax	none
Other Income (Describe)		Other Special Debt	none

Description of items listed in Section 1

Life Insurance Held (Give face amount of policies - name of company and beneficiaries)

Metropole whole life insurance - face amount $120,000 - beneficiary Elaine Your - wife

SUPPLEMENTARY SCHEDULES

Section 2. Notes Payable to Banks and Others

Name and Address of Holder of Note	Amount of Loan: Original Bal.	Amount of Loan: Present Bal.	Terms of Repayments	Maturity of Loan	How Endorsed, Guaranteed, or Secured
	$	$	$		

SBA FORM 413 (8-67) REF: ND 520-1 EDITION OF 1-67 MAY BE USED UNTIL STOCK IS EXHAUSTED (OVER)

Figure 6.11 SBA Form 413: personal financial statement.

Section 3. Other Stocks and Bonds: Give listed and unlisted Stocks and Bonds *(Use separate sheet if necessary)*

No. of Shares	Names of Securities	Cost	Market Value Statement Date Quotation	Amount
100	S-T-S Dev. Co.	$18 share	$29/share	2,000

Section 4. Real Estate Owned. *(List each parcel separately. Use supplemental sheets if necessary. Each sheet must be identified as a supplement to this statement and signed). (Also advises whether property is covered by title insurance, abstract of title, or both).*

Title is in name of John and Elaine Your	Type of property Residential
Address of property (City and State) 85 Ole Fifty-Five Trail Chevy, Minn.	Original Cost to (me) (us) $ 80,000 Date Purchased 1974 Present Market Value $ 150,000 Tax Assessment Value $ 68,000
Name and Address of Holder of Mortgage (City and State)	Date of Mortgage 1974 Original Amount $ 68,000 Balance $ 60,000 Maturity 25 yrs. Terms of Payment 308.73/Month

Status of Mortgage, i.e., current or delinquent. If delinquent describe delinquencies

Current

Section 5. Other Personal Property. *(Describe and if any is mortgaged, state name and address of mortgage holder and amount of mortgage, terms of payment and if delinquent, describe delinquency.)*

None Listed

Section 6. Other Assets. *(Describe)*

None Listed

Section 7. Unpaid Taxes. *(Describe in detail, as to type, to whom payable, when due, amount, and what, if any, property a tax lien, if any, attaches)*

None

Section 8. Other Liabilities. *(Describe in detail)*

None

(I) or (We) certify the above and the statements contained in the schedules herein is a true and accurate statement of (my) or (our) financial condition as of the date stated herein. This statement is given for the purpose of: *(Check one of the following)*

☐ Inducing S.B.A. to grant a loan as requested in application, of the individual or firm whose name appears herein, in connection with which this statement is submitted.

☐ Furnishing a statement of (my) or (our) financial condition, pursuant to the terms of the guaranty executed by (me) or (us) at the time S.B.A. granted a loan to the individual or firm, whose name appears herein.

Signature   John Your   Signature   9/20/83   Date

Page 2   ☆ U.S. G.P.O. 1978-721-287/429 REG.# 3-I

Figure 6.11 *(Continued)*

SBA LOAN NO. ____________

COMPENSATION AGREEMENT FOR SERVICES IN CONNECTION WITH APPLICATION AND LOAN FROM (OR IN PARTICIPATION WITH) SMALL BUSINESS ADMINISTRATION

This undersigned representative (attorney, accountant, engineer, appraiser, etc.) hereby agrees that the undersigned has not and will not, directly or indirectly, charge or receive any payment in connection with the application for or the making of the loan except for services actually performed on behalf of the Applicant. The undersigned further agrees that the amount of payment for such services shall not exceed an amount deemed reasonable by SBA (and, if it is a participation loan, by the participating lending institution), and to refund any amount in excess of that deemed reasonable by SBA (and the participating institution). This agreement shall supersede any other agreement covering payment for such services.

A general description of the services performed, or to be performed, by the undersigned and the compensation paid or to be paid are set forth below. If the total compensation in any case exceeds $300 (or $50 for: (1) regular business loans of $15,000 or less; (2) all disaster home loans; or (3) all economic opportunity loans), or if SBA should otherwise require, the services must be itemized showing each date services were performed, time spent each day, and description of the service rendered on each day listed. If necessary, the statement of services may be continued on the reverse side of this form, or attached as a rider hereto.

The undersigned Applicant and representative hereby certify that no other fees have been charged or will be charged by the representative in connection with this loan, unless provided for in loan authorization specifically approved by SBA.

DESCRIPTION OF SERVICES

Amount Heretofore Paid $ 275.00

Additional Amount to be Paid $ -0-

Total Compensation $ 275.00

(Parts 103, 104, and 122 of Title 13 of the Code of Federal Regulations contain provisions covering appearances and compensation of persons representing SBA applicants. Section 103.13-5 authorizes the suspension or revocation of the privilege of any such person to appear before SBA for charging a fee deemed unreasonable by SBA for the services actually performed, charging of unreasonable expenses, or violation of this agreement. In addition, whoever commits any fraud, by false or misleading statement or representation, or by conspiracy. shall be subject to the penalty of any applicable Federal or State statute.)

Dated 20 Sept. , 19 80

J. Kracks and Korn
Attorney-at-Law
239 South Street
Cheng, Minn.
(Representative)

By ____________

The Applicant hereby certifies to SBA that the above representations, description of services and amounts are correct and satisfactory to Applicant.

Dated 20 Sept. , 19 80

Yourcompany
1010 Twentypenny Lane
Chevy, Min.
(Applicant)

By ____________

The participating lending insitution hereby certifies that the above representations of service rendered and amounts charged are reasonable and satisfactory to said lender.

Dated ________, 19___

____
(Lender)

By ____________

NOTE: Foregoing certificate must be executed, if by a corporation, in corporate name by duly authorized officer and duly attested; if by a partnership, in the firm name, together with signature of a general partner.

**SBA REVIEW BY ____________ TITLE ____________ DATE ________

SBA FORM 159 (10-74) REF SOP 20 50 PREVIOUS EDITIONS ARE OBSOLETE.

WHITE TO SBA, YELLOW TO BORROWER, PINK TO BORROWER'S REPRESENTATIVE GPO 895-748

Figure 6.12 SBA Form 159: compensation agreement for services in connection with application and loan from (or in participation with) the SBA.

only by the owner of the business, and "None" is written across the top section where the professional's name and address would go.

Other Forms

Other forms could include government compliance forms, request for assistance forms, and so on. Each local SBA office may require something different. Ask the local office for a complete set of forms, then read the forms and instructions carefully.

Chapter Seven
Presenting the Loan Proposal

To get your loan approved, you have to sell yourself and your business to the bank or the SBA. Your loan proposal is your sales presentation.

If the loan proposal has been prepared as this book suggests, the banker will probably be impressed with the work as well as with you. The fact that you did the research and financial analysis yourself proves to the banker that you know more about running a business than the average businessperson.

This chapter discusses how to give the loan proposal the best physical appearance, how to get appointments with lenders, and how to best present your proposal to a lender. It also tells you what to do between the time the proposal is first presented and when the loan is made.

There are four parts in presenting the loan proposal:

1. Loan proposal appearance.
2. Setting up appointments with lenders.
3. Making the presentation.
4. Procedures after the presentation.

PHYSICAL APPEARANCE OF THE LOAN PROPOSAL

You might think that if you have a competent loan proposal using industry data and carefully researched sales figures, with completed government forms, it wouldn't matter what the proposal looks like. This is not true. In a world of appearances how something looks on the outside may be just as important to people as what is contained inside. The lender is more impressed with a proposal that is typewritten, professionally duplicated and reduced, and bound than with one that is in a manila folder with handwritten schedules.

The Yourcompany sample loan proposal in Appendix II shows the typical style of a loan proposal.

The basic concerns for preparing a proposal that will have the best appearance include:

Typing, style, and proposal layout.
Duplicating, binding, and tabs.

Typing, Style, and Proposal Layout

The loan proposal should be typed double-spaced except for financial schedules, which should be single-spaced. The text of the loan proposal should be indented 2½ to 3½ inches from the left side of the page. In this indented space place headings for the various sections of the loan summary such as Application, Purpose, Repayment, and so on.

The monthly projected income statement should have all 12 months typed on a single legal-sized sheet, which may be reduced to 8½″ × 11″. Monthly cash flow projection should also be typed on just one page. Never continue a financial schedule over two pages.

Figure 7.1 is a copy of a first page typewritten. The example was typed on a standard 8½ × 11 page.

The page size can be either standard letter size (8½ × 11) or legal size (8½ × 13), but do not mix sizes.

The SBA and most other government forms are legal size. So are leases, corporation papers, and other legal documents. However, income tax, most pages from magazines, and financial statements are letter size. There are two alternatives:

John Your, President
Yourcompany
1010 Twentypenny Lane
Chevy, Minn.
Phone: 411/222-2222

Application: $200,000 partially secured term loan payable over six (6) years in seventy-two (72) monthly installments of $3,705 including interest at ten percent (10%) per annum. A ninety percent ($180,000) loan guarantee is requested under the special criteria of the SBA 7a program.

Purpose: To enable John Your and his partners to expand operations of a wholesale-retail computer sales company located at the above address.

Funds from the loan will be used as follows:

Purchase fixed assets:		
Equipment	$35,000	
Furniture	5,000	
Improvements	10,000	$ 50,000 (1)
Create current assets:		
Working capital	45,000	
Inventory	60,000	
Prepayments	1,400 (2)	106,450
Repay debt		42,550 (3)
Total SBA loan required		$200,000

Figure 7.1 Proposal summary.

1. If you decide that you want the entire loan proposal to be *legal size*, then duplicate all the letter-size documents on legal-size paper.
2. If you decide to use *letter-size* paper, you will have to have the government forms and legal documents reduced photographically (by a professional duplicator) to the smaller size.

The proposal should begin with a blank sheet of paper for the first page, followed by a table of contents, the loan summary, the market analysis, the exhibits in numerical order, and the government forms. Another blank sheet of paper should end the proposal.

The table of contents shows the order in which the material will appear in the proposal. The sample loan proposal in Appendix II has a table of contents that can serve as an example.

Duplicating, Binding, and Tabs

After the draft of the loan proposal has been typed and checked for typographical and mathematical errors (especially in the figures and financial schedules), it can be duplicated and put in order.

Make at least three copies of the loan proposal besides the original. One copy is for the bank, the second is for you, and the third is a protection copy in case one becomes lost or another copy is needed quickly. Have these copies and any reductions done by a professional duplicator on bond paper.

When the copies are made, put each proposal together in its proper order and place dividers with tabs in front of each exhibit. If you have a market analysis and a loan summary, each should be marked with a divider. Indicate government forms with a tabbed divider.

The pages should be bound between two heavy covers. For example, you can use Vellobind, a binding where two stiff sheets of paper are put on the front and back of the proposals. The proposal and covers are then attached by plastic posts that go through holes made in the pages.

Costs

What does it cost to prepare the proposal in a typed, duplicated, tabbed, and bound form? In general, the greater the number of pages, the greater the costs. Although binding is about the same cost regardless of size, typing and duplicating costs increase with the number of pages in the proposal.

Typing costs range from \$0.75 to \$1.75 per page. Good typists may be listed in the classified ads of college newspapers. The average loan summary and market analysis should be no more than 40 pages. The cost for typing should be between \$30 and \$70 for the average proposal.

Duplicating costs may be as little as 4 cents per page in many areas and is seldom more than 10 cents per page for the work of a professional duplicator. Because the average proposal complete with exhibits runs about 150 pages, the cost varies from between \$4.50 and \$15.00 per proposal. If you have reductions done, it will cost more.

The average total cost for typing, duplicating, indexing, and binding three copies of a loan proposal runs between \$45 and \$90.

SETTING UP APPOINTMENTS WITH LENDERS

Call the bank or agency, find out who handles your type of loan, and make an appointment.

Before you arrange for the appointment, however, you must find the right bank. SBA loans require either bank participation or evidence of bank rejection.

The two main steps in receiving the proper hearing for your loan proposal are:

1. Choosing the right bank.
2. Creating receptivity to your application.

Choosing the Right Bank

When choosing a bank, you should consider the following questions:

Does the bank participate in the SBA program? Is it the bank's policy to make SBA loans?

How experienced is the bank in making these loans? (Has the bank made only two SBA loans or as many as 2,000 SBA loans?)

Does the person at the bank who handles these loans have experience doing so?

Many banks do not participate in the SBA loan program. It is better to discover this *before* you make an appointment.

Banks that have the most experience in making SBA loans are the best banks to try. A bank with little experience might cause delays in submitting the loan proposal to the SBA. However, a bank with a lot of experience might be picky and systemized and might not give all good loan applications a chance. The best idea is to call a loan counselor at the SBA to find out which banks have the most experience and which will give you the best hearing.

Note. Regardless of whether the bank you now deal with makes loans under this program, it is customary to give your current bank the first chance at your loan.

The first thing a "stranger" bank will ask you when you make the loan presentation is, "Have you submitted this to your bank yet?" If your answer is no, the interview may end right there.

Creating Receptivity to Your Application

After you find the right bank to process your loan proposal, the next step is to make sure that the banker is receptive to your application.

A lender is most impressed by someone who has already proved that he or she is "a good bank customer." A good bank customer is someone who (1) keeps good balances in his or her checking account (not too many overdrafts), (2) has been with the bank for some period of time (at least three years), and (3) has some credit with the bank already (auto loan, business loan, etc.).

The best bank customer is the one who has demonstrated all of these but also knows the names of the branch manager, assistant branch manager, and others at the bank.

If you are approaching a new bank solely for the purpose of getting an SBA loan, some planning is required to ensure receptivity to your application. One method is to have yourself recommended by a third party whom the banker respects. This third party could be a friend of yours who has an account at the stranger bank, your own banker, a member of the stranger banker's social club, or someone you know who works for that bank (but perhaps in a different area).

If you don't know anyone at the bank or anyone who has contacts there, try talking to your industry association or the local chamber of commerce. This will give you some credibility.

Remember: Do not call up a bank that is unfamiliar to you and make an appointment to see someone without first getting a third-party introduction. The more of these introductions you can arrange, the better the receptivity when you make the loan presentation.

MAKING THE PRESENTATION

You now have a handsome loan proposal and a receptive banker. The next step is to set up the appointment and sell the lender on your proposal. There are four elements of the presentation:

1. Appointment times and days.
2. Your personal appearance.
3. The proper course of the discussion.
4. Immediate follow-up procedures.

Appointment Times and Days

It is best to make an appointment with a bank early in the week. Fridays are the worst days because this is when bankers have their longest lines and the most transactions. Monday is a good day; on Mondays banks generally receive their customers' dollar deposits from weekend sales. The number of transactions is not too large, but the dollar deposited is larger than on any other day. You can also have a longer appointment on a Monday because the bank is not as busy.

The best time for appointments is lunch time. This gives the banker and you an opportunity to get to know each other and will allow you to have a discussion in a relaxed atmosphere. Other favorable times are early in the morning when the bank has just opened and late in the day when the bank is about to close. Bankers remain at the bank long after the bank doors are locked and get to work at least an hour before the doors open. Early morning appointments are good because by opening time the branch manager has taken care of his daily chores and he is still fresh. The last hour in the appointment day is favorable because the bank will soon be closed and the employees are more relaxed.

Note. No matter what day or time you make the appointment, call at least three days—preferably a week—in advance to make the appointment. This allows you to have the best appointment time and indicates to the banker that you are professional.

Your Personal Appearance

You probably think, "I should be able to look and act as I want to." That's true. But you may be creating problems for yourself if you do.

For a bank appointment, a man should wear a very conservative suit, preferably a three-piece one. Dark colors are best. Wear a light, unpatterned shirt and a nice, expensive-looking tie. Why the somber, conservative appearance? Remember, a banker is giving you the bank's money, and his or her position is on the line if you default. A conservative dress is an assurance he or she can see.

Women should also dress conservatively. You want to look like the type of woman a banker would trust to manage the bank's money.

First appearances are important to a banker, so if you have to look and act differently than you ordinarily do, practice first.

The Discussion of Your Loan Proposal

It is impossible to give you a precise understanding of how to discuss your loan proposal with the banker, but here are some general guidelines.

1. Be relaxed. If you can't *be* relaxed, then *act* relaxed.
2. Let the lender review your loan proposal while you sit quietly.
3. Let the lender ask you a question to start the discussion.
4. Answer all questions as thoroughly as you can.
5. If you do not know the answer to a particular question, admit it. Don't try to act as if you understand.
6. In your replies try to use as many financial buzzwords as you can.
7. Mention the negative aspects of your business as well as the positive ones. The banker already knows many of the negatives of most businesses. Let him know that you do, too.
8. It is better to say nothing than trip yourself up. The only real substitute for brains is *silence*.
9. If you are married and have a family, casually bring up that fact in the conversation. People with families are generally considered more creditworthy than single people without families.
10. Try not to take the whole thing too seriously.

Don't expect the banker to act excited about your business. Even when bankers are excited, they never show it. It seems to be an unwritten banker code. The best reaction that you can hope for is that the banker will be smiling and relaxed when you are finished.

When the banker acts unconcerned about your loan proposal, does not ask many questions, and the interview is shorter than 15 minutes, indications are that things are going poorly.

Bankers generally like to "sit" on a loan proposal for several days before they make a decision. This gives them time to review the proposal, read it over, and get a better idea if it is a good loan. Generally speaking, the worse your chance for approval, the faster your loan will be returned. After the proposal is presented there is nothing you can do for about a week. Wait until the banker contacts you.

Immediate Follow-up Procedures

In the two weeks after you submit your loan proposal, follow these procedures:

1. On the day after the appointment write a letter to the banker summarizing the discussion and thanking the banker for his or her time.
2. If you *do not* hear from the bank within one week, call the banker and ask if any other documents are required for the loan proposal. Remember, do not put pressure on the bank. It may harm your case.

If the banker requests more documents or wants the projections reworked, this is a favorable sign. It indicates that the bank is interested.

3. When you are asked by the banker for more information or for corrections, provide them *immediately*. Quick action on your part will help your loan chances tremendously.

PROCEDURES AFTER THE LOAN PRESENTATION

After submitting the loan proposal, the following must be taken into consideration:

Time and timing (how long and when).
Bank's steps for approval.
What to do if the loan is denied by the bank.
Keeping track of your loan proposal.

Time and Timing

A collateralized business loan made on the bank's standard loan program may take only one to two weeks. An SBA loan may take from three to seven months to be approved.

In Los Angeles and in other major urban areas, the SBA processes its guarantee loans in two or three weeks. However, it usually takes at least two months from the time you submit your loan to the bank before it is placed with the SBA because of the documentation that the branch manager must prepare and because of approvals that must be obtained from his or her superiors.

If your loan is declined by two banks and you submit it to the SBA for a direct loan—a lower interest rate—the process can take from six months to two years.

Bank's Steps for Approval

The reason the bank takes so long to process an SBA-guaranteed loan is summed up in two words: *documentation* and *authorization*.

If your loan proposal is well prepared, the banker will not have to do an inordinate amount of work before the proposal is submitted to the SBA, but he or she will have to do some.

The banker has to fill out the SBA Form 4-I before the loan can be accepted by the SBA for a guarantee. The form requires from four to six hours of the banker's time for completion.

The banker may have to prepare a credit memorandum for senior officers who must approve the loan before it can be submitted to the SBA.

Credit information reports are ordered from agencies such as TRW Credit or Dun and Bradstreet. If the applicant—person or business—has a credit file with the bank, that is checked and a written summary is prepared.

All this documentation must be completed when the banker is not busy with his other duties—approving car loans, supervising staff, making management reports, carrying on other bank business. Many bankers have time to do their SBA work only on weekends.

Most branch managers have a limit on how much they can lend on their own authority. The maximum amount that a branch manager can lend on his or her "signature" varies between $25,000 and $200,000.

Not only do branch managers have a limit on what they can loan, but in most cases so do their superiors. It is possible that a $500,000 SBA-guaranteed loan might have to be approved by the branch manager (or credit committee) and perhaps even by the president of the bank.

Since the only person who will see you is the branch manager, his or her credit memorandum and your loan proposal have to be strong.

What If the Loan Is Denied

If your loan application is declined by the first bank, follow these steps:

1. Get a written reason for being turned down.
2. Try to restructure your loan proposal so that whatever objections the banker had will no longer exist.
3. Resubmit your loan to the first bank and simultaneously make an appointment with another bank to submit your loan package.

The *written explanation* for rejecting your loan is important for three reasons: (1) It allows you to adjust your proposal so that the specific deficiencies may be eliminated. (2) It tells you what problems you may have when you submit your proposal to another bank. (3) It is required if you intend to submit your proposal directly to the government lender. The SBA requires that your loan application be declined by one or two lenders (depending on population of your area) before you are allowed to apply for a direct loan.

Redo your proposal to answer each problem presented in the banker's rejection letter. For example, if your expenses were considered too low, increase them on the projection. If your debt-to-worth ratio is unacceptable—you don't have enough money in the business—invest more money or property and let this be reflected in the loan proposal. In short, give the bankers what they want, and they will give you what you want.

Next, *resubmit* your loan to the same lender. To decline your loan a second time, the lender will have to find new reasons, which you have now made more difficult. Remember, *if they cannot turn you down, they have to accept you*.

It is not a question of whether your loan will be approved, but a question of time and patience.

If the second bank declines your loan, go to a third after you have again corrected your proposal. If the third bank turns down your loan, correct your proposal and submit it again. At the same time submit it to the SBA. And so on. *Don't give up!* You *will* get your money in time.

Keeping Track of Your Loan Proposal

When you submit your loan proposal to a bank or the SBA, it is extremely difficult to know how it is progressing. About the only way you can find out about your loan is to call the banker—no more than once a week—and inquire. Remember, do not pressure the lender, merely inquire.

PHILOSOPHY OF PREPARING AND SUBMITTING A LOAN PROPOSAL

We cannot tell you anything else to carry you through this long process of approval except to give you three pieces of philosophy that have helped us and others in similar situations. They are:

The documentation is the proof.

Whatever is not forbidden is required.

It is not a matter of whether or not you will get the loan; it is a matter of time.

The Documentation Is the Proof

Because of the banker's limited time, he or she will depend on your support for the loan analysis—that is, *if* it is supported by third-party information. If you say that your sales will be $1 million per year because of population, expendable income, and so on, you should have copies of census tracts and other documentation in your proposal. If you have all this, the bank will accept your documentation as proof of predicted sales.

If you provide enough documentation, you *prove* that the loan is a good investment for the bank.

However, if the banker receives negative information on your credit report or finds that some of your documentation is patently wrong, *that* documentation becomes the proof.

Whatever Is Not Forbidden Is Required

Dr. Murry Gell-Mann, the inventor of a subatomic structure theory called the "quark theory" and a winner of the Nobel Prize, said the following, "Whatever is not forbidden is required." He was referring to subatomic theory. If there was nothing to disprove the existence of subatomic particles such as quarks, then quarks exist. But allow us to apply this to bankers and loans and restate it: "If a bank or the SBA cannot find a reason to decline your loan, they must approve it." The SBA has in its regulations about five reasons for declining a loan. If none of these reasons apply, then it must approve your loan.

If a bank declines your loan because you are not pledging your home as collateral or because the business does not have enough equity, and you *do* pledge your home and invest more money, the bank must reconsider lending you the money. The point is that you have to eliminate all the negatives. Then the loan *must* be approved.

It Is Not a Matter of Whether or Not You Will Get the Loan; It Is a Matter of Time

We have never known anyone, no matter how poor his or her personal or business situation, who did not receive a loan if he or she tried long enough and hard enough. If you continue to remedy your weak points, eventually you will receive the loan.

Persistence alone will teach you many things. Don't give up. You will receive your money. Good Luck!

Chapter Eight

SBA and Business

During the past hundred years or so, the United States Department of Justice has spent a great deal of time and money on antitrust suits against large corporations and monopolies. Shortly after World War II, Congress decided there was another way to discourage monopolies and promote competition. Instead of spending all its time, effort, and expense on "trust busting," it decided to develop and assist the country's small business concerns. Out of this idea, and the lengthy congressional process, evolved the Small Business Administration.

In 1953 Congress enacted the Small Business Act, and established the SBA as an independent federal agency to advise and assist the nation's small businesses. The SBA was to have four major responsibilities:

1. To provide financial assistance.
2. To provide management, service, and technical assistance.
3. To license and regulate small business investment companies.
4. To ensure small concerns a fair portion of government procurement contracts.

These services are available to all eligible small business concerns. Each of these categories and the programs offered are discussed in the following chapters.

In this chapter we discuss general details about SBA financial assistance and SBA management assistance programs. Chapters 9 and 10 are about the categories of loan assistance (disaster loans, direct loans, guarantee loans, etc.) and company eligibility requirements to get these loans. Chapter 11 outlines SBA procurement assistance. Other government loan programs are discussed in Chapter 12.

SBA FINANCIAL ASSISTANCE

SBA loans have helped thousands of small firms get started, expand, grow, and prosper.

By law, the agency may not make a loan if a business can obtain funds from a bank or other private source. Your business must first seek private financing before applying to the SBA. If your company is located in a city of more than 200,000, you must apply to two banks and they must both turn you down before you can apply for a direct SBA loan.

The SBA's specific lending objectives are to (1) stimulate small business in deprived areas, (2) promote minority enterprise opportunity, and (3) promote small business contribution to economic growth. The SBA, by the direction of Congress, also has as its primary goal the preservation of free, competitive enterprise to strengthen the nation's economy.

All applicants for loans must agree to comply with SBA regulations prohibiting discrimination in employment or services to the public based on race, color, religion, national origin, sex, or marital status.

Following is a list of SBA offices:

Main Office
U.S. Small Business Administration
1441 L Street, N.W.
Washington, D.C. 20416
202-653-6544

District Offices

ALABAMA

Birmingham
U.S. Small Business Admin.
908 S. 20th St., Suite 202
Birmingham, Alabama 35205
205-254-1344

ALASKA

Fairbanks
U.S. Small Business Admin.*
Federal Building & Courthouse
P.O. Box 14, 101 12th Ave.
Fairbanks, Alaska 99701
907-452-1951

ARIZONA

Phoenix
U.S. Small Business Admin.
112 North Central Avenue
Phoenix, Arizona 85004
602-261-3611

ARKANSAS

Little Rock
U.S. Small Business Admin.
611 Gaines St., Suite 900
Little Rock, Arkansas 72201
501-378-5871

CALIFORNIA

Fresno
U.S. Small Business Admin.*
1229 N Street
P.O. Box 828
Fresno, Calif. 93712
209-487-5000

Los Angeles
U.S. Small Business Admin.
350 S. Figueroa St., 6th Floor
Los Angeles, Calif. 90071
213-688-2956

Sacramento
U.S. Small Business Admin.*
2800 Cottage Way
Sacramento, Calif. 95825
916-484-4726

San Diego
U.S. Small Business Admin.
U.S. Federal Building, Room 4-S-33
880 Front Street
San Diego, Calif. 92188
714-293-5440

San Francisco
U.S. Small Business Admin.
211 Main Street
Fourth Floor
San Francisco, Calif. 94105
415-556-7490

COLORADO

Denver
U.S. Small Business Admin.
721 19th St., Room 426A
Denver, Colo. 80202
303-837-0111

CONNECTICUT

Hartford
U.S. Small Business Admin.
One Financial Plaza
Hartford, Conn. 06103
203-244-3600

DELAWARE

Wilmington
U.S. Small Business Admin.*
844 King Street
Federal Building, Room 5207
Wilmington, Del. 19801
302-573-6294

DISTRICT OF COLUMBIA

U.S. Small Business Admin.
1030 15th St., N.W., Suite 250
Washington, D.C. 20417
202-655-4000

FLORIDA

Coral Gables
U.S. Small Business Admin.
2222 Ponce De Leon Blvd., 5th Fl.
Coral Gables, Fla. 33134
305-350-5521

*Limited assistance available.

Jacksonville
U.S. Small Business Admin.
Federal Building, Room 261
400 West Bay Street
Jacksonville, Fla. 32202
904-791-3782

Tampa
U.S. Small Business Admin.*
700 Twiggs Street, Room 607
Tampa, Fla. 33602
813-228-2594

GEORGIA

Atlanta
U.S. Small Business Admin.
1720 Peachtree St., N.W.
6th Floor
Atlanta, Ga. 30309
404-881-4325

GUAM

Agana
U.S. Small Business Admin.*
Pacific Daily News Building
Room 507
Agana, Guam 96910
671-477-8420

HAWAII

Honolulu
U.S. Small Business Admin.
300 Ala Moana Blvd.
P.O. Box 50207
Honolulu, Hawaii 96850
808-546-8950

IDAHO

Boise
U.S. Small Business Admin.
1005 Main St., 2nd Floor
Continental Life Building
Boise, Idaho 83702
208-384-1096

ILLINOIS

Chicago
U.S. Small Business Admin.
Federal Building, Room 437
219 S. Dearborn Street
Chicago, Ill. 60604
312-353-4528

Springfield
U.S. Small Business Admin.*
One North, Old State Capitol Plaza
Springfield, Ill. 62701
217-525-4416

*Limited assistance available.

INDIANA

Indianapolis
U.S. Small Business Admin.
575 N. Pennsylvania St.
Room 522 New Federal Building
Indianapolis, Ind. 46204
317-269-7272

IOWA

Des Moines
U.S. Small Business Admin.
New Federal Bldg., Room 749
210 Walnut Street
Des Moines, Iowa 50309
515-284-4422

KANSAS

Wichita
U.S. Small Business Admin.
Main Place Building
110 East Waterman Street
Wichita, Kansas 67202
316-267-6311

KENTUCKY

Louisville
U.S. Small Business Admin.
600 Federal Place, Room 188
Louisville, Kentucky 40202
502-582-5971

LOUISIANA

New Orleans
U.S. Small Business Admin.
1001 Howard Avenue
Plaza Tower—17th Floor
New Orleans, La. 70113
504-589-2611

Shreveport
U.S. Small Business Admin.*
U.S. P.O. & Courthouse Bldg.
500 Fannin Street
Shreveport, La. 71163
318-226-5196

MAINE

Augusta
U.S. Small Business Admin.
Federal Building, Room 512
40 Western Avenue
Augusta, Maine 04330
207-622-6171

MARYLAND

Towson
U.S. Small Business Admin.
Oxford Building
8600 LaSalle Rd., Room 630
Towson, Md. 21204
301-962-4392

MASSACHUSETTS

Boston
U.S. Small Business Admin.
150 Causeway St., 10th Floor
Boston, Mass. 02114
617-223-2100

Holyoke
U.S. Small Business Admin.*
302 High St., 4th Floor
Holyoke, Mass. 01040
413-536-8770

MICHIGAN

Detroit
U.S. Small Business Admin.
McNamara Building, Room 515
477 Michigan Avenue
Detroit, Mich. 48226
313-226-6075

Marquette
U.S. Small Business Admin.*
Don H. Bottum University Center
540 W. Kaye Avenue
Marquette, Mich. 49855
906-225-1108

MINNESOTA

Minneapolis
U.S. Small Business Admin.
Plymouth Building
12 South 6th Street
Minneapolis, Minn. 55402
612-725-2362

MISSISSIPPI

Biloxi
U.S. Small Business Admin.*
Gulf National Life Insur. Bldg.
111 Fred Haise Blvd., 2nd Floor
Biloxi, Miss. 39530
601-435-3676

Jackson
U.S. Small Business Admin.
Petroleum Building, Suite 690
200 E. Pascagoula St.
Jackson, Miss. 39201
601-969-4371

MISSOURI

Kansas City
U.S. Small Business Admin.
1150 Grand Avenue
5th Floor
Kansas City, Mo. 64106
816-374-5557

St. Louis
U.S. Small Business Admin.
One Mercantile Center, Suite 2500
St. Louis, Mo. 63101
314-425-4191

*Limited assistance available.

MONTANA

Helena
U.S. Small Business Admin.
618 Helena Ave., Box 4819
Helena, Montana 59601
406 449 5381

NEBRASKA

Omaha
U.S. Small Business Admin.
Empire State Building
Nineteen and Farnam Streets
Omaha, Neb. 68102
402-221-4691

NEVADA

Las Vegas
U.S. Small Business Admin.
301 E. Stewart—Box 7527
Las Vegas, Nevada 89101
702-385-6011

Reno
U.S. Small Business Admin.*
50 S. Virginia Street
Room 308
Reno, Nevada 89505
702-784-5477

NEW HAMPSHIRE

Concord
U.S. Small Business Admin.
55 Pleasant Street, Room 213
Concord, N.H. 03301
603-224-4041

NEW JERSEY

Newark
U.S. Small Business Admin.
970 Broad St., Room 1635
Newark, N.J. 07102
201-645-2434

NEW MEXICO

Albuquerque
U.S. Small Business Admin.
Patio Plaza Bldg., Room 320
5000 Marble Avenue, N.E.
Albuquerque, N.M. 87110
505-766-3430

NEW YORK

Albany
U.S. Small Business Admin.*
Twin Towers Bldg., Room 921
99 Washington Avenue
Albany, N.Y. 12210
518-472-6300

Buffalo
U.S. Small Business Admin.*
Federal Building, Room 1311
111 West Huron Street
Buffalo, N.Y. 14202
716-846-4301

Elmira
U.S. Small Business Admin.*
180 State Street, Room 412
Elmira, N.Y. 14901
607-773-4686

New York City
U.S. Small Business Admin.
Federal Office Bldg., Room 3100
26 Federal Plaza
New York, N.Y. 10007
212-264-4355

Rochester
U.S. Small Business Admin.*
Federal Building
100 State Street
Rochester, N.Y. 14614
716-263-6700

Syracuse
U.S. Small Business Admin.
Federal Building—Room 1073
100 South Clinton Street
Syracuse, N.Y. 13260
315-423-5370

NORTH CAROLINA

Charlotte
U.S. Small Business Admin.
230 S. Tryon St., Suite 700
Charlotte, N.C. 28202
704-372-0711

Greenville
U.S. Small Business Admin.*
215 S. Evans Street, Room 206
Greenville, N.C. 27834
919-752-3798

NORTH DAKOTA

Fargo
U.S. Small Business Admin.
Federal Building, Room 218
653 2nd Avenue, North
Fargo, N.D. 58102
701-237-5771

OHIO

Cincinnati
U.S. Small Business Admin.
Federal Office Bldg., Room 5524
550 Main Street
Cincinnati, Ohio 45202
513-684-2814

*Limited assistance available.

Cleveland
U.S. Small Business Admin.
1240 East 9th St., Room 317
Cleveland, Ohio 44199
216-522-4180

Columbus
U.S. Small Business Admin.
Federal Bldg., U.S. Courthouse
85 Marconi Boulevard
Columbus, Ohio 43215
614-469-6860

OKLAHOMA

Oklahoma City
U.S. Small Business Admin.
200 N.W. 5th St., Suite 670
Oklahoma City, Okla. 73102
405-231-4301

OREGON

Portland
U.S. Small Business Admin.
1220 S.W. Third Ave., Fed. Bldg.
Portland, Oregon 97204
503-221-2682

PENNSYLVANIA

Bala Cynwyd
U.S. Small Business Admin.
1 Bala Cynwyd Plaza, Suite 400
East Lobby—231 St. Asaphs Rd.
Bala Cynwyd, Pa. 19004
215-597-3311

Harrisburg
U.S. Small Business Admin.*
1500 North 2nd Street
Harrisburg, Pa. 17102
717-782-3840

Pittsburgh
U.S. Small Business Admin.
Federal Building, Room 1401
1000 Liberty Avenue
Pittsburgh, Pa. 15222
412-644-2780

Wilkes-Barre
U.S. Small Business Admin.*
Penn Place
20 N. Pennsylvania Avenue
Wilkes-Barre, Pa. 18702
717-826-6497

PUERTO RICO

Hato Rey
U.S. Small Business Admin.
Chardon and Bolivia Streets
Hato Rey, P.R. 00919
809-753-4218

RHODE ISLAND

Providence
U.S. Small Business Admin.
57 Eddy Street, 7th Floor
Providence, R.I. 02903
401-528-4580

SOUTH CAROLINA

Columbia
U.S. Small Business Admin.
1801 Assembly Street
Room 131
Columbia, S.C. 29201
803-765-5376

SOUTH DAKOTA

Rapid City
U.S. Small Business Admin.*
Federal Building, Room 246
515 9th Street
Rapid City, S.D. 57701
605-343-5074

Sioux Falls
U.S. Small Business Admin.
National Bank Bldg., Room 402
8th & Main Avenue
Sioux Falls, S.D. 57102
605-336-2980

TENNESSEE

Knoxville
U.S. Small Business Admin.*
Fidelity Bankers Bldg., Room 307
502 S. Gay Street
Knoxville, Tenn. 37902
615-637-9800

Memphis
U.S. Small Business Admin.*
Federal Building
167 North Main St., Room 211
Memphis, Tenn. 38103
901-521-3588

Nashville
U.S. Small Business Admin.
404 James Robertson Parkway
Suite 1012
Nashville, Tenn. 37219
615-251-5881

TEXAS

Corpus Christi
U.S. Small Business Admin.*
3105 Leopard Street
Corpus Christi, Tex. 78408
512-888-3011

Dallas
U.S. Small Business Admin.
1100 Commerce St., Room 3C36
Dallas, Tex. 75242
214-749-3961

El Paso
U.S. Small Business Admin.*
4100 Rio Bravo, Suite 300
El Paso, Texas 79901
915-543-7200

Harlingen
U.S. Small Business Admin.
222 East Van Buren Street
Harlingen, Texas 78550
512-423-8934

Houston
U.S. Small Business Admin.
One Allen Center, Suite 705
500 Dallas Street
Houston, Texas 77002
713-226-4341

Lubbock
U.S. Small Business Admin.
Federal Office Bldg. & U.S. Courthouse,
Room 712
1205 Texas Avenue
Lubbock, Texas 79401
806-762-7011

San Antonio
U.S. Small Business Admin.
727 E. Durango, Room A-513
Federal Building
San Antonio, Texas 78206
512-229-6250

UTAH

Salt Lake City
U.S. Small Business Admin.
Federal Building, Room 2237
125 South State Street
Salt Lake City, Utah 84138
801-524-5800

VERMONT

Montpelier
U.S. Small Business Admin.
Fed. Bldg., 87 State St., Rm. 204
Montpelier, Vermont 05602
802-229-0538

VIRGINIA

Richmond
U.S. Small Business Admin.
Federal Building, Room 3015
400 N. 8th Street
Richmond, Virginia 23240
804-782-2617

VIRGIN ISLANDS

St. Thomas
U.S. Small Business Admin.*
U.S. Federal Building
Veterans Drive—Room 283
St. Thomas, V.I. 00801
809-774-8530

*Limited assistance available.

WASHINGTON

Seattle
U.S. Small Business Admin.
Federal Building, Room 1744
915 Second Avenue
Seattle, Wash. 98174
206-442-5534

Spokane
U.S. Small Business Admin.
Courthouse Building, Room 651
Spokane, Wash. 99210
509-456-3777

WEST VIRGINIA

Charleston
U.S. Small Business Admin.*
Charleston National Plaza
Suite 628
Charleston, W. Va. 25301
304-343-6181

Clarksburg
U.S. Small Business Admin.
Lowndes Building, Room 301
109 N. Third Street
Clarksburg, W. Va. 26301
304-623-5631

WISCONSIN

Madison
U.S. Small Business Admin.
122 W. Washington Ave., Rm. 713
Madison, Wisc. 53703
608-252-5261

Milwaukee
U.S. Small Business Admin.*
Federal Building
Room 246
517 East Wisconsin Avenue
Milwaukee, Wisc. 53202
414-291-3941

WYOMING

Casper
U.S. Small Business Admin.
Federal Building, Room 4001
100 East B Street
Casper, Wyo. 82601
307-265-5550

*Limited assistance available.

Purpose of Loans

The SBA extends financial assistance to small manufacturers, wholesalers, retailers, service establishments, and other firms when financing is not otherwise available on reasonable terms. Loans are made to:

1. Finance construction, conversion, or expansion of facilities.
2. Finance the purchase of equipment, facilities, machinery, supplies, or materials.
3. Supply working capital.
4. Effect change of ownership.

Advantages of an SBA Loan

SBA loans have several advantages over standard bank financing. The SBA offers lower interest rates and has longer terms available. Most important, the leverage factor is higher. That is, with a commercial bank loan a newly established firm may usually borrow only an amount equal to the equity in the business. For example, if a new business has $15,000 in equity, the bank will lend $15,000 and no more. For a business that has been in existence for more than a year, the amount of the loan could be twice the equity.

The SBA ordinarily guarantees loans that are anywhere from three to five times the amount of the business equity. The same $15,000 equity could bring $45,000 to as much as $75,000 depending on the type of business involved. With an Economic Opportunity Loan, the same equity may bring loans of five to seven times the amount, depending on the kind of loan proposal made. This means that if you are starting a new business, you can, by applying through the SBA, get a much larger loan than if you applied to the bank directly without SBA assistance.

Guaranteed and Direct Loans

There are two types of SBA loans available: guaranteed (participation) and direct. The 7 (a) (bank-guaranteed) participation loan is the most extensively used. Your bank makes this loan, and the SBA guarantees 90% of the amount in event of default. For example, if a bank loans your business $200,000, the bank will receive $180,000 from the SBA if you fail to pay off the loan. The SBA may guarantee up to $350,000 or, in special situations, up to $500,000. The SBA has a set of objectives, any *two* of which must be met in order to justify the $500,000 guarantee. The objectives are:

1. Construction of medical facilities whose need has been certified by the appropriate local authority.
2. Conservation or production of energy.
3. Creation or preservation of jobs.
4. Performance of a specific government contract.
5. Stimulation of the economy in labor surplus areas.
6. Conservation of natural resources.
7. Improvement of mass transit facilities.
8. Economic development of depressed urban or rural areas.
9. Assistance to broadcasting and cable television operations.
10. Revitalization of SBA-designated neighborhood business areas.

There are two types of SBA participation loans available: immediate and guaranteed.

Immediate Loans. With an immediate participation loan, the lending institution makes the loan and the SBA purchases upon disbursement its agreed percentage of the loan. The SBA's participation, however, cannot exceed 75% of the loan amount or $150,000, whichever is less.

Guaranteed Loans. Here the participating institution makes and disburses the entire loan, and the SBA guarantees that if the loan should go into default, it will purchase an agreed-upon percentage of the unpaid balance of the loan within a stated period.

Direct Loans. Direct loans from the SBA cannot exceed $150,000 and at times may not be available at all because of federal fiscal restraints. In exceptional circumstances, if certain standards are met, this ceiling may be waived by regional directors. These exceptions are the same as those for the $500,000 maximum guarantee loan.

A direct loan may be granted more than once, but generally you cannot apply within six months of the receipt of a prior SBA loan. At times there are long waiting lists for the direct loans and they only will be granted as money becomes available. Direct loans usually have lower interest rates than participation loans.

Maturity

Your loan may run for as long as 10 years. However, those portions of the loans used for acquiring real property or constructing facilities may have a maturity of 20 years. Working capital loans, on the other hand, are limited to a six-year duration.

Interest Rates

The maximum interest rate chargeable for SBA loans is set periodically. Ideally the rate is high enough to induce financial institutions to participate while still having reasonably priced credit available to small businesses. The SBA rate is the maximum that cannot be exceeded on fixed-rate loans. There is no given formula to determine the maximum rate, and there is no minimum rate.

Participating banks have the option of making variable-rate loans. That is, if agreed to by both parties, the loan may stipulate a fluctuating interest rate. For loans maturing in less than seven years, the spread may be to 2.25 points above the base rate. If the loan term is seven years or longer, the spread may increase to 2.75 points. The base rate must be the prime rate, as regularly published in the media, or the SBA "Optional Peg Rate," which is published quarterly in the *Federal Register*. The original note rate may not exceed the SBA maximum rate in effect at the time of acquisition and must remain in force for one full calendar quarter. After that, the rate may fluctuate quarterly.

Collateral

Security for a loan normally consists of one or more of the following:

A mortgage on land, a building, and/or equipment.

Assignment of warehouse receipts for marketable merchandise.

A mortgage on chattels such as showcases, automobiles, or heavy equipment.

Guarantees or personal endorsements, and in some instances assignments of current receivables.

A pledge or mortgage on inventories usually is not satisfactory collateral unless the inventories are stored in a bonded or otherwise acceptable warehouse.

Repayment

As with any personal loan or mortgage, SBA loans are repaid in equal monthly installments including principal and interest. Exceptions are made when the borrower's income is received on an annual or seasonal basis. It should also be noted that all or any part of a loan may be prepaid before maturity without incurring any penalty whatsoever.

Problem Loan Servicing. If, on your guaranteed loan, payments become 60 days delinquent, the participating bank notifies the SBA. With direct loans the SBA is immediately aware of delinquencies. In either case the problem is referred to Problem Loan Servicing. It will contact you and try to determine what is needed to enable your company to meet its financial obligations. An analysis of the situation may result in a change of the loan repayment schedule. Depending on individual circumstances, different approaches will be tried. Management assistance may be prescribed if it is determined that difficulties are due to improper administration.

The SBA wants to see your business remain in operation. A time extension or a moratorium on principal payment may be offered as help, sometimes up to a full year.

Liquidation. If the loan goes into default, it is transferred to liquidation. Here again, if there is a possibility of pulling the company through, the SBA will negotiate new payment schedules. It may want to reorganize the assets for sale of the business to new owners. Liquidation proceedings are begun only after the debt is determined uncollectable by conventional means. The SBA will seek possession of the collateral pledged, such as equipment and machinery, fixtures, and so forth. In the case of bankruptcy the loan automatically goes into default, and the SBA files its claim against the assets.

MANAGEMENT ASSISTANCE

Establishing a business is relatively easy; keeping it going is another matter altogether. Fortunately the SBA can help you stay afloat by giving you management assistance at any time.

The SBA management assistance programs are keyed to encourage the establishment, growth, and success of small businesses.

The SBA identifies management problems, develops alternative solutions, and helps to implement and expand business plans with the help of management assistance officers who staff the agency's counseling program. For individual counseling, the SBA also relies heavily on national volunteer organizations such as SCORE (Service Corps of Retired Executives) and ACE (Active Corps of Executives). Counseling on problems of marketing, accounting, product analysis, production methods, and research and development is given in SBA field offices. Advice and training are also offered at no charge to people considering going into business on their own.

Management assistance programs and other SBA-sponsored help include the following:

- The Small Business Institute
- Service Corps of Retired Executives (SCORE)
- Active Corps of Executives (ACE)
- Call Contracting Program
- International trade
- Management training
- University business development center
- Management publications

The Small Business Institute

The SBA's newest management assistance resource is the Small Business Institute (SBI). With the cooperation of faculty, senior students, and graduate students of nearly 400 of the nation's leading schools of business provide long-term counseling and assistance at no charge to small business owners.

Although participation in the SBI program is primarily for SBA clients who are loan recipients and holders of special government "set-aside" contracts, business owners who wish to avail themselves of the service should contact the management assistance officer at the nearest SBA office. The officer will determine your eligibility.

Service Corps of Retired Executives (SCORE)

SCORE is an organization of more than 6,000 retired business executives, both men and women, who volunteer their services to help small business owners solve their problems. The collective experience of these SCORE volunteers spans the full range of American enterprise.

Assigned SCORE counselors visit the owners in their places of business. Through careful observation, an analysis is made of each business and its problems. Once the problem is determined, several alternatives are available. The SCORE volunteer may be able to develop a solution or he or she may call for other volunteer assistants who in turn may also request outside consulting from the local SBA office. Finally, a plan is offered to correct the trouble and help the owner through the critical period. This service is provided at no cost to the small business owner.

Local chambers of commerce can often help you get in touch with SCORE volunteers. Or you can call the local SBA office for a referral to the nearest SCORE chapter.

Active Corps of Executive (ACE)

ACE augments SCORE's services and keeps management counseling continually updated. Its members are active executives from all major industries, professional and trade associations, educational institutions, and many of the professions. More than 2,500 ACE members throughout the country volunteer specialized kinds of expertise not usually found in every SCORE chapter.

Call Contracting Program

For existing businesses with specific problems that require uncommon or specialized qualifications, the Call Contracting Program may be the answer. This program provides both management and technical assistance ranging from junior and senior accounting to complex engineering advice from professional consultants. If your firm has a problem the SBA staff and its volunteer consultants in the area are not equipped to handle, they will assign a call contractor, and there will be no charge for the service. The contractor will come to your place of business as a consultant, study the problem, and make recommendations for its solution.

The SBA maintains this counseling service for small firms that require it. The professional consultants who provide this assistance must meet strict standards and are selected through competitive bidding or careful negotiation. At least one of these contractors is located in each of the SBA's ten regions, and some regions have several. To find out if you are eligible for the Call Contracting Program, either as a recipient of the counseling or as a consultant, contact the management assistance officer at the nearest SBA office.

International Trade

The SBA works closely with the Department of Commerce, The Export-Import Bank, the Overseas Private Investment Corporation, and other government and private agencies to provide small businesses with advice and information on export opportunities. The underlying purpose is to increase small business participation in international trade. Here again, contact your local SBA office for further information.

Management Training

To reach the greatest possible number in the small business community, the SBA cosponsors management training programs with universities, colleges, distributive education units, trade and professional associations, chambers of commerce, and local business organizations. In some communities management training is also offered over commercial and educational television stations.

To meet local needs, the SBA's management training program encompasses four types of training for present and prospective small business owners: courses, conferences, problem clinics, and prebusiness workshops.

Courses. Management courses provide classroom training on a variety of subjects. Courses may be general surveys of several different areas of business management or a series of in-depth sessions on a single subject. Instructors may be teaching staff members of educational institutions or may be professionals—such as management consultants, bankers, lawyers, accountants, and others—who have teaching ability in addition to expertise in a particular subject.

Instructors are selected and paid by the cosponsoring organizations. The owner-student is usually charged only a nominal fee to cover expenses.

Conferences and Problem Clinics. A conference is usually a one-day or evening session—although it may be held on parts of two or three days—for a group of 50 to 100. It covers a single management subject and normally features speakers, panel discussions, question-and-answer periods, and work sessions.

In a problem clinic small groups of owner-managers under the guidance of a leader or moderator give intense, in-depth treatment to a single subject.

Much of the discussion is based on the participants' own knowledge and experience. The SBA and its cosponsors act as catalysts to bring together people with common interests, such as expanding marketing areas, crime prevention, or personnel training in specific types of businesses.

Prebusiness Workshops. Prebusiness workshops are designed for persons who are interested in operating their own business or for those who have been in business for a year or less. They may be one-day sessions or a series of evening meetings totaling six to eight hours.

The purpose of the workshops is to help prospective owner-managers make a careful analysis of what is involved in starting and managing a small business. Workshops deal with fundamentals of good management that are applicable to any type of business. They are not intended to give in-depth training. Rather thay provide a management orientation and a guide for preparation by prospective owners before a business is started.

Training Materials. The SBA makes available a variety of materials for its cosponsored management training programs. These include prebusiness workshop packages, instructor's manuals, 16 millimeter sound and color movies, transparencies for overhead projection, and a "Guidebook for Coordinators of Management Training for Small Business." This booklet provides detailed information to help cosponsors plan, promote, and implement small business management training programs in cooperation with the SBA.

University Business Development Center

The University Business Development Center (UBDC), is one of the ways the SBA encourages private sector organizations to seek new ways to serve the small business community. UBDC is designed to draw together the total resources of a university, including faculty and students, and to make them available to new and existing small businesses. UBDC also includes other government agencies that have pertinent campus programs and additional volunteers from the private sector. If there is a university near you, check your nearest SBA office. There may be a UBDC in your area.

Management Publications

The services of professional management consultants are readily available to big business firms but are rarely within the means of the small business owners.

To help them keep abreast of modern management techniques and maintain efficient management policies, SBA issues about 300 publications on problems of interest to a cross sections of management and presents facts and figures in brief, readable, nontechnical form. Professionals in many businesses contribute their work as a public service to small firms. Management assistance publications that are distributed free through SBA offices include the following leaflet series:

> *Management Aids for Small Manufacturers* is a series dealing with functional problems of small plants; it also concentrates on subjects of interest to administrative executives.
>
> *Small Marketers Aids* are guides for retail, wholesale, and service firms.
>
> *Small Business Bibliographies* are reference sources for individual types of businesses that apply most directly to counseling.

The following series of booklets are for sale at nominal prices from the Superintendent of Documents, U.S. Government Printing Office, Washington, D.C. 20402:

> *Small Business Management Series* is devoted to more comprehensive discussions of special management problems of small concerns. More than 35 volumes have been published.
>
> *Starting and Managing Series* describes problems of starting and managing specific types of small enterprises. Only the first volume, *Starting and Managing a Small Business of Your Own,* does not deal with a specific type of business. Representative titles are *Starting and Managing a Small Shoestore* and *Starting and Managing a Small Drive-In Restaurant.*

Nonseries booklets are also available. They discuss management subjects that do not fit into the series categories, such as *Managing for Profits* and *Buying and Selling a Small Business.*

Chapter Nine

Categories of Loan Assistance

Among the many types of available loan assistance are the following:

Economic Opportunity Loan (EOL) for economically and/or socially disadvantaged persons owning small business concerns.

Displaced Business Loans for small business concerns displaced by governmental projects including, but not limited to, road projects and urban renewal.

Economic Injury Loans for businesses which have been injured as a result of federal regulations or other actions such as environmental acts, water pollution control acts, occupational safety acts, consumer protection acts, closing of military installations, and so on.

Disaster Loans to individuals and businesses after federally declared natural or other physical disasters occur.

Handicapped Assistance Loans (HAL) for small business owners who are physically handicapped or nonprofit organizations where at least 75% of the man hours performed in the production of goods and services are by handicapped individuals.

Loans for seasonal lines of credit.

Contract loans to complete specific contracts.

Energy loans.

Loans to local and state development loan companies to help small businesses within their areas of operation.

Loans to Small Business Investment Companies (SBIC) and Minority Enterprise Small Business Investment Companies. Loans to SBICs have different criteria than other programs and they will be discussed separately. SBICs provide both equity and debt financing for small business concerns.

Type of Loan*	Purpose	Who May Apply
7 (a) Business Loan	To assist firms to finance construction, conversion or expansion; to purchase equipment, facilities, machinery; to acquire working capital; and effect change of ownership. Loans are direct or in participation with banks.	Small businesses
Economic Opportunity Loans	To assist firms operated by those who have marginal or	Low-income or disadvantaged

Type of Loan	Purpose	Who May Apply
	submarginal incomes, or those who have been denied equal opportunity because of race, color, or creed.	persons desiring to strengthen or establish a small business
Displaced Business Loans	To assist firms displaced by federally aided construction programs.	Small businesses
Economic Injury Loans	To assist firms suffering economic injury resulting from: (1) a major or natural disaster declared by the President or Secretary of Agriculture, (2) federal, state, or local urban renewal or highway construction programs, (3) inability to market or process a product because of disease or toxicity resulting from natural or undetermined causes.	Small businesses
Occupational Safety and Health Loans	To enable firms to meet the requirements of the Occupational Safety and Health Act of 1970, and standards set up by that law, either on a voluntary basis or because they received a notice of deficiency.	Small businesses
Consumer Protection Loans	To assist firms engaged in meat, poultry, or egg processing to comply with various federal and state laws.	Small businesses
Strategic Arms Economic Injury Loans	To assist firms economically injured as the result of cutbacks in federal projects relating to the development of strategic arms or the installation of such arms or facilities.	Small businesses
Economic Dislocation Loans	To assist firms in areas of economic dislocation.	Small businesses
Disaster Loans	To assist disaster victims to rebuild homes or restore business establishments damaged in SBA declared disaster areas to their pre-disaster condition.	Individuals, business concerns, nonprofit organizations
Handicapped Assistance Loans (HAL)	To assist business owners who are physically handicapped or nonprofit organizations where at least 75% of the man hours performed are by handicapped	Handicapped owners of small concerns; Nonprofit organizations

Type of Loan	Purpose	Who May Apply
	individuals in the production of goods and services.	
Seasonal Line of Credit Program	To assist seasonal types of business.	Small businesses
Contract Loan Program	To assist firms in completing specific contracts.	Small businesses
Energy Loans	To assist firms to purchase small business firms or manufacture, distribute, or service any of these energy measures: solar energy equipment, photovoltaic cells, energy conserving devices, wood or waste energy production devices, hydroelectric energy equipment, wind energy conversion equipment, and services necessary to aid citizens in using the above.	Small businesses
Development Company Loans	To assist small firms by helping to establish and finance the operation of state and local small business development companies that make loans to small firms for equity capital, plant construction, conversion, or expansion.	State and local development companies
Small Business Investment Companies; Minority Enterprise Small Business Investment Companies (SBIC/MESBIC)	To stimulate and supplement the flow of private equity capital and long-term loan funds available for business.	Small businesses

*Apply for each of these loans at the nearest SBA office.

ECONOMIC OPPORTUNITY LOANS (EOL)

The purpose of this program is to make funds available on reasonable terms to small business concerns located in areas with high levels of unemployment or low income individuals. Also included are small businesses owned by, or to be started by, persons who have been socially and economically disadvantaged. The rate of unemployment and the degree of economic disadvantage are flexible and are not tied to any particular number or set of numbers.

The business must be at least 51% owned by persons who (1) have an individual annual family income—other than welfare—that is not sufficient for the basic needs of the family, or (2) because of economic and social disadvantage, have been denied access to adequate financing on reasonable terms through the normal lending channels.

Eligibility is granted for all honorably discharged veterans, especially from the

Vietnam era, who are unable to obtain financing on reasonable terms either from the usual commercial sources or other SBA funding programs.

The EOL has a direct loan program, but there are also participation loans available. However, SBA participation may not exceed $100,000 or 90% of the loan, whichever is less.

Repayment will be required at the earliest feasible date. Working capital loans have a maturity of 10 years. Terms up to 15 years are provided when loan proceeds are for realty and other fixed assets. Grace periods for payment of principal may be given. Interest payments must be made as soon after the loan is disbursed as possible and will be required during any grace period. A fluctuating repayment schedule may be established for seasonal businesses.

There are no specific requirements for the collateral for the loan. Inadequate collateral cannot be used as a reason to turn down the loan unless the applicant refuses to pledge whatever worthwhile collateral is available.

The SBA may require that the applicant accept management assistance as a condition of the loan.

DISPLACED BUSINESS LOANS AND ECONOMIC INJURY LOANS

These are loans made to small business concerns that have been put in a disadvantaged position because of government policy or a federal resource emergency or shortage. Assistance is for business concerns that are economically injured because of being displaced by, located in, or adjacent to a federal urban renewal area, highway, or other construction. If your firm qualifies, the funds may be used for necessary working capital to carry the business until normal operations resume, replacement cost of realty, generally re-establishing business, including purchases of new property, machinery, and equipment, or the purchase of a new business. Upgrading is allowed up to 50% of the total cost to be for land and 33.3% for buildings.

Strategic Arms Economic Injury Loans

These loans go to small business concerns suffering injury because of loss of federal support for any project due to an international agreement limiting the developing of strategic arms or the installation of their facilities. Loan proceeds may be used for working capital and to meet financial obligations which the applicant would have been able to meet if federal support for the strategic arms project had not been lost.

Base Closing Assistance Loans

These loans are available to small businesses who have suffered or will suffer economic injury as a result of the federal government closing a major military installation under the jurisdiction of the Department of Defense. Also included are injuries from a severe reduction in the size and scope of operations at a major military installation. These loans provide working capital and funds to pay financial obligations not being met because of reduced income.

Economic Dislocation Loans

These loans are available to small concerns in an area of economic dislocation. There is a $100,000 maximum and funds may not be used to reduce the exposure of any other lender. To be eligible, the governor of a state must certify to the SBA (a) that small business concerns within the state have suffered substantial economic injury as a result of an economic dislocation, and (b) that these concerns are in need of financial assistance which is not available on reasonable terms. Initiated in 1977, the program was used to aid homeowners in Los Angeles County, California who had lost their houses during the brush fires of November 1978. This program can also be used by private individuals.

SPECIAL LOANS

Occupational Safety and Health Loans

These loans aid small businesses that wish, either voluntarily or because of a notice of deficiency, to comply with the Occupational Safety and Health Act of 1970. The concerns must show substantial economic injury caused by their inability to conform to the OSHA standards without SBA assistance. Those complying voluntarily must submit a report of a licensed professional engineer or architect along with the loan application. Loans are for additions or alterations in the equipment, facilities, or operating methods of the business that are needed for compliance. Working capital may be requested to replace amounts used for compliance costs.

Consumer Protection Loans

These are available to small firms operating in meat, poultry, or egg processing. Loan proceeds are to effect additions to or alterations in the equipment, facilities, or methods of operations so that they meet requirements established by the Eggs Products Inspection Act of 1970, the Wholesome Meat Act of 1967, and the Wholesome Poultry Act of 1968. Firms are eligible for assistance if they demonstrate that they are likely to suffer substantial economic injury without SBA assistance. To qualify they must produce a notice of deficiency from an inspection authority showing that they do not conform with current requirements. Loan proceeds can be used only for changes considered necessary by the U.S. Department of Agriculture or appropriate state agency.

Coal Mine Health and Safety Loans

These loans assist small coal mines to make additions to or alterations in the equipment, facilities, or operating methods to meet the requirements of the Federal Coal Mine Health and Safety Act of 1969. Again, the applying firms must demonstrate substantial economic injury without SBA assistance. Funds can be used to replace working capital expended for compliance, to furnish funds when construction is involved and operations curtailed, to meet continuing fixed costs, to help finance start up costs, and to finance changes in operating methods required by examining authorities.

The SBA must receive a notice of deficiency from the Bureau of Mines and an opinion that the changes applied for will bring the mine into full compliance.

Water Pollution Control Loans

These loans are available to companies that must comply with the Federal Water Pollution Control Act. Funds are to be used for additions or alterations in the equipment or facilities, including construction of pretreatment facilities and interceptor sewers or operating methods. Again, economic injury from lack of SBA assistance must be shown.

DISASTER LOANS

The SBA is authorized to make or guarantee loans where necessary to victims of floods, riots, civil disorders, and other catastrophes such as hurricane, tornado, drought, fire, earthquake, and so on.

Physical Disaster Loans

Physical disaster loans may be made to home or property owners, businesses of any size, and nonprofit institutions. Financial assistance may be extended to rehabilitate or replace property damaged or lost as a result of a declared disaster. While repayment ability must be shown, the emergency conditions which accompany any disaster result in less stringent credit analysis, especially in the smaller loan amounts.

Although there are no specific ceilings on loan amounts, the SBA has set various administrative ceilings. Usually loan proceeds cannot be more than the actual physical damage. However, funds can be used to repay interim financing used to alleviate the disaster-caused injury. Physical disaster loans made to small businesses may provide working capital, the payment of operating expenses, and any purpose under the 7 (a) program, subject to some limitations. Working capital loans are limited to operating expenses and working capital losses resulting from the disaster.

The Small Business Act does not contain specific requirements for collateral as security for a disaster loan. The SBA does, however, require applicants to pledge whatever collateral they can furnish.

Economic Injury Disaster Loans

This program is limited solely to small business concerns. Firms are eligible when the President or Secretary of Agriculture or the SBA determines that a specific geographical area has sustained a major natural disaster. Interest rates and terms are similar to those of physical disaster loans. The applicant must demonstrate economic injury. These loans may be used to provide (a) working capital to carry the concern until normal operations are resumed, and (b) payment of financial obligations that applicants are not able to meet because of the disaster. No funds may be used for dividends, bonuses, or disbursements to owners, partners, officers, or stockholders not directly related to the performance of services.

Aid to Major Sources of Employment

These loans were authorized under the Disaster Relief Act of 1970 to enable industrial or commercial enterprises that are major sources of employment in a declared disaster area, but that are not operating because of the disaster, to resume operations. The goal is to restore the economic viability of the disaster area.

A major source of employment is defined as (a) a concern which employs 10% or more of the entire work force of a geographically identifiable community, no larger than a county, or (b) a concern which employs 10% or more of the total work force in an industry within the major disaster area, or (c) any business firm within the major disaster area which employs 1000 or more employees.

Emergency Energy Shortage Loans

These loans assist small businesses which have been or are likely to be seriously affected by a shortage of fuel, electrical energy, energy producing resources, or raw or processed materials. Proceeds of the loans may be used to:

1. Meet business obligations which otherwise could have been met.
2. Finance changes in operating methods to convert to an adequate energy supply source.
3. Finance changes in operating methods to allow for the continued existence of the business.
4. Furnish funds to meet continuing fixed costs.
5. Refinance short term debt.
6. Pay off long-term debts.
7. Provide working capital.
8. Refund burdensome loans from other lenders.

Product Disaster Loans

This program authorizes the SBA to assist small firms to reestablish or continue their business when they have suffered economic injury as a result of diseased or toxic products, through natural or undetermined causes. Low interest rates and the same maximum maturity as the physical disaster loans apply to this program.

Loans may be used to provide working capital to support the business until sales can resume. Funds may be also used to replace or expand equipment if it is necessary to properly process a product to insure fitness for human consumption. Unrealized net profit or a drop in sales that is not disaster related may not be considered in determining economic injury.

HANDICAPPED ASSISTANCE LOANS (HAL)

HAL-1 is a loan to a nonprofit organization where at least 75% of the working hours are performed by handicapped individuals. The loans are limited to nonprofit sheltered workshops and similar organizations, to enable them to produce and provide marketable goods and services. Funds can not be used for subsidization of wages of low producers, health and rehabilitation agencies, community fund raising drives, private donors, grants, or bequests. The SBA prohibits duplication of the work or activity of any other Federal department or agency unless expressly stipulated.

HAL-2 loans are for eligible small business concerns owned by handicapped persons. They may be used to establish, acquire or operate a small business.

SEASONAL LINE OF CREDIT PROGRAM

This program provides financial assistance of a maximum of $500,000 for guarantees and $100,000 for EOL direct loans for seasonal types of businesses such as toy manufacturers, tourist bureaus, and outdoor ice skating rinks. These firms must meet SBA eligibility requirements and must have been in business for at least 12 months prior to the loan application.

CONTRACT LOAN PROGRAM

This Contract Loan Program offers financial assistance on specific contracts, up to the amount of the cost of labor and materials needed to complete the contract, but the loan may not exceed the $500,000 guarantee. Firms may be construction contractors, manufacturers, and service contractors providing specific services under an assignable contract. Firms must have been in operation for at least 12 months.

ENERGY ORIENTED LOANS

This is one of the newest programs offered by the SBA, effective since January 4, 1979. The SBA will provide assistance to small concerns to finance plant construction, conversion, or expansion (including land acquisition), or to start up and acquire equipment, facilities, machinery, supplies, or materials. All this is to enable the company to design or engineer, manufacture, distribute, market, install, or service any of the following energy measures:

1. Solar thermal energy equipment.
2. Photovoltaic cells and related equipment.
3. A product or service whose primary purpose is the conservation of energy through devices that increase the energy efficiency of systems using fossil fuels.
4. Equipment which produces energy from wood, biological waste, grain, or other biomass energy sources.
5. Equipment that co-generates energy from industrial waste.
6. Hydroelectric power equipment.
7. Engineering, architectural, consulting, or other professional services to aid citizens in utilizing any of the above measures.

LOANS TO STATE AND LOCAL DEVELOPMENT COMPANIES

The SBA is authorized to make loans to state and local development companies in order to stimulate small business development. These funds may be used to provide private equity capital and long-term loans.

Local development companies (LDCs) may be organized by local chambers of commerce or simply by groups of local citizens. A bank may be involved in the formation of an LDC.

An LDC must be incorporated in the state where it operates and must operate in a specific area. At least 75% of the persons owning and controlling the LDC must either live or do business in the area of operation. No more than 25% of the ownership or control may be held by a single individual or his or her affiliates if they have financial interest in either the project being developed or the small business being helped. The LDC must have a minimum of 25 stockholders or members.

Before the SBA approves a loan, the development company must produce evidence that funds are not available from banks or other private sources. Generally, a development company is required to provide from its own funds 20% to 30% of the project cost.

Loans to LDCs may be made for the following purposes:

1. Helping a development company buy land.
2. Building a new factory.
3. Acquiring machinery and equipment.
4. Expanding or converting an existing plant or constructing new space.

Chapter Ten
Loan Eligibility Requirements

To be eligible for SBA financial assistance, certain standards must be met. Your firm must be a small business concern and have certain credit ratings. The Small Business Administration publishes regulations providing details on qualifying size standards. These are available at any SBA office.

A small business concern, as defined by the SBA for its loan purposes, is one that is independently owned and operated and one that is not dominant in its field of operation. There are further size standards based on number of employees, dollar volume of business, and type of business. Examples include the following:

Construction. Any construction concern is classified as small if its average income does not exceed between $5 million and $9.5 million for the preceding 3 fiscal years. The dollar limits depend on the type of construction company (grading, electrical, etc.).

Manufacturing. A manufacturing concern is considered to be *small* if its number of employees does not exceed 250 persons, and *large*—and therefore ineligible for SBA loans—if its number of employees exceeds 1500 persons. Companies that employ over 250 people should contact their local SBA field office to see if they qualify.

There is one exception, though, and that is a manufacturing company primarily engaged in the food canning and preserving industry. It is considered small if its employees do not exceed 500 persons, exclusive of agricultural labor as defined in subsection (k) of the Federal Employment Tax Act.

Retail. Any retail concern is classified as small if its annual sales do not exceed $2 million. Certain industries or subindustries can have sales in excess of $2 million and still be considered a small business. The exceptions include:

1. Clothing stores (men's and boy's, women's ready-to-wear, or family)—$2.5 million
2. Shoe stores—$2.5 million
3. Household appliance and radio/television stores—$2.5 million
4. Variety stores—$3 million
5. Farm equipment dealers—$4.5 million
6. Motor vehicle dealers, new and used—$6.5 million
7. Department stores, grocery stores, and meat, meat and fish, or seafood markets—$7.5 million

Services. A service business is considered small if:

1. Its annual sales do not exceed $1.5 million to $10 million, depending on the type of service industry.
2. It is engaged primarily in the following industries and the annual sales do not exceed the dollar amounts shown: hotel-motel—$3 million; power laundry—$3 million; motion picture production or services—$8 million; rendering general engineering services—$3.5 million.
3. It is engaged primarily in owning and operating a hospital and its capacity does not exceed 150 beds. Convalescent and nursing homes or medical and dental laboratories are classified under the $1.5 million annual sales restriction.

Shopping Centers. Any concern primarily engaged in operating shopping centers is considered small and therefore eligible for SBA assistance if:

1. Assets do not exceed $8 million.
2. Net worth does not exceed $4 million.
3. Average net income does not exceed $400,000. The average net income is to be calculated without the benefit of any carry-over loss.
4. Not more than 25% of the gross leasable area is let to concerns that are larger than the SBA's small business size standards.

Transportation and Warehousing. If a firm is primarily engaged in passenger and freight transportation or warehousing it is considered small if:

1. Annual sales do not exceed $1.5 million.
2. It is primarily engaged in the air transportation industry and the number of its employees does not exceed 1000.
3. It is primarily engaged in grain storage with not more than 1 million bushel capacity in owned and leased facilities and its annual sales do not exceed $1.5 million.
4. It is primarily engaged in trucking, warehousing, packaging and crating, and/or freight forwarding, and annual sales do not exceed $6.5 million.

Wholesale. Any wholesaling concern is considered small if annual sales do not exceed $9.5 million. There are exceptions. Firms in some lines of wholesaling can have annual sales of $14.5 million to $22 million. If you are a wholesaler, check with the SBA to see if you qualify. Similarly, if your concern has annual sales over $9.5 million, contact the SBA to verify qualification. If your business is primarily engaged in wholesaling but is also engaged in manufacturing, your business qualifies under both the manufacturing and the wholesaling standards.

Farming and Agriculture Related Industries. Companies engaged in the production of food and fiber, ranching and raising of livestock, agriculture, and all other farming and agriculture related industries are eligible, but annual sales cannot exceed $1 million.

Recreational Enterprises. Amusement enterprises are also eligible for SBA assistance. However, they must be open to the public, and properly licensed by appropriate state or local authorities.

Special Exceptions. There are special exceptions to the dollar volume standards used in determining business size. If your company generates at least 50% of its business in the specified states or territories, it can have a larger dollar volume and still qualify by SBA standards. Businesses in these areas may exceed the maximum annual sales for their categories by a certain percentage amount:

Area	% of Gross Sales Allowed Over Maximums Set in Part 121
Alaska	25.0
Hawaii	12.5
Virgin Islands	10.0
Puerto Rico	7.5
Guam	7.5

For example, the SBA defines as small a shoe store with annual sales of $2.5 million. In Hawaii, a shoe store can have annual sales of $2.8 million and still qualify for a small business loan.

Part 121 of the SBA Rules and Regulations is the section that establishes size standards. As changes in the national economy occur, these standards are updated.

Contractor and Real Estate Financing

In contracting and real estate businesses an SBA loan must be used to finance the construction or rehabilitation, or the acquisition and prompt rehabilitation (costing more than one third of the purchase price), of residential or commercial property. Loans for the construction and sale of real estate are available for up to 36 months. During part of this time, the building may be rented out.

A contractor must meet SBA size standards. The concern may be a construction contractor, contractor, or builder who has shown "managerial and technical ability in construction or renovating projects of comparable size."

Only 20% of the total loan amount may be used to buy unimproved vacant property. Collateral cannot be "less than a second lien as security." All liens on the property must be equal to less than 80% of the fair market value of the completed project.

Not more than 5% of the SBA loan can be for offsite improvements such as street, curbs, water or sewer mains, or other improvements that "benefit the entire development." Loan repayment must be from the sale of the property to "parties not affiliated with the borrower" (*Federal Register*, Vol. 43, No. 201, October 17, 1978).

The contractor must give to the participating lender, bank, or the SBA, *letters* from all of the following sources as to the value of, or services for, the project.

1. A mortgage lender.
2. An independent licensed real estate broker.
3. An independent architect, appraiser, or engineer.

The mortgage lender must state whether or not permenent mortgage money is usually available to qualified borrowers to purchase real property (similar buildings or homes) in the vicinity.

The real estate broker must state whether or not there is a sales market for that type of building as compared with other similar buildings. The broker must have a minimum of 3 years experience in that specific location and area.

The architect, appraiser, or engineer must agree to make construction inspection and to certify documents to support interim construction loan disbursements. The loan applicant will bear the cost of these inspection and certifications.

The interest and maximum loan amount are the same as other SBA direct or guaranteed loans.

GENERAL CREDIT REQUIREMENTS

After meeting the Small Business Administration size standards, a loan applicant still must comply with credit and other policy requirements.

A loan applicant must:

Be of good character.

Have enough experience and knowledge to operate a business successfully.

Have a minimum equity position of 20% of the total assets of the business.

Show that the proposed loan is secured by sufficient collateral (usually less than 100%) to assure repayment.

Show that the past earnings record and future prospects of the firm indicate ability to repay the loan and other fixed debt, if any, out of profits.

Be able to provide from his or her own resources sufficient funds to have a reasonable amount at stake to withstand possible losses, particularly during the early stages if the venture is in a new business.

INELIGIBLE APPLICATION

Because it is a public agency using taxpayer's funds, the SBA has an unusual responsibility as a lender. It therefore will not make loans:

Other Funds Available. If funds are otherwise available on reasonable terms
(a) from private financial institutions,
(b) from the sale, at fair prices, of assets not needed by the concern in the conduct of its business or not reasonably necessary to its growth,
(c) through the use of personal credit and/or resources of the owner, partners, management, or principal stockholders,
(d) from other government agencies that supply credit specifically for that particular type of business, or
(e) from other known sources of credit.

Payouts. If the loan is for the purpose of
(a) paying off creditor(s) who are inadequately secured and in a position to sustain a loss,
(b) providing funds for distribution or payment to the owner, partners, or shareholders,
(c) refunding a debt to a small business investment company, or
(d) replacing working capital that was used for any of these purposes.

Speculation. If the loan proceeds will be used in speculation in any type or real or personal property, tangible or intangible. It is also forbidden to use SBA funds to free company money for speculation.

Nonprofit. If the applicant is a religious organization or nonprofit enterprise. Exceptions are for cooperatives that carry on a business activity in order to obtain profits for their members in the operation of their otherwise eligible small business concerns.

Media. If the business is a newspaper, magazine, book publishing company or distribution enterprise. Radio, cable, or television broadcasting companies do qualify.

If any of the applicant's or principal's gross income is derived from gambling activities. Exceptions are for concerns with less than one-third of their gross income from sales of official state lottery tickets under a state license, or from gambling activities in those states where such activities are legal within the State.

Lending. If the concern is primarily engaged in lending or investments. Also ineligible are otherwise approved concerns using funds to finance investments not related or essential to the enterprise.

Monopoly. If the granting of financial aid will encourage monopoly.

Relocation. If the business is going to use the loan proceeds to relocate for other than sound business purposes.

Distribution Sales. If the business is a multilevel sales distribution plan. Typically this plan involves sales of soft goods such as cosmetics, household cleaners or utensils on a door-to-door or house party basis. The profit is made by recruitment of distributors.

Government. If the sole proprietor, partner, officer, director or stockholder (with 10% or more interest), or member of the stockholder's household is a federal government employee with a grade of GS-13 or above, or a major or lieutenant commander, or higher in the military. A business is also ineligible if a partner or holder of 10% of the stock is a member of Congress or an employee of the legislative or judicial branch of the government, or a member of their household. Exceptions are made for the Disaster Loan Program.

If there are questions concerning the eligibility of your particular business, contact the local SBA office.

SBA SPECIAL ASSISTANCE FOR VETERANS

If you are a veteran, no matter what your age or when you served, or you are the dependent of a veteran, the SBA gives you special attention. At every district and branch office of the SBA, a special Veterans Affairs Officer has been designated to facilitate the delivery of SBA services to veterans.

The SBA provide veterans the following assistance:

Prompt processing of all loan applications.

Extension of maximum loan maturity to veterans.

Liberal interpretation of the present deferment policy on direct loans.

No-decline policy solely because of inadequate collateral.

Hints for Selling to the United States Government*

1. Determine which of the many government agencies may buy the products or services that you can furnish by:

   (a) Obtaining the *U.S. Government Purchasing and Sales Director* (available from the Superintendent of Documents, U.S. Government Printing Office, Washington, D.C. 20402.

*These hints were provided to the authors by the SBA.

(b) Subscribing to the *Commerce Business Daily* which lists proposed procurement, sales, and contract awards (May be ordered from the Superintendent of Documents, U.S. Government Printing Office, Washington, D.C. 20402).

(c) Contacting military installations and the larger federal civilian agencies in your area to determine if they purchase products or services that you can furnish.

2. Secure placement on all appropriate bidders' lists so as to receive invitations for bid, or requests for proposals from the agencies when they require additional supplies or service. Do this by:

(a) Requesting the appropriate form for obtaining placement on bidders' lists from each purchasing office which buys items or services which you can provide.

(b) Completing in detail the form which is sent to you (probably Standard Form 129 or DD Form 558-1).

(c) If the purchasing office does not send a list of items to be checked, or if the exact items or services that can be furnished are not specified on the list, attach a separate sheet containing:

(1) The specific name of each item or service which you are now producing.

(2) Defense items or services which you have produced (since World II).

(3) Additional items or services which your firm is capable of producing and which you wish to furnish.

(Describe fully each item or service on this attached sheet and, if possible, refer to the number of the federal or other specification which it meets or can be made to met.)

(d) Transmitting the completed form to the purchasing office accompanied by a letter which mentions your attached list and asks that you be informed about which bidder's lists your firm has been placed on.

(e) Requesting confirmation again of the exact bidder's lists on which your firm has been placed if no reply is received in a reasonable period of time. (*Your firm may not be on any bidder's list unless you are so informed in writing, and ordinarily will be placed only on bidder's lists for the items or services which you have specified*).

3. Bid competitively each time you learn of a suitable purchase.

(a) Figure your costs *closely*. Government business is very competitive.

(b) Respond to each invitation for bid or request for proposal sent you by the purchasing office by:

(1) Submitting a bid or proposal, or

(2) Writing that you are unable to bid on the transaction but wish to remain on the active bidder's mailing list for the particular item or service. Otherwise your firm may be dropped from the bidder's list.

4. Direct your efforts toward selling only those items or services for which you can compete or are qualified to produce.

5. Screen the *Commerce Business Daily* which lists contract awards and subcontracting opportunities or comparable commercial publications for new bidding opportunities.

Chapter Eleven
SBA Procurement Assistance

Procurement Assistance, the 8 (a) program, assists small business concerns owned by socially and economically disadvantaged persons. The aim of this program is to help these firms achieve a competitive position in the marketplace.

Section 8 (a) of the Small Business Act authorizes the SBA to enter into contracts with the United States government and any federal department, agency, or office having procurement powers.

The SBA works closely with purchasing agencies of the federal government and with the nation's leading contractors in developing policies and procedures that will lead to a greater number of contracts for small business concerns.

This authority, together with other financial, technical, and management resources at its disposal, allows the SBA to contract with other federal departments and agencies to supply their goods, services, and construction needs. In turn, the SBA then subcontracts the actual performance of the work to 8 (a) companies. The firms that are awarded 8 (a) contracts can receive free management and technical help in the planning and operating stages of the business.

The major areas in which the SBA helps small firms within the procurement and technical assistance program include:

Prime contracts
Subcontracts
Certificates of competency
Property Sales Program
Technology assistance

Each government agency has its own goals in awarding small business, minority, and 8(a) contracts. Private sector companies with government contracts also have stipulations concerning these businesses. Roughly 20% of all government contracts are earmarked for small and minority business by law. This means that the procurement would be restricted to small business firms only, and a large business would not be permitted to submit bids or proposals on the procurement. Socially and economically disadvantaged firms account for about .7% and .8% of all government purchases. The Carter Administration set goals in 1979 to raise this amount to 2% to 2.5%. The SBA actively requests government contracts and these contracts are also referred by participating agencies.

ELIGIBILITY

Eligibility is limited to small business concerns that must be owned and controlled by a person or persons who can demonstrate lack of opportunity to develop a competitive position in the economy because of social *and* economic disadvantages. Socially disadvantaged groups include, but are not limited to, Black Americans, Native Americans, Spanish Americans, Oriental Americans, Eskimos, and Aleuts. A recently discharged veteran of the Armed Forces may be considered socially disadvantaged. But being a member of one of these groups is not the only requirement to enter into the 8 (a) program. Nor is a small business owner required to belong to any of these groups to be socially disadvantaged. Language barriers for recent immigrants could be a contributing factor. Handicapped persons are also considered to be socially disadvantaged. However, economic disadvantage must also be demonstrated. Contact the SBA for details.

Disadvantaged persons must presently own and control the firm. The concern may be a proprietorship, or may be 51% owned by disadvantaged person(s).

APPLICATION FOR PROCUREMENT ASSISTANCE

If you wish to apply for procurement assistance, you contact the nearest total SBA office for an interview to determine:

1. If your firm is eligible.
2. If the federal government or others purchase the product or service your firm provides.
3. If there is sufficient financial support among the purchasers to provide contracts during participation in the 8 (a) program.
4. If your concern can be helped through this program.

After establishing social and economic disadvantage, you must submit an extensive business plan. These forms are available from the local SBA office (see Appendix I. "SBA Business Plan and Qualifications Resume").

Information from the business plan is then sent to Washington. There the products/services offered are compared with the federal national buying agencies to identify any likely financial support during the next fiscal year. Your firm itself may identify support as the SBA makes this information available. A commitment is then needed from those agencies who have a use for your firm's products/services.

If the business plan and program participation is approved, and the procurement item(s) are required by the federal agencies, your firm will be given instruction for preparing a proposal. With this proposal, the SBA may negotiate on your firm's behalf with other federal agencies.

When negotiating 8(a) contracts, the SBA has several options to help your company complete the work successfully. These options are used only when necessary and are determined on a case by case basis. They include:

Advance payments
Progress payments
Business development expense/Price support

Advance Payments

If your firm needs initial working capital to enter into the contract, the SBA will lend, interest free, the amount required. A repayment schedule is made, taking in account the terms of the contract.

Progress Payments

The SBA may set up with the buying agency the terms of interim payments as work progresses on the contract.

Business Development Expense

This is a price support given by the SBA. If the price of the buying agency is lower than the price your 8(a) concern will accept, the SBA examines the financial data behind each party's figures. If each side is justified in its demands, the SBA will pay the price difference to the 8 (a) firm.

These three program features are the major reason firms would like to participate in the 8 (a) program. These advantages are not available when making competitive bids on ordinary small business set-asides. (Set asides are contracts that are restricted to small businesses—that is "set-aside" from the others.)

The SBA does not intend to make the 8 (a) firms depend on these features. Their intention is for these programs to help firms become economically viable, and then remove firms from the program entirely.

SUBCONTRACTING

After negotiation of a prime contract, the SBA will make the formal subcontract to your firm. Once your business becomes the subcontractor, you are allowed to subcontract a portion of the work. However, you must perform no less than 30% of the work yourself. This rule is flexible, and a greater or lesser percentage might be determined on a case by case basis.

The SBA will try to locate additional contracts necessary to fulfill your firm's business plan. The business must actively market its regular products/services at the same time.

Participation in the 8 (a) program ceases when the goals of the business plans are met. Participation may also cease if the SBA determines that the goals will not be met because of inadequate subcontracting opportunities.

The SBA will not act as prime contractor for 8(a) companies if (a) government requests for one item are excessive in relation to total federal buying of that item, (b) the contract has already been designated for small business bidding, (c) a small concern may suffer a major hardship if contracting goes to the 8 (a) program, and (d) there is reasonable assurance that a disadvantaged small business can win the contract through competitive bidding.

The SBA cannot guarantee any 8 (a) concern subcontracts in any amount since it is totally dependent upon other federal procuring agencies. The SBA only pledges its "best efforts" to support the firms approved for 8 (a) participation.

SUBCONTRACTING PROGRAM

The Small Business Act also provides that the SBA develop a subcontracting program to (1) enable small business concerns to be considered fairly as subcontractors and suppliers to businesses performing as prime contractors under government contracts, (2) insure that these prime and subcontractors will consult through the SBA procurement agency, and (3) enable the SBA to obtain from any government agency information concerning subcontracting by its prime contractors and their subcontractors.

Federal procurement regulations divide purchase into two categories: those ranging from $10,000 to $500,000, and those over $500,000. Contracts which fall into the first category include a "best efforts" clause. The prime contractor must award the maximum amount of subcontracting to small business that he "finds to be consistent with the efficient performance" of the contract. In procurements over $500,000, the contractor is required to maintain a complete small business subcontracting program with specific responsibilities.

CERTIFICATES OF COMPETENCY PROGRAM (COC)

If a contracting officer proposes to reject the low bid of a small business firm because of questions regarding the firm's ability to perform the contract—either because of capacity or credit—the case is referred to the SBA. Their personnel then contact the company concerned to inform them of the impending decision. They also offer an opportunity to apply for a COC. If this certificate is granted, it would require the award of the contract in accordance to the Small Business Act.

The COC program is carried out by a specialized SBA field staff of individuals with technical engineering backgrounds in cooperation with financial specialists. On receiving the COC application, a team of financial and technical personnel is sent to the firm to survey its potential. Credit ratings, past performance, management capabilities, management schedules, and the prospects for obtaining financial help or equipment are considered.

If the financial position of the firm is weak, if important equipment is absent, or if the management effort is inadequate, the regular assistance programs of the SBA (loans, management counseling, assistance in locating equipment, etc.) may be applied to strengthen capability. If it appears that the firm has the credit and productive capacity required to fulfill the contract—with or without SBA assistance—the team's finding will be presented to a review committee.

If the committee's decision is negative and the COC is denied, both the firm and the procuring agency are notified. If the decision is affirmative and the contract is less than $250,000, a COC is then issued. For procurements in excess of that amount, an affirmative recommendation is forwarded to Washington, D.C., to a higher review committee. If the committee's decision is negative, the firm and the procuring agency are informed. If approved, a COC is sent to the procuring agency. By the terms of the Small Business Act, the COC is conclusive on questions of capacity and credit and the contract must be awarded.

A COC is valid only for the specific contract for which it is issued. A business concern that is capable of handling one contract may not be qualified for another. Each case is considered separately. Each case is considered only if and after the government contracting officer has made a negative decision because of the small business's capacity and/or credit. Firms may not apply before bid acceptance is determined. Firms cannot apply if they have been disqualified for reasons other than capacity or credit.

Most important is that a final decision is reached by the SBA within *15* working days of the original referral.

PROPERTY SALES PROGRAM

You may be able to pick up needed personal and real property at bargain basement prices by buying from the federal government. This property is surplus to federal needs, and is authorized for sale in accordance with public law. SBA cooperates with other federal agencies to channel a fair share of the property and resources to small business. However, the SBA does not itself sell real or personal property, except property held as collateral for loans that have been foreclosed because of default.

The SBA's property sales assistance to small business consists of (1) providing counsel to small business on matters pertaining to government property sales, and (2) helping small business obtain a fair share of government property sales.

Five categories of federal property are covered by the program:

Timber and related forest products
Strategic materials from the National Stockpile
"Royalty Oil"
Leases involving rights to minerals, oil and vegetation
Surplus real and personal property

Timber and Related Forest Products

Timber is regularly sold from the federal forests managed by the Forest Service, U.S. Department of Agriculture, and the Bureau of Land Management. The SBA and the sale agencies jointly set aside timber sales for bidding by small concerns when it appears that under open sales, small business would not obtain its fair share.

Local district offices of the Forest Service also offer smaller timber sales. These sales are normally purchased by small business and are not usually reviewed for set asides.

Strategic Materials from the National Stockpile

The Office of Preparedness, General Services Administration, regulates the procurement and disposal of strategic materials in accordance with law. Whenever a stockpile requirement is lowered, any surplus may be sold.

In instances where small business may find it difficult to purchase its fair share because of the large size of the lots, the agencies may agree to divide materials into smaller parcels and/or set aside a reasonable amount for exclusive bidding by small business.

Royalty Oil

Royalties due the government under leases of federal oil rights for the exploration of oil may be accepted by the Secretary of the Interior in the form of oil or money. If the Secretary decides to accept oil instead of money, the oil is called "royalty oil."

When the Secretary of the Interior feels that sufficient supplies of crude oil are not available in the open market to small business refineries, he can give preference to these refineries. The royalty oil is for their processing or use in the refineries and is not for resale.

The SBA refers qualified small business refineries to the Geological Survey, U.S. Department of the Interior, and assists small concerns in obtaining royalty oil.

Leases Involving Rights to Minerals, Oil, and Vegetation

The federal government is an extensive owner of mineral rights and oil rights. Leases to recover these minerals and oil are normally competitively sold by the government.

The SBA and the sales agency may jointly set aside a reasonable amount of leases for bidding by small concerns when it appears that under open bidding small business would not obtain its fair share.

Surplus Real and Personal Property

The federal government disposes of property for which it sees no immediate future need.

The two agencies of the government principally concerned with surplus personal property sales are the Department of Defense and the General Services Administration. Scheduled sales are widely publicized and are normally competitive bid sales. The SBA helps small business to locate and obtain this property.

TECHNOLOGY ASSISTANCE PROGRAM

The SBA Technology Assistance Program consists of three subprograms:

Technology assistance
Research and development assitance
Experimental projects

Each is aimed at improving the ability of small high-technology firms to compete more effectively for federal government contracts.

Technology Assistance

This program assists small business concerns to obtain the benefits of research and development performed by other federal agencies under government contracts or at government expense. The SBA provides services designed to acquaint small businesses with available technology and to aid in the selection of that portion which is relevant. This service has led to many industrial applications for small firms. Industrial firms have reduced their research and development schedules by 2 to 4 months with considerable savings by eliminating duplication of available technology. Other firms, through efficient design and adoption of available technology in production, have increased sales and profits.

The SBA and other professional personnel help the concern define its technical problems and needs. Then the SBA locates from the numerous sources available technology in the form of data, or a technical expert that will consider the problem. The SBA will also provide relevant technical data, sometimes sharing in the cost. Contact the SBA regional office for more information.

Research and Development Assistance

This program provides small research and development and technology-oriented firms with a means of obtaining information on contract opportunities. The principal means of obtaining contract opportunities for such small firms is the SBA *Science, Engineering, Research and Development Directory* published each year. The Directory is widely circulated among all Federal Government agencies procuring research and development. It is also circulated among major Government prime contractors for subcontract opportunities. The SBA also uses the Directory among its regions and as a source reference for its prime contracts and subcontracts programs. Firms wishing to be listed should contact the SBA regional office.

Experimental Projects

This program is aimed at improving the ability of small high-technology firms to compete more effectively for federal government contracts. From time to time, the SBA develops and carries out experimental programs aimed at improving the source location process, the associated procurement methods, and the method of transferring technology and similar topics. The experiments are generally carried out in cooperation with other federal agencies and are small in terms of the effort and funds involved. These efforts are under the direction of Technology Assistance Division in Washington, D.C.

Chapter Twelve
Other Government Loans

Government loans are numerous. For businesses that qualify, they are generally the best deal going. The problem is that they change from time to time. Each new administration stresses different industries. President Jimmy Carter created several loan programs for energy businesses. The Ronald Reagan administration all but dismantled the programs created by Carter. And so it goes. The two strongest loan programs, practically unaffected by presidential administrations over the years, are the programs of the SBA and those of the Farmers Home Administration and the Export-Import Bank, which are discussed in this chapter. It is a good idea to check with the particular government agency you wish to apply to *before* you try to submit your proposal. U.S. congressional representatives are usually a lot of help in these matters.

PROCESSING TIME

Government loans take a long time to process. It is always a matter of months and sometimes it can be years. Delays, rewrites of proposals, and submission of additional information are common. Expect the loans to take a minimum of two months, and don't be surprised if the time for approval drags out for more than a year.

GOVERNMENT AGENCIES AND TYPES OF LOANS

The following is a list of all the government agencies and the types of loans they make to businesses.

Type of Loan	Purpose	Who May Apply	Where to Apply
Small Business Administration			
Business loans	To assist small firms to finance construction, conversion, or expansion; to purchase equipment, facilities,	Small businesses	Nearest SBA field office

Type of Loan	Purpose	Who May Apply	Where to Apply
	machinery, supplies, or materials; and to acquire working capital. Loans are direct or in participation with banks		
Economic opportunity loans	To assist small firms operated by those who have marginal or submarginal incomes or those who have been denied equal opportunity (Title IV of the Economic Opportunity Act)	Low-income disadvantaged persons desiring to strengthen or establish a small business	Nearest SBA field office
Disaster loans	To assist disaster victims to rebuild homes or restore business establishments damaged in SBA-declared disaster areas to their predisaster condition	Individuals, business concerns, and nonprofit organizations	Nearest SBA field office
Economic injury loans	To assist concerns suffering economic injury resulting from: (1) a major or natural disaster declared by the president or secretary of agriculture; (2) federal or state or local urban renewal or highway construction programs; (3) inability to market or process a product because of disease or toxicity resulting	Small business firms suffering such economic injury	Nearest SBA field office

Type of Loan	Purpose	Who May Apply	Where to Apply
	from natural or undetermined causes		
Development company loans	To assist small firms by helping to establish and finance the operation of state and local small business development companies that make loans to small firms for equity capital, plant construction, conversion, or expansion.	State and local development companies	Nearest SBA field office
Energy loans	To assist small firms to purchase other small business firms or manufacture, distribute, or service any of these energy measures: solar energy equipment, photovoltaic cells, energy-conserving devices, wood or waste energy-production devices, hydroelectric energy equipment, wind energy conservation equipment, and services necessary to aid citizens in using the above	Businesses engaged in or preparing to engage in production of vehicles that use fuel other than gasoline	Department of Energy, Washington, D.C.
Economic Development Administration (EDA)			
Business or public loans	To aid unemployment and underemployment	States or components, nonprofit organizations,	Administrator, EDA, Washington, D.C. 20230

Type of Loan	Purpose	Who May Apply	Where to Apply
	areas in their economic development	and private borrowers	
Trade Adjustment Assistance Center (TAAC)	To provide financial and technical assistance to import-damaged businesses	Businesses damaged by imported products	Administrator, EDA, Washington, D.C. 20230
Export-Import Bank of the United States (Eximbank) and Overseas Private Investment Corporation			
Export-Import Bank of the United States (Ex-Im Bank): To assist in financing U.S. foreign trade through the following programs (in all cases, advance commitments are available without charge)	Authorizing the Foreign Credit Insurance Association (FCIA) to issue policies covering commercial and/or political risks on short- and medium-term credit extended by U.S. exporters to their overseas customers	Exporters or banks	Exporters' insurance agent or broker, or directly to FCIA, 1 World Trade Center, 9th Floor, New York, N.Y. 10048
	Guaranteeing payment of medium-term export paper purchased without recourse by commercial banks	Commercial banks, Edge Act Corporations, and Agreement Corporations	Commercial banks apply to Eximbank (exporter applies to his bank)
	Direct loans to overseas buyer of U.S. goods and services, enabling them to pay cash to the U.S. exporters	Overseas buyers or interested exporters	Eximbank, Washington, D.C. 20571
	"Discount" loans against eligible export debt obligations held by commercial banks, providing liquidity and, where necessary, more competitive interest rates to banks financing U.S. exports	Commercial banks, Edge Act Corporations, and Agreement Corporations	Eximbank, Washington, D.C. 20571

Type of Loan	Purpose	Who May Apply	Where to Apply
Overseas Private Investment Corporation (OPIC)			
Private enterprise development	OPIC offers a variety of services to private U.S. companies interested in establishing new businesses or expanding present facilities in less developed countries. These services include investment information and counseling; preinvestment and project development financing; project insurance against the risks of currency inconvertibility, expropriation, and war, revolution or insurrection; and project financing through loan guarantees and direct dollar and local currency loans	U.S. citizens or corporations, partnerships, or associations substantially and beneficially U.S.-owned	OPIC, Washington, D.C. 20527
Commodity Credit Corporation (Department of Agriculture)			
Agricultural	To provide nonrecourse loans on commodities stored on the farm or in commercial warehouses in order to provide price support and enable farmers to carry out an orderly marketing program	Producers, producer associations	The local county office of the Agricultural Stabilization and Conservation Service
	To expand or build farm storage facilities or to buy	Farmers	The local county office of the ASCS

Type of Loan	Purpose	Who May Apply	Where to Apply
	drying equipment for use with stored commodities		
Farmers Home Administration (Department of Agriculture)			
Business and industry loans	Guaranteed loans with no maximum amount to start business or expand business in rural areas of less than 50,000 population.	Business firms and nonprofit corporations	Local FMHA office
Operating	To family farmers for land improvement, equipment, labor, and development resources necessary to successful farming including the development of recreational and other nonfarm enterprises to be operated on the farms.	Operators of farms not larger than family farms	Local Farmers Home Administration office
Farm ownership	To buy, improve, or enlarge farms and to provide essential services including buildings and land for nonfarm enterprises needed to supplement farm incomes.	Farmers and ranchers who are or will become operators of not larger than family farms	Local FMHA office
Irrigation	Loans to develop irrigation systems, drain farmland, and carry out soil conservation measures	Groups of farmers and ranchers	Local FMHA office
Grazing and forest lands	Loans for shifts in land use to develop grazing areas and forest lands	Groups of farmers and ranchers	Local FMHA office

Type of Loan	Purpose	Who May Apply	Where to Apply
Rural housing	To construct and repair needed homes and essential farm buildings, purchase previously occupied homes, or buy sites on which to build homes	Farmers and other rural residents in open country and rural communities of not more than 5,500	Local FMHA office
Rural rental housing	Loans to provide rental housing for the rural elderly and for younger rural residents of low and moderate income	Individuals, profit corporations, private nonprofit corporations	Local FMHA office
Housing for labor	Loans to finance housing facilities for domestic farm labor	Individual farmers, groups of farmers, and public or private nonprofit organizations	Local FMHA office
Conditional commitments	Assurance to builder or seller that homes to be constructed or rehabilitated will meet FMHA lending requirements if built as proposed and that the agency would be willing to make loans to qualified applicants who may want to buy homes	Individual, partnership, or corporations engaged in construction of homes	Local FMHA office
Disaster	Emergency loans in designated areas where natural disasters such as floods and droughts have brought about a temporary need for credit not	Farmers	Local FMHA office

Type of Loan	Purpose	Who May Apply	Where to Apply
	available from other sources		
Farm Credit Administration (An independent agency that supervises nationwide farmer-owned and controlled Farm Credit System)			
Banks for cooperatives	To provide complete loan service for farmer cooperatives	Farmers cooperatives	Bank for cooperatives serving area
Federal land banks	To provide long-term mortgage credit to purchase, enlarge, or to improve farms, to refinance debts, and other purposes	Farmers (full-time or part-time) and farming corporations	Federal land bank association serving area
Production	To provide shortand intermediate-term credit for farm production, farm home, or farm family purposes	Farmers (both full-time and part-time) and farming corporations	Production credit association serving area
Solar Energy Research Institute (SERI)	Fund businesses for research and development on solar energy	Businesses and corporations engaged in solar research and development	SERI Golden, Colo. 80401
U.S. Department of Agriculture (USDA)	Grant money for experimentation in agricultural energy projects	Businesses, corporations, and nonprofit organizations engaged in energy research	USDA, ARS energy research, Beltsville, Md. 20706
The Maritime Administration			
Shipbuilding	To insure construction loans and/or mortgages to aid in financing the construction, reconstruction, or reconditioning of vessels	Private ship owners	Maritime Administration, Washington, D.C. 20235
Natural Resource Loans, Department of Interior			
Bureau of Indian Affairs	To encourage industry and	Indians, Eskimos, and Aleuts	The Indian Agency Superintendent

Type of Loan	Purpose	Who May Apply	Where to Apply
	income producing enterprises and for the education of certain Indians needing funds for that purpose		or a local Indian relending organization
Geological survey	To encourage domestic minerals exploration by providing financial assistance on a participating basis	Individuals, partnerships, and corporate enterprises	Field offices and Washington, D.C., Office of Minerals Exploration, Geological Survey
Bureau of Commercial Fisheries	To assist in strengthening the domestic fishing industry, loans are made to finance and refinance the cost of purchasing, constructing, equipping, maintaining, repairing, or operating new or used commercial fishing vessels or gear	U.S. citizens, as defined in Section 2 of the Shipping Act, 1916, as amended, who have the qualifications necessary to operate and maintain the vessel or gear to be used	Division of Loans and Grants of a regional office of the Bureau of Commercial Fisheries, U.S. Dept. of Interior
Bureau of Reclamation	Loans and grants for the development of small reclamation projects, primarily for irrigation, in the 17 western states and Hawaii	Nonfederal entities having authority to contract with the U.S. under federal reclamation law; no individuals	Regional Offices of Bureau of Reclamation

WHAT ARE GOVERNMENT REQUIREMENTS?

Guidelines differ from agency to agency. The factor that remains consistent is that the programs help create employment. Agencies fund businesses that banks and other financial institutions are not able to fund because the loan is too big or too risky or does not fall into traditional bank policy guidelines.

ECONOMIC DEVELOPMENT AGENCY

Most people have never heard of the Economic Development Agency (EDA), but it may be a valuable lending source for businesses, especially those businesses damaged by imports. The EDA, part of the Department of Commerce, has different programs from time to time, most of them geared toward creating employment. Direct loans have a $5 million maximum limit, but a company could get as much as $5 million more, for a total of $10 million. For loan guarantees, the maximum is $10 million per loan and $20 million per company.

Eligibility

In the past EDA loans were made for one purpose: to upgrade an area economically by job creation. Recently the EDA developed a program to help businesses suffering losses as a result of competition from imported goods.

Firms that suffer loss of sales and other damage from products imported into the United States qualify for financial and technical assistance from the EDA through Trade Adjustment Assistance Centers (TAAC) located throughout ten western states. This assistance is offered by the EDA, authorized by the Trade Act of 1974. Past assistance has been given to the following industries that have been hard hit by imports: apparel, textiles, footwear, handbags, consumer electronics, steel, industrial fasteners, fisheries, and others.

General eligibility requirements are as follows:

The applicant's industry cannot be experiencing a long-run overcapacity situation.

The project must be consistent with the EDA-approved Overall Economic Development Program (OEDP) for the area.

Each applicant has to be approved by an agency of the state or political subdivision directly concerned with economic development.

At least 15% of the total eligible project cost must be supplied as equity capital or as a subordinated loan.

At least one-third of the 15% is to be supplied by the state or a community or an area organization.

The EDA encourages the applicant to borrow as much as possible of the project cost, above the first 15%, from private lending institutions. These loans can be repaid before the federal loan and may be secured by a first lien.

The EDA makes a preliminary review to determine whether the project is feasible. The agency may obtain advice from other government agencies with expertise in the business involved.

TAAC Loan Program

To qualify for TAAC assistance, a firm first must be certified by the EDA as having been harmed by imports. Certification requires the following information:

Description of the business.

Identification of owners and any affiliates or subsidiaries.

Definition of the articles produced.

Data on company sales, production, and employment. (Some of these figures should have declined as a result of import damage.)

List of customers who shifted their purchases to foreign sources.

Supporting documents, including certified financial statements and tax returns.

Following certification, which can take up to three months, a firm can receive technical assistance from a TAAC specialist or contract consultant who will diagnose the company's problems and opportunities, begin preparation of an adjustment plan and loan application if required, and address problems recognized by the firm's management.

To qualify for any loan, a borrower must have been refused funds from at least two financial institutions.

There is no limit on the size of the company that can receive TAAC assistance. Most companies helped to date have had between 20 and 100 employees and an average $5 million in sales.

The whole process takes as little as three months or as much as 12 months before funding is given.

Loan Terms

There is a $10 million limitation on the amount the EDA can loan, but it may not lend more than 65% of the cost of land, buildings, and machinery and equipment. Maturity of the loan is as much as 25 years. Interest rates are determined by the cost of government borrowing. The EDA must have at least a second lien position on the fixed assets being purchased. The EDA also guarantees up to 90% of a loan made by a bank that meets EDA criteria.

TAAC financial assistance may be provided or guaranteed by the EDA if the company meets the EDA's financial criteria. Funding obtained from private or EDA or other government sources may be used for any purpose in the firm's approved recovery plan.

Funds may be used for working capital, expenditures for plant, machinery, and equipment; and diversification out of import-affected areas into more promising lines of business.

The maximum guaranteed loan is $3 million, with the Department of Commerce guaranteeing 90% of the face value. The maximum direct loan is $1 million. Processing a loan application generally takes from three to six months.

Interest rates charged on direct loans are set every quarter by the secretary of treasury to correspond to the market yield on U.S. securities of comparable maturity, plus a charge to cover administrative costs and probable losses under the program.

For loan guarantees, the interest rate is limited to the maximum rate the participating financial institution may establish for SBA loans.

The length of the loan depends on the purposes for which the loan is made and the ability of the firm to repay it. Loans have a maximum maturity of 25 years.

List of Department of Commerce Offices

The following is a list of the Department of Commerce offices in the United States:

ALABAMA

Birmingham
Gayle C. Shelton, Jr., Director
Suite 200-201, 908 South 20th Street
Birmingham, Ala. 35205
205-254-1331

ALASKA

Anchorage
Sara L. Haslett, Director
412 Hill Building
632 Sixth Avenue
Anchorage, Alaska 99501
907-265-5307

ARIZONA

Phoenix
Donald W. Fry, Director
Suite 2950 Valley Bank Center
201 North Central Avenue
Phoenix, Ariz. 85073
602-261-3285

ARKANSAS

•Little Rock (Dallas, Texas District)
1100 North University
Suite 109
Little Rock, Ark. 72207
501-378-5157

•Denotes trade specialist

CALIFORNIA

Los Angeles
Eric C. Silberstein, Director
Room 800, 11777 San Vicente Boulevard
Los Angels, Calif. 90049
213-824-7591

•San Diego
233 A Street, Suite 310
San Diego, Calif. 92101
714-293-5395

San Francisco
Philip M. Creighton, Director
Federal Building
Box 36013, 450 Golden Gate Avenue
San Francisco, Calif. 94102
415-556-5860

COLORADO

Denver
Norman Lawson, Director
Room 165, New Customhouse
19th & Stout Street
Denver, Colo. 80202
303-837-3246

CONNECTICUT

Hartford
Richard C. Kilbourn, Director
Room 610-B, Federal Office Building
450 Main Street
Hartford, Conn. 06103
203-244-3530

FLORIDA

Miami
Roger J. LaRoche, Director
Room 821, City National Bank Building
25 West Flagler Street
Miami, Fla. 33130
305-350-5267

•Clearwater
128 North Osceola Avenue
Clearwater, Fla. 33515
813-446-4081

•Jacksonville
815 South Main Street, Suite 100
Jacksonville, Fla. 32207
904-791-2796

•Tallahassee
Collins Building, Room G-20
Tallahassee, Fla. 32304
904-488-6469

GEORGIA

Atlanta
David S. Williamson, Director
Suite 600
1365 Peachtree Street, NE
Atlanta, Ga. 30309
404-881-7000

Savannah
James W. McIntire, Director
222 U.S. Courthouse & P.O. Box 9746
125-29 Bull Street
Savannah, Ga. 31402
912-232-4321

HAWAII

Honolulu
John S. Davies, Director
4106 Federal Building, P.O. Box 50026
300 Ala Moana Boulevard
Honolulu, Hawaii 96850
808-546-8694

ILLINOIS

Chicago
Gerald M. Marks, Director
1406 Mid Continental Plaza Building
55 East Monroe Street
Chicago, Ill. 60603
312-353-4450

INDIANA

Indianapolis
Mel R. Sherar, Director
357 U.S. Courthouse & Federal Office Building
46 East Ohio Street
Indianapolis, Ind. 46204
317-269-6214

IOWA

Des Moines
Jesse N. Durden, Director
817 Federal Building
210 Walnut Street
Des Moines, Iowa 50309
515-284-4222

KENTUCKY

•Frankfort (Memphis, Tennessee District)
Capitol Plaza Office Tower, Room 2425
Frankfort, Ky. 40601
502-875-4421

LOUISIANA

New Orleans
Edwin A. Leland Jr., Director
432 International Trade Mart
2 Canal Street
New Orleans, La. 70130
504-489-6546

•Denotes trade specialist

MAINE

•Portland (Boston, Massachusetts District)
Maine State Pier
40 Commercial Street
Portland, Maine 04111
207-773-5608

MARYLAND

Baltimore
Carroll F. Hopkins, Director
415 U.S. Customhouse
Gay and Lombard Streets
Baltimore, Md. 21202
301-962-3560

MASSACHUSETTS

Boston
Francis J. O'Connor, Director
10th Floor, 441 Stuart Street
Boston, Mass. 02116
617-223-2312

MICHIGAN

Detroit
William L. Welch, Director
445 Federal Building
231 West Lafayette
Detroit, Mich. 48226
313-226-3650

•Grand Rapids
350 Ottawa Street, NW
Grand Rapids, Mich. 49503
616-456-2411/33

MINNESOTA

Minneapolis
Glenn A. Matson, Director
218 Federal Building, 110 South Fourth Street
Minneapolis, Minn. 55401
612-725-2133

MISSISSIPPI

•Jackson (Birmingham, Alabama District)
P.O. Box 849
1202 Walter Sillers Building
Jackson, Miss. 39205
601-969-4388

MISSOURI

St. Louis
Donald R. Loso, Director
120 South Central Avenue
St. Louis, Mo. 63105
314-425-3302-4

•Kansas City
Room 1840, 601 East 12th Street
Kansas City, Mo. 64106
816-374-3142

•Denotes trade specialist

MONTANA

•Butte (Cheyenne, Wyoming District)
225 South Idaho Street, Room 101
P.O. Box 3809
Butte, Mont. 59701
406-723-6561, Ext. 2317

NEBRASKA

Omaha
George H. Payne, Director
Capitol Plaza
Suite 703A, 1815 Capitol Avenue
Omaha, Neb. 68102
402-221-3665

NEVADA

Reno
Joseph J. Jeremy, Director
777 West 2nd Street, Room 120
Reno, Nev. 89503
702-784-5203

NEW JERSEY

Newark
Clifford R. Lincoln, Director
4th Floor, Gateway Building
Market Street & Penn Plaza
Newark, N.J. 07102
201-645-6214

NEW MEXICO

Albuquerque
William E. Dwyer, Director
505 Marquette Avenue NW, Suite 1015
Albuquerque, N.M. 87102
505-766-2386

NEW YORK

Buffalo
Robert F. Magee, Director
1312 Federal Building
111 West Huron Street
Buffalo, N.Y. 14202
716-846-4191

New York
Arthur C. Rutzen, Director
Room 3718, Federal Office Building
26 Federal Plaza, Foley Square
New York, N.Y. 10007
212-264-0634

NORTH CAROLINA

Greensboro
Joel B. New, Director
203 Federal Building
West Market Street, P.O. Box 1950
Greensboro, N.C. 27402
919-378-5345

OHIO

Cincinnati
Gordon B. Thomas, Director
10504 Federal Office Building
550 Main Street
Cincinnati, Ohio 45202
513-684-2944

Cleveland
Charles B. Stebbins, Director
Room 600, 666 Euclid Avenue
Cleveland, Ohio 44114
216-522-4750

OKLAHOMA

•Oklahoma City (Dallas, Texas District)
4020 Lincoln Boulevard
Oklahoma City, Okla. 73105
405-231-5302

OREGON

Portland
Lloyd R. Porter, Director
Room 618, 1220 Southwest 3rd Avenue
Portland, Oreg. 97204
503-221-3001

PENNSYLVANIA

Philadelphia
Patrick P. McCabe, Director
9448 Federal Building
600 Arch Street
Philadelphia, Pa. 19106
215-597-2850

Pittsburgh
William M. Bradley, Trade Specialist-in-Charge
2002 Federal Building
1000 Liberty Avenue
Pittsburgh, Pa. 15222
412-644-2850

PUERTO RICO

San Juan (Hato Rey)
Enrique Vilella, Director
Room 659-Federal Building
San Juan, P.R. 00918
809-753-4555, Ext. 555

RHODE ISLAND

•Providence (Boston, Massachusetts District)
1 Weybossett Hill
Providence, R.I. 02903
401-277-2605, Ext. 22

•Denotes trade specialist

SOUTH CAROLINA

Columbia
Philip A. Ouzts, Director
2611 Forest Drive
Forest Center
Columbia, S.C. 29204
803-765-5345

•Charleston
Suite 631, Federal Building
334 Meeting Street
Charleston, S.C. 29403
803-577-4361

TENNESSEE

Memphis
Bradford H. Rice, Director
Room 710, 147 Jefferson Avenue
Memphis, Tenn. 38103
901-521-3213

•Nashville
4014 Aberdeen Road
Nashville, Tenn. 37216
615-297-5233

TEXAS

Dallas
C. Carmon Stiles, Director
Room 7A5, 1100 Commerce Street
Dallas, Tex. 75242
214-749-1515

Houston
Felicito C. Guerrero, Director
2625 Federal Building
Courthouse, 515 Rusk Street
Houston, Tex. 77002
713-226-4231

•San Antonio
University of Texas at San Antonio
Division of Continuing Education
San Antonio, Tex. 78285
512-229-5875

UTAH

Salt Lake City
George M. Blessing, Jr., Director
1203 Federal Building
125 South State Street
Salt Lake City, Utah 84138
801-524-5116

VIRGINIA

Richmond
8010 Federal Building
400 North 8th Street
Richmond, Va. 23240
804-782-2246

•Fairfax
8550 Arlington Boulevard
Fairfax, Va. 22031
703-560-6460

WASHINGTON

Seattle
Judson S. Wonderly, Director
Room 706, Lake Union Building
1700 Westlake Avenue North
Seattle, Wash. 98109
206-442-5615

WEST VIRGINIA

Charleston
Roger L. Fortner, Director
3000 New Federal Building
500 Quarrier Street
Charleston, W. Va. 25301
304-343-6181, Ext. 375

WISCONSIN

Milwaukee
Russell H. Leitch, Director
Federal Building/U.S. Courthouse, 517
East Wisconsin Avenue
Milwaukee, Wis. 53202
414-291-3473

WYOMING

Cheyenne
Lowell O. Burns, Director
6022 O'Mahoney Federal Center
2120 Capitol Avenue
Cheyenne, Wyo. 82001
307-778-2220, Ext. 2151

OFFICE OF MINORITY BUSINESS ENTERPRISE REGIONAL OFFICES

Charles McMillan
Regional Director
Office of Minority Business Enterprise
U.S. Department of Commerce
1371 Peachtree Street, NE, Suite 505
Atlanta, Ga. 30309
404-881-5091

Henry Zuniga
Regional Director
Office of Minority Business Enterprise
U.S. Department of Commerce
1412 Main Street, Room 1702
Dallas, Tex. 75202
214-749-7581

Ramon V. Romero
Regional Director
Office of Minority Business Enterprise
U.S. Department of Commerce
Federal Building, Room 15045
450 Golden Gate Avenue
San Francisco, Calif. 94102
415-556-7234

Daniel V. Lemanski
Regional Director
Office of Minority Business Enterprise
U.S. Department of Commerce
55 East Monroe Street, Suite 1438
Chicago, Ill. 60603
312-353-8375

Newton S. Downing
Regional Director
Office of Minority Business Enterprise
U.S. Department of Commerce
Federal Office Building
26 Federal Plaza, Room 1307
New York, N.Y. 10007
212-264-3262

Luis Encinias
Acting Regional Director
Office of Minority Business Enterprise
U.S. Department of Commerce
1730 K Street, NW Suite 420
Washington, D.C. 20006
202-634-7897

OVERSEAS PRIVATE INVESTMENT CORPORATION

If your company is involved in international trade, especially if you want to franchise your product or service overseas, it might be helpful to look up the Overseas Private Investment Corporation:

OVERSEAS PRIVATE INVESTMENT CORPORATION

The U.S. Government, through the Overseas Private Investment Corporation (OPIC), is prepared to offer qualified U.S. businesses appropriate guidance, counseling, and financial support in determining how and where to invest in undeveloped countries. Insurance protection and financial services are also available during project development and operation. OPIC is the agency through which the Federal Government encourages and assists U.S. private overseas investments, including, in some circumstances, distributorships owned by U.S. manufacturers which are consistent with both the United States and the developing nations' economic interests. The agency places special emphasis on projects sponsored by small and medium sized American business investors.

OPIC is an independent, financially self-sustaining agency of the U.S. Government, and its contracts are backed by the full faith and credit of the United States. Its two principal operating units are the Insurance and Finance Departments, organized primarily along regional geographic lines. Within each department an officer is assigned specifically to assist small and minority U.S. companies. OPIC's only office is in Washington, D.C.; however, its staff works closely with U.S. Embassy economic and commercial officers abroad.

All applications for OPIC insurance or financing are carefully reviewed to assure their consistency with host country aims and U.S. foreign economic policy. Approved projects must offer potential benefit to the host country in such areas as job creation, skills training, import savings, export earnings, and tax revenues. They also are reviewed to assure that the United States gains net benefits in expanded trade, employment, access to needed materials, and investor earnings.

For OPIC purposes, an eligible U.S. investor, project sponsor or lender is a U.S. citizen, a U.S. entity at least 50 percent beneficially owned by U.S. citizens, corporations or partnerships, or a foreign firm at least 95 percent owned by U.S. citizens or firms.

Opportunity Identification and Evaluation

Two of the most difficult problems facing the potential investor abroad are: (1) evaluation of the investment climate and (2) identification of potential investment opportunities.

In an effort to broaden its facilities for identifying and publicizing appropriate investment opportunities, OPIC has introduced a new approach to country studies and project identification.

Target Missions

Target missions are conducted with on-the-spot studies by OPIC officials in selected countries. These are followed by investor identification and project brokering in the United States designed to match potential projects with qualified investors. OPIC then organizes group visits by U.S. business executives to selected countries. There they meet host country officials, local business persons and U.S. embassy personnel, and review areas of investment opportunity. These missions have been received enthusiastically by medium and smaller-size companies.

Feasibility Studies

On a selective basis, OPIC can also enter into cost-sharing arrangements with a U.S. firm to investigate and study the feasibility of an opportunity which that firm has identified through its own resources. To encourage investment in poor countries, feasibility study funds are available to companies of specific size* in host countries having a specified per capita income*. However, smaller U.S. firms are eligible for feasibility survey assistance in all countries in which OPIC operates. To receive such assistance, the U.S. firm must have a sound operating record, and demonstrate that it has the managerial, technical and financial competence to implement the project if it proves feasible.

The maximum OPIC participation is $50,000 or up to 75 percent of the total eligible costs of the study as formally budgeted and agreed upon by the firm and OPIC, whichever is less. If a project results from the study, the costs of the study are expected to be capitalized as part of the overall project costs. If a decision not to invest is reached, OPIC will reimburse the sponsor for that portion agreed upon.

Project Financing

As a source of medium and long-term funds for project financing in countries where conventional financial institutions are often reluctant or unable to lend on such a basis. OPIC can provide a portion of a project's debt requirements. OPIC's financing commitment in a new venture is usually 35 to 45 percent of total project costs. It cannot exceed 50 percent.

OPIC participates in project financing through:

Loans from its Direct Investment Fund, generally ranging from $200,000 to $3 million, repayable over a term from 5 to 12 years following a suitable grace period, with interest rates depending on OPIC's assessment of the financial and political risks involved.

Guarantees of loans made by private U.S. financial institutions from $2 to $25 million;

A combination of these financing instruments.

In all cases, the project must be commercially and financially sound. It must be within the demonstrated competence of the proposed management and the U.S. investor, who must have a proven record of success in the particular business as well as a significant financial risk in the enterprise. The project must be approved by the host country.

OPIC encourages joint ventures between local citizens and U.S. firms. However, in projects involving OPIC financing, U.S. investors must own at least 25 percent of the voting shares or equivalent risk-taking interest and the U.S. sponsor is expected to have a continuing management role. (There is no minimum U.S. equity participation required in connection with OPIC insurance protection.)

Special Assistance for Small Business

The 1978 amendments to OPIC's charter call for preferential measures to encourage investment by U.S. small and medium-sized companies interested in the growing market potential of the developing nations.

Consistent with this mandate, OPIC provides several specific services to smaller U.S. companies, defined as those not ranked in the "Fortune 1000", that are not available to larger companies. These include a reduced insurance registration fee, OPIC payment for the services of licensed insurance brokers to smaller companies in obtaining OPIC insurance, grants for certain project reconnaissance travel, expanded funding of up to 75% of agreed costs of feasibility studies, assumption by OPIC of certain legal or consultant's fees incurred in establishing or operating a project, assistance in setting up financial controls, and support of private U.S. voluntary organizations and cooperatives in developing small-scale private enterprises. (Call 1-800-424-OPIC.)

Application Process

In all cases, to be eligible for OPIC services, investors should contact OPIC early in the planning stages so they can become familiar with initial project design. In order for an investment to be eligible for insurance, the investor must obtain a Registration Notice from OPIC before the investment is made or irrevocably committed to the project.

For further information, call 1-800-424-OPIC.

DEPARTMENT OF AGRICULTURE LOANS

The Department of Agriculture does not make loans just to farmers. It makes loans to nonfarm enterprises in rural communities, providing funding for, among other things, swimming facilities, tennis courts, riding stables, vacation rental cottages, lakes and ponds for fishing and boating, docks, camping or picnic grounds, repair shops, roadside markets, service stations, grocery stores, and water and waste disposal systems. Its stated aim is to make loans to "promote development of business and industry . . . in towns or cities of below 50,000 population."

The Farm Credit Administration

The Farm Credit Administration is a division of the Department of Agriculture and supervises 12 land banks that make long-term mortgage loans to be used for agricultural purposes. A loan may not exceed 65% of the value of the agricultural facilities.

The Farmers Home Administration

The Farmers Home Administration (FmHA) loans to businesses, farmers, and rural residents and communities. Some loan programs are strictly for individuals and their families. Some involve associations of people. Still other loans are made to partnerships, corporations, or public bodies.

Most of the loan programs fall into two categories:

1. Guaranteed loans made and serviced by a private lender.
2. Insured loans originated, made, and serviced by the agency personnel. Notes are sold to investors, and interest is based on the current cost of federal borrowing.

Programs and Eligibility Requirements

Business and Industrial Loan. This is the most important program for most businesspeople. The FmHA during 1978 channeled $1 billion in capital to about 1,500 businesses ranging from motel entrepreneurs to textile-manufacturing companies. The FmHA made a $33 million loan to American Cotton Growers of Littlefield, Texas, to build a cotton mill; $16.7 million to Robin International of Greenville, Mississippi, to build a rice mill; and $7.5 million to Copper Mountain, Inc., of Copper Mountain, Colorado, to expand a ski resort.

This program has no minimum or maximum set on a loan. Recently the dollar amount of the loans averaged $900,000.

The major restriction on the loan is that it cannot go to a business in a city with a population in excess of 50,000 people. The loans are not made to finance purchases of ongoing businesses or to refinance debt.

The FmHA guarantees 90% of the money required to start the business. The business contributes 10% of the necessary capital, the bank 90%. The bank's portion of the loan is guaranteed 100%.

Final maturity of the loan may be up to 30 years for land and buildings, 15 years for fixtures, machinery and equipment, and seven years for working capital.

The application is submitted to a commercial bank, which contacts the FmHA. The business and industry specialist at the state level has the authority to grant loans of up to $1 million. Amounts over $1 million must be approved by headquarters in Washington, D.C.

Nonfarm Enterprise Loans. The FmHA makes loans to family farmers for developing and operating nonfarm enterprises, including repair shops, service stations, restaurants, grocery stores, welding shops, roadside stands, kennels, cabinet shops, riding stables, sporting goods stores, beauty shops, custom services, camping sites, and barbershops.

To qualify the applicant must:

1. Be the owner and operator of a larger-than-family farm or a tenant on such a farm.
2. Personally manage the nonfarm operation.

Loans are made for up to $50,000 for one to seven years for equipment and operating capital. Loans of up to $100,000 at 5% interest for up to 40 years are available for real estate.

OTHER GOVERNMENT LOANS

Energy Loans and Grants

Since the Department of Energy's budget was cut back severely, most of its loan programs have been disbanded. There are, however, two important agencies that provide money for energy-related projects: the Solar Energy Research Institute (SERI) and the U.S. Department of Agriculture.

Solar Energy Research Institute. SERI originated with Solar Energy Research and Development Act of 1974 and is managed under contract by the Midwest Research Institute. It focuses on ongoing solar technology development efforts, and its current programs stress photovoltaic, biogas development.

To be added to its mailing list, for contract solicitations, and for *In Review: A SERI Monthly Update*, a publication describing SERI's activities, write

SERI
Documentation Distribution
1617 Cole Boulevard
Golden, Colo. 80401

U.S. Department of Agriculture. Most projects are solicited from state agricultural experimentation stations, the Agricultural Research Service, university labatories, or private industry. But the USDA also accepts unsolicited proposals for energy-related ideas for agricultural application. Programs have been funded for $25,000 to $50,000 over a five-year period since 1977.

For more information on any of the programs, contact your county office of the

Agricultural Stabilization and Conservation Service (listed under "U.S. Government" in the telephone book) or write to:

United States Department of Agriculture
ARS Energy Research Coordinator
ARS-USDA, Room 219 North
ARC West
Beltsville, Md. 20706

Maritime Administration

The Maritime Administration guarantees loans for shipbuilding or refinancing U.S. flag vessels constructed or reconstructed in U.S. shipyards. It guarantees 100% of the loan.

To apply, the businessperson must obtain Form MA-163, the application, from the local Maritime Administration office and return 12 copies of the application with a $100 filing fee.

The Department of the Interior

The Department of the Interior administers loans and loan guarantees for American Indian businesspersons (Bureau of Indian Affairs); businesses engaged in domestic mineral exploration (Geological Survey); and for fishermen and fishing industries for the purchase, construction, equipping, maintaining and repairing, and operation of fishing vessels (Bureau of Commercial Fisheries).

ASSISTANCE FROM THE EXPORT-IMPORT BANK

The Export-Import Bank of the United States is an independent government agency, the main aim of which is to facilitate exporting U.S. goods and services. This agency is politically sensitive, and in recent years funds for their programs have been drastically cut back. Much assistance, however, is still available from this agency. Following is a description published by the agency:

The Export-Import Bank of the United States (Eximbank) is a financially self-sustaining independent U.S. Government agency. Its primary purpose is to facilitate the export of U.S. goods and services. This is accomplished through a variety of financing programs, several being particularly well suited for use by small exporters.

The need for export financing to be competitive in foreign markets is an established fact of business life. Often the availability of credit can be as important as pricing in penetrating an overseas market, particularly in many of the lesser developed countries. The natural reluctance of U.S. banks and exporters to extend credit to unknown foreign buyers in developing markets can be largely overcome through the protection offered by Eximbank programs.

Eximbank-supported financing is a natural extension of domestic financing and marketing operations, and it is a complementary marketing tool to those offered by other U.S. Government agencies. For example, Small Business Administration (SBA) financing support . . . can be used to expand a company's production facilities to meet foreign demand. It can also be used to finance basic overseas market development costs and to purchase materials and labor required to perform an export sales contract. SBA financing programs can be used to assist the small exporter up to the point that Eximbank financing programs are needed to support qualified export sales.

Similarly, the eventual establishment of a strong sales network overseas often leads to investment in selected markets. Once a company has successfully set up a marketing operation in a country, it might decide to invest in assembly and warehousing operations there—in order to obtain lower shipping and tariff costs—and to expand sales through a local partner. In such situations, Eximbank will work in close partnership with Overseas Private Investment Corporation (OPIC) to put together an appropriate export and investment financing package.

Small Business Advisory Service

To encourage smaller export firms, Eximbank maintains a Small Business Advisory Service to provide information on the availability and use of export credit insurance, guarantees, discount loans, and foreign bank credits supporting the sale of U.S. goods and services abroad. Direct telephone inquiries are welcome. The Small Business Advisory Service can be reached at (202) 566-8990.

Briefing Programs

Eximbank offers a regular Briefing Program which is open to representatives from the small business and banking communities. Conducted on a weekly basis at the Bank headquarters in Washington, D.C., the program includes both group briefings and one-on-one discussions about direct application of Eximbank programs. In addition to the briefings conducted at the Bank, Eximbank officers regularly meet with groups and individual business people when traveling throughout the country. To obtain additional information on the briefing program and scheduled travel of Eximbank officers, write the Office of Public Affairs or telephone (202) 566-8990.

Financial Support Programs

Each of Eximbank's financing programs is available for use by any U.S. firm, regardless of size. Better known than most is the Direct Lending Program which is designed to provide long term financing for large industrial projects or multimillion dollar product sales. Small suppliers often benefit from subcontracts in these sales, but they seldom are involved as primary suppliers.

The Commercial Bank Exporter Guarantee Program

Similar to the medium-term insurance policy, the Guarantee facility covers direct sale of U.S. capital and quasi-capital goods to foreign buyers. In contrast to the insurance program, however, the Guarantee program is operated through a direct network of U.S. commercial banks. Over 280 national and regional banks participate in this program, guaranteeing transactions which currently have a median contract value of approximately $180,000.

To use this program, the small exporter would apply to its bank for financing of overseas sales. The bank in turn would apply to Eximbank for Guarantee coverage of the commercial and political risks involved in extending credit to designated overseas buyers.

The advantage of this program to the small exporter is that the commercial bank administers the coverage, thereby relieving the exporter of a large portion of the paperwork.

The Small Business Guarantee Program

Similar to the coverage offered under the small business insurance policy, Eximbank will cover 100% of the political risk and 95% of the commercial risk involved in the financed portions for medium-term sales. These guarantees, which came into effect July 1, 1978, are offered to eligible small business exporters at the same rates as regular guarantee coverage to established exporters. Eximbank made a series of administrative modifications to its guarantee program in mid-1978, which should make the program appeal to a broader range of banks by providing sufficient incentives for those banks to finance small business transactions.

The Cooperative Financing Facility

The Cooperative Financing Facility (CFF) helps make credit available to small and medium-size foreign buyers of U.S. goods and services, through banks in their own countries. The CFF is a line of credit extended from Eximbank to foreign banks for the purpose of financing 42.5 percent of local buyers' purchases of U.S. capital equipment, quasi-capital equipment and services. A 15 percent cash payment is required and the other 42.5 percent is provided from the local banks' own resources or other borrowings at market rates of interest.

An advantage of this program for small U.S. exporters is that they can inform foreign customers of the CFF lines being extended to their own local banks. At that point, the small exporter can leave the financing arrangements to the individual buyers and their banks. The local CFF bank would be expected to be familiar with the customer's credit standing and market conditions, enabling it to reach a decision quickly on a credit request. Over one half of CFF loan authorizations approved yearly are for less than $100,000.

As of mid-1978, Eximbank had 95 CFF lines of credit in 28 foreign markets, primarily those designated as "developing countries."

Discount Loan Program

Under the Discount Loan Program, Eximbank will agree to buy eligible fixed-rate medium-term export debt obligations from U.S. commercial banks. With this assurance, Eximbank has given tangible support to banks—particularly the smaller ones—which offer fixed-rate loans in the medium-term area.

Optional Coverages

In mid-1978, Eximbank initiated a "Switch Cover Option" for its Medium-Term Insurance, Bank Guarantee, Discount Loan, and CFF programs. This option was designed to assist U.S. exporters selling through distributors and dealers overseas. Under the option, eligible U.S. equipment which has been exported to a dealer under a floor-planning scheme, could be insured, guaranteed or financed under the name of the ultimate end user if he/she is found to be creditworthy. Extension of the switch cover option is made on a case-by-case basis depending upon the distributor, the products and usage.

The Small and Minority Bank Pilot Project

Eximbank began in mid-1978 a new pilot program to bring a selected number of qualified small and minority banks into its regular financing network. The program incorporates extensive training of the participating bank lending officers both in

Washington and with larger sponsoring commercial banks throughout the country. As part of the program, Eximbank officers provide direct counseling to the lending officers and their local business clients.

Application Process

The first step small exporters should take in exploring the availability of export financing is to contact their own bank. If it is one of the larger regional banks, it may have its own international department or at least a loan officer responsible for handling foreign transactions. If it is a smaller bank, or one not yet involved in international trade, it will have a correspondent relationship with one or more banks experienced in the international area. In either case, the bank should be able to assist its client in the initial steps necessary to set up an export financing program.

When an exporter's bank is not conversant with international financing, or unable to provide assistance through correspondent banks, the exporter should directly contact Eximbank's Small Business Advisory Service for advice in determining sources and availability of financing. Alternate sources of information on Eximbank/FCIA export financing programs can be obtained from the nearest FCIA regional office or the field offices of the U.S. Department of Commerce or the U.S. Small Business Administration.

Inquiries for further information on the Export-Import Bank of the United States should be directed to:

Office of Public Affairs
Export-Import Bank of the United States
811 Vermont Avenue, N.W.
Washington, D.C. 20571
(202) 566-8990

Or you may call *toll free* to our Small Business Advisory Service at (800) 242-5201.

SUMMARY

There are several government loan programs besides the Small Business Administration. Practically every government agency has some loan program, but the requirements for the programs and the programs themselves vary from time to time. We have given brief descriptions of programs that are currently in place. It is always a good idea to contact the agency before you start preparing the loan presentation.

Remember, if you qualify for government programs, getting the loan is primarily a matter of persistence and patience.

Appendix One

SBA Business Plan and Qualifications Résumé

BUSINESS PLAN AND QUALIFICATIONS RÉSUMÉ
(Each item should be completed, if none or not applicable so state.)

I. Firm Identification:

Name ____________________

Trade Name ____________________

Address ____________________
Street P.O. Box

____
City County State Zip

Business Phone ________ ________ Home Phone ________ ________
Area Code Number Area Code Number

Type of Business ____________________ SIC Code ____________

Employees Identification Number ____________ Tax Exemption No. ________

Number of Employees: ____________ as of ____________

Indicate if supply, service, construction or concession ____________

Month and Year Business Established ____________

Fiscal Year Ends ____________

Is concern organized for profit? Yes ☐ No ☐

Is concern associated in any way with a nonprofit organization?
Yes ☐ No ☐

If yes, specify name of non-profit organization and the nature of the association ________

____

Does concern and affiliates meet small business size standard as defined in Part 121 SBA Rules and Regulations? Yes ☐ No ☐
If answer is *no*, Divestiture Agreement must be submitted.

II. List other types and locations of business in which firm is or has recently been engaged.

Type of Business ____________________

Address of Facility ____________________

____

Presently Operating: Yes ☐ No ☐ If operating, how long? __________

III. Ownership:

A. Type of Ownership

Sole proprietorship ☐
Partnership ☐ (Attach copy of partnership agreement.)
Corporation ☐ (Attach copy of certificate from Secretary of State, Articles of Incorporation, and By-Laws.)

If corporation: Total no. of shares authorized: ____________________
Total no. of shares issued: ____________________

B. Is concern owned and controlled by one or more persons who have been deprived of the opportunity to develop and maintain a competitive position in the economy because of social or economic disadvantage?

Yes ☐ No ☐

C. Name and address of all stockholders and/or partners and their ethnic identification; i.e., Aleuts, Black American, Eskimo, Indian, Oriental, Spanish-American, White American, etc.

Name	Address	*Number and Class of Shares	Office Held	Ethnic Ident.

*Attach copy of Stock Certificate(s) issued

D. Attach copy of all Divestiture and/or Ownership Agreements.

E. Attach personal financial statement on above principles (SBA Form 413 may be used to submit this statement).

F. SBA Form 912, "Statement of Personal History," must be completed according to the instructions contained therein and submitted with this Business Plan and Qualifications Resume.

G. Show names of social and/or economic disadvantage persons listed in III C above. Give a narrative summary of cultural, social, chronic economic circumstances, and background on each to support disadvantaged status. (Continue on separate sheet as necessary.)

Name: ______________________________

Narrative summary:

Name: ______________________________

Narrative summary:

Name: ______________________________

Narrative summary:

Name: ______________________________

Narrative summary:

H. List all entities that owners, directors, officers, partners, and managers of applicant have a financial interest in or hold a management or board position. If none, so state.

Name of Entity	Name of Person	Position Held	% or Ownership

I. Have any of the above firms received or applied for 8(a) approval:
Yes ☐ No ☐ If yes, identify ______________________________

IV. *Company History:* (Narrative of purpose, chronological development, problems, and successes)

V. Product or service: (Narrative of characteristics, uses and applicability to commercial market. Nature of work performed with own forces, area of operations.)

VI. A. Management (A copy of this form must be completed by all directors, officers, and senior management personnel.)

1. Name ______________ 2. Age ______ 3. Sex ______

4. Marital Status ______________ 5. Social Security Number ______

6. Military Serial Number ______________________

7. Present position (Include description of duties)

8. Other jobs and positions held and salaries

9. Formal schooling

10. Technical training and qualifications

11. Management training

12. Military experience

(a)

Branch of Service	Place of Service	Period of Service	MOS	Rank
______	______	______	______	______
______	______	______	______	______

(b) Service schools attended and date of attendance

____

____

____

B. List professional, management, and technical resource support to be received by your company. (Attach copies of all Management and Technical Support Agreements.)

Name	Address	Phone	Service Performed	Compensation to be Paid
______	______	______	______	______
______	______	______	______	______
______	______	______	______	______
______	______	______	______	______

C. Diagram organization chart of firm.

VII. *Marketing*

A. Market area:

B. Market potential:

C. Commercial customers:

D. Government customers: (Include name and phone number of contracting officers and small business specialist contacted.)

E. Competitors:

F. Advantage over competitors:

G. Pricing and bidding procedures (attach sample of pricing and bidding documents):

H. Sales forecast by product or service category:

I. *Sales and distribution plan:* (Including advertising pricing, credit terms, etc.)

J. Business plan graph (reflect commercial and non 8(a) Government sales, 8(a) projected support, and break even point).

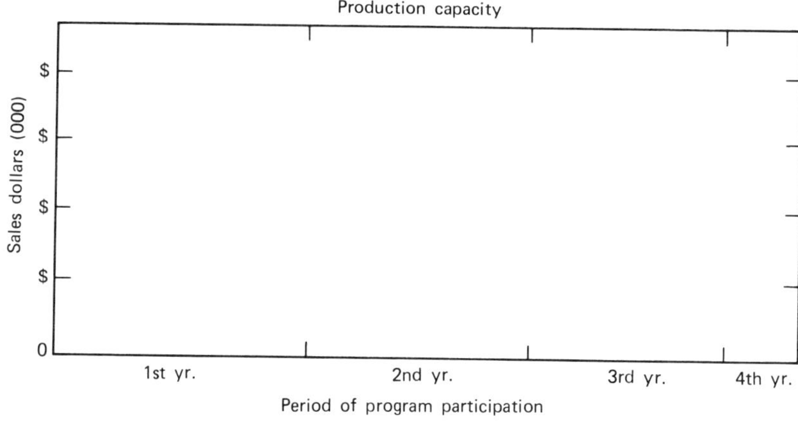

K. Break even chart (reflect income from sales, fixed cost, variable cost, and break even point).

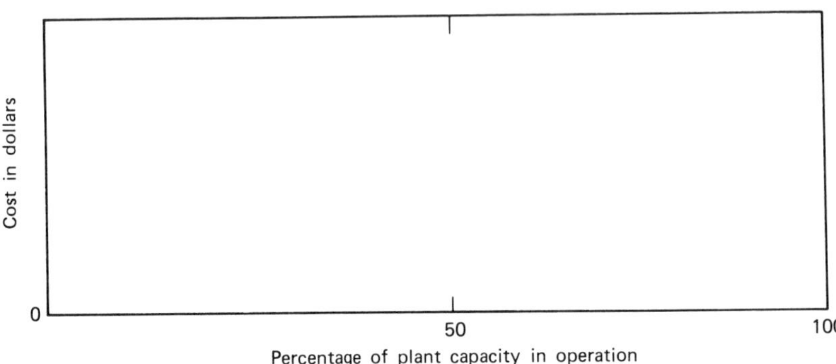

VIII. *Production*

A. Plant: (Include location, total square footage, and layout and sketch of office and storage areas. Also include copy of lease deed or proposed lease.)

B. Equipment:

Quantity	Description	Age	Buying or Leasing	Cost

C. *Equipment layout and production flow plan:*

D. Supervisory personnel (names and responsibilities):

E. *Labor skill and source (detailed list by classification, number, and pay rate):*

Skill Classification	Number	Pay Rate	Source

F. *Materials used, source of supply, and average delivery time:*

G. *Shipping facilities and accessibility to transportation:*

H. *Quality control system:*

I. *Workforce classified as disadvantaged and training programs:*

J. *Expansion capability:*

IX. *Operational plan:*

X. *Financial*

Attach year-end and current business balance sheet on applicant and affiliates, year-end and current profit and loss statements on applicant and affiliates, aging of accounts receivable and payables on applicant, monthly cash flow for twelve months on applicant and annual detail projection for two years on applicant.

A. *Sales History:* (applicant)

	FY_______	FY_______	FY_______	Year-end to Date as of_______
Commercial	_______	_______	_______	_______
Government 8(a)	_______	_______	_______	_______
Government other	_______	_______	_______	_______
Total____________	_______	_______	_______	_______

B. Profits or losses (Applicant)

FY_______	FY_______	FY_______	Year-end to Date as of_______
__________	__________	__________	_______________

C. Projection (applicant)

	1st Year	2nd Year	3rd Year	4th Year
8(a) projected support	_______	_______	_______	_______
Commercial sales	_______	_______	_______	_______
Other government	_______	_______	_______	_______
Total	_______	_______	_______	_______

Note: Projected 8(a) support should decline with each progressive year. Commercial and other government sales should increase.

D. *Condensed balance sheets (applicant):*

Current as of________		FY Ending 19________	
C/A________	C/L________	C/A________	C/L________
F/A________	LT/L________	F/A________	LT/L________
O/A________	N/W________	O/A________	N/W________
TOTAL________	________	________	________

FY Ending 19_______		FY Ending 19_______	
C/A________	C/L________	C/A________	C/L________
F/A________	LT/L________	F/A________	LT/L________
O/A________	N/W________	O/A________	N/W ________
TOTAL________	________	________	________

Key: C/A—current assets O/A—other assets LT/L—long term liabilities
F/A—fixed assets C/L—current liabilities N/W—networth

E. *Sales history (affiliates):*

Name of Affiliate ______

	FY ____	FY ____	FY ____	Year end to date of ____
Commercial	____	____	____	____
Government	____	____	____	____
TOTAL	____	____	____	____

F. *Condensed balance sheets (affiliates):*

Name of Affiliate ______

Current as of ____		FY Ending 19____	
C/A ____	C/L ____	C/A ____	C/L ____
F/A ____	LT/L ____	F/A ____	LT/L ____
O/A ____	N/W ____	O/A ____	N/W ____
TOTAL ____	____	____	____

FY Ending 19____		FY Ending 19____	
C/A ____	C/L ____	C/A ____	C/L ____
F/A ____	LT/L ____	F/A ____	LT/L ____
O/A ____	N/W ____	O/A ____	N/W ____
TOTAL ____	____	____	____

XI. Other Pertinent Information:

A. *Contracts or jobs in-house:*

Customer & Representative	Description	Amount ($)	% Completed	Scheduled Completion
____	____	____	____	____
____	____	____	____	____
____	____	____	____	____
____	____	____	____	____
____	____	____	____	____
____	____	____	____	____

B. *Average monthly billings*—$ ______:

C. *Record of surety and fidelity bonds:*

Date	Job or Person	Type of Bond	Amount	Surety Company	Agent or Agency

D. Contracts or jobs completed within the last two years:

Customer	Description	Amount ($)

E. *Schedule of insurance:*

Company	Coverage	Amount	Expiration Date	Agent or Agency

F. *Bank and trade reference:*

Name and Address	Contact Person and Position
__________	__________
__________	__________
__________	__________
__________	__________

G. *Availability of credit and financial assistance:*

Source	Amount	Terms	Degree of Commitment (Attach any documentation of commitment)
______	______	______	__________
______	______	______	__________
______	______	______	__________

H. *List of loans or loan guarantees provided by the Small Business Administration:*

Name and Address of Lender	Loan Number	Original Amount of Loan	Amount Outstanding
__________	______	______	______
__________	______	______	______
__________	______	______	______
__________	______	______	______

I. *Outline of business Goals: (necessary to become competitive)*

Annual Sales	$______	Current Ratio ______	to ______
Annual Profits	______	Debt to Net ______ Worth Ratio	to ______
Bondability	______	Estimated number of ___ years to become competitive	to ______

J. *Additional equipment necessary to conduct competitive business:*

Description	Purchase Cost	Lease Cost
__________	$__________	$______
__________	__________	______

____________	____________	________
____________	____________	________
____________	____________	________
____________	____________	________
____________	____________	________
____________	____________	________
TOTAL	$____________	$________Per Mon

K. *Other resources needed to become competitive:*

Type	Amount	Anticipated Source
____________	____________	____________
____________	____________	____________
____________	____________	____________

L. *Licenses and certificates in effect:*

Type	Amount	Place of Issue
____________	____________	____________
____________	____________	____________
____________	____________	____________

M. List trade association and other organizations of which company is a member:

N. Labor agreements in effect:

O. Contracts with suppliers:

P. List law suits in force or pending:

Q. Patents, royalties, etc.:

R. Product research and development:

S. Annual sales volume in dollars required for company to breakeven: $________

VII. Statement of Cooperation:

I understand that if approved for participation in the 8(a) Program I will assume certain obligations as listed below. I understand and agree that if I do not meet these obligations, Small Business Administration may, in its sole discretion, remove me from further participation. I further understand that SBA cannot assure the availability of 8(a) contracts to my company, either now or in the future.

I pledge to use my best efforts to develop my business by actively soliciting business (either commercial or competitive Federal) in accordance with the projections made in my business plan.

I pledge to provide SBA with timely and accurate financial information which will consist of at least quarterly profit or loss statements and semi-annual balance sheet. The income from 8(a) contracts is to be shown separately from other income. If requested, I will provide such other information as may be required.

To the best of my ability, I will put into practice the business methods and advice provided to me by Small Business Administration. I will discuss with appropriate SBA personnel any major changes or long-term commitments prior to entering into such commitments.

I will conduct my business affairs in an ethical manner.

I hereby certify that I have not paid fees to third parties, whether directly or indirectly, in the process of obtaining 8(a) subcontracts. If such fees have been paid, or contracted to be paid, I attach full details of such agreement.

I further certify that the statements contained in this application and attachments are true and correct to the best of my knowledge and belief.

________________________ ________________________

Signature of Authorized Officer of Firm | Title

____

Date

Technical and Management Assistance Agreement:

The undersigned requests the SBA to provide technical and management assistance in connection with this Business Plan and Qualifications Resume. It is understood that said assistance shall be performed free of charge. I hereby authorize SBA to furnish information and data contained in the Business Plan and Qualifications Resume to those persons providing this company with technical and management assistance. All information will be treated in strict confidence.

In consideration of this assistance, I hereby waive all claims arising therefrom against SBA and aforereferenced persons.

________________________ ________________________

Signature of Authorized Officer of Firm | Title of Officer | Date

Appendix Two

Sample SBA Loan Proposal for Yourcompany

The sample loan proposal in this appendix shows the typical loan summary for an SBA loan. The loan summary is for Yourcompany, an example that we have been using throughout this book.

Most of the sections of this sample loan summary have been presented elsewhere in the book.

Also included in this appendix is a table of contents for the sample loan summary which indicates the items that are typically included in a completed loan proposal. The presentation here does not include the documents for Exhibits I through IV. The SBA forms that would go with this loan summary to complete the proposal are shown in Chapter 9.

Loan Summary
- Application
- Purpose
- Ownership
- Repayment
  - Comparative and Projected Annual Financial Statements
  - Monthly Projected Income Statement
  - Monthly Projected Cash Flow
  - Notes to the Projections
- Personal Data
  - Résumés of Partners
  - Personal Financial Statements of Partners
- Collateral
- Pro-Forma and Comparative Balance Sheets and Ratios

Exhibit I. Business financial aging of accounts receivable and payable statements and written estimates of equipment, improvements and furniture requested

Exhibit II. Partnership papers, copy of business license, business lease and distributorship agreements

Exhibit III. Personal data including résumés, personal financial statements, and trust deeds on residences

Exhibit IV. Personal income tax last three years, all partners

Exhibit V. SBA Forms 912, 4, 413, and 159

PROPOSAL SUMMARY

John Your, President
Yourcompany
1010 Twenty Penny Lane
Chevy, Minn.
Phone: 411/222-2222

Application: $200,000 partially secured term loan payable over six (6) years in seventy-two (72) monthly installments of $3,705 including interest at ten percent (10%) per annum. A ninety percent ($180,000) loan guarantee is requested under the special criteria of the SBA 7a program.

Purpose: To enable John Your and his partners to expand operations of a wholesale-retail computer sales company located at the above address.

Funds from the loan will be used as follows:

Purchase fixed assets:			
Equipment	$35,000		
Furniture	5,000		
Improvements	10,000		$ 50,000 (1)
Create current assets:			
Working capital	45,000		
Inventory	60,000		
Prepayments	1,450	(2)	106,450
Repay debt			42,550 (3)
Total SBA loan required			$200,000

Footnotes:

(1) Equipment, furniture and improvement estimates appear in Exhibit I.

(2) Prepayments include $1,000 for telephone deposits and $450 for utility deposits.

(3) Debt repayment is for $55,000 note owed Gold Bank, 20 Tops Drive, Jewel, Minn. The interest rate is 14% payable in four years at $1502.96 per month. Present balance is $43,550. Better cash flow calls for a substitution of a lower-interest longer-term loan.

Ownership: Yourcompany is a partnership with the following owners:

John Your
85 Ole Fifty-five
Chevy, Minn.

Owner of 50% of the company

Tath Tacki 1222 Fromp Chevy, Minn.	Owner of 30% of the company
Ed Syrup 7211 Last Street Chevy, Minn.	Owner of 20% of the company

Repayment: The ability to repay the proposed loan is demonstrated in the following annual comparative and projected financial statements, monthly projected income statement, monthly cash flow, and accompanying footnotes.

YOURCOMPANY
Comparative and Projected Financials

	12/31/80 12 Month Tax Return	12/31/81 12 Month Tax Return	12/31/82 12 Month Tax Return	7/30/83 7 Month P&L	7/30/83 12 Month Annualized	12 Month Projected
Sales	420,000	490,000	600,000	380,000	648,817	650,000 (1)
Cost of sales	264,600	318,500	369,000	235,673	402,267	408,850 (2)
Gross profit	155,400	171,500	231,000	144,327	246,550	241,140
Operating expense						(3)
Salaries	50,000	73,000	85,000	58,480	100,000	100,000 (3A)
Payroll tax	5,500	9,350	8,250	6,433	11,000	11,000 (3B)
Rent	6,000	7,000	9,000	5,263	9,000	9,000 (3C)
Office supplies	1,000	1,200	1,400	702	1,200	1,300
Bad debt	-0-	400	500	263	450	400
Advertising	1,000	4,000	5,000	3,216	5,500	5,750
Depreciation	4,000	5,000	6,000	3,909	6,000	10,300 (3D)
Utilities	1,200	1,300	1,300	760	1,500	1,400
Phone	1,800	2,000	2,100	1,228	2,100	2,100
Accounting and Legal	1,200	1,400	1,800	1,053	1,800	1,800
Auto and Travel	500	1,000	1,900	1,170	2,000	2,100
Miscellaneous	150	200	250	117	200	200
Interest	-0-	1,500	1,750	1,023	1,750	2,000 (3E)
Total operating expense	72,350	105,250	125,350	83,217	142,300	147,350
Net profit	83,050	66,250	105,650	61,110	104,250	93,800 (3)
Add: depreciation	4,000	5,000	6,000	3,909	N/A	10,300 (3D)
Cash inflow	87,050	71,250	111,650	65,019		104,100
Less: Owners draw	12,000	14,000	18,000	11,600		24,000
Income tax	29,067	19,875	47,542	18,333	N/A	42,210 (4)
Principal loan repayment	-0-	1,860	2,176	1,430		24,460 (5)
Cash outflow	41,067	35,735	67,718	31,363		90,670
Cash margin	45,983	35,515	43,932	33,656		13,430
Commonized percentage						
Sales	100.0	100.0	100.0	100.0		100.0
Cost of sales	63.0	65.0	61.5	62.0	N/A	62.9
Gross profit	37.0	35.0	38.5	38.0		37.1
Operating expense	17.2	21.5	20.9	21.9		25.0
Net profit	19.8	13.5	17.6	16.1		12.1

YOURCOMPANY
Monthly Projections

	1984 Jan.	Feb.	March	April	May	June	July	Aug.	Sept.	Oct.	Nov.	Dec.	Total Year
					Projected Income Statement								
Sales	53,840	54,408	55,534	56,204	56,522	46,748	57,438	53,310	53,664	53,840	54,158	54,334	650,000 (6)
Cost of sales	33,865	34,223	34,931	35,352	35,552	39,404	36,130	33,532	33,755	33,865	34,065	34,176	408,850 (2)
Gross profit	19,975	20,185	20,603	20,852	20,970	17,344	21,308	19,778	19,909	19,975	20,093	20,158	241,150
Operating expense	12,279	12,279	12,279	12,279	12,279	12,279	12,279	12,279	12,279	12,279	12,280	12,280	147,350 (3)
Net profit	7,696	7,906	8,324	8,573	8,691	5,065	9,029	7,499	7,630	7,696	7,813	7,878	93,800
					Projected Cash Flow								
Collections	53,996	54,214	53,879	54,351	55,422	56,137	56,490	56,725	57,369	53,723	53,629	53,822	659,757 (7)
SBA loan proceeds	200,000												200,000
Cash inflow	253,996	54,214	53,879	54,351	55,422	56,137	56,490	56,725	57,369	53,723	53,629	53,822	859,757
Disbursements:													
Cost of sales	33,865	34,223	34,931	35,352	35,552	29,404	36,130	33,532	33,755	33,865	34,065	34,176	408,850 (2)
Operating expense (−depreciation)	11,421	11,421	11,421	11,421	11,421	11,421	11,421	11,421	11,421	11,421	11,420	11,420	137,050 (8)
Owner's draw	2,000	2,000	2,000	2,000	2,000	2,000	2,000	2,000	2,000	2,000	2,000	2,000	24,000
Income tax	-0-	-0-	10,552	-0-	-0-	10,552	-0-	-0-	10,553	-0-	-0-	10,553	42,210 (4)
Principal loan repayment	2,038	2,038	2,038	2,038	2,038	2,038	2,038	2,038	2,039	2,039	2,039	2,039	24,460 (5)
Loan disbursements	155,000	-0-	-0-	-0-	-0-	-0-	-0-	-0-	-0-	-0-	-0-	-0-	155,000
Total disbursements	204,324	49,682	60,942	50,811	51,011	55,415	51,589	48,991	59,767	49,325	49,524	60,188	791,570 (9)
Cash flow monthly	49,672	4,532	(7,063)	3,540	4,411	722	4,901	7,734	(2,398)	4,398	4,105	(6,366)	
Cash flow cumulative	49,672	54,204	47,141	50,681	55,092	55,814	60,715	38,449	66,051	70,449	74,554	68,188	

COMMENTS RE PROJECTED ITEMS

(1) *Sales $650,000* are based on historical trends of the company. Sales in the last full year of operation were $600,000. Annualized sales based on 7/30/83 seven-month sales of $380,000 and adjusted by the Business Equipment Industrial Production index from the *Survey of Current Business* are expected to be $648,817.

(2) *Cost of sales $408,850* is based on 62.9% of sales. This percentage represents a weighted average s sales, which has varied from 61.5% (12/31/82) to 65% (12/31/81).

(3) *Operating expense $147,350* is based on historical and expected expenses of the company. Several expenses are explained individually as follows:

(3A) *Salaries* are for all nonmanufacturing personnel including two secretaries, production supervisor, engineer, bookkeeper, and office manager.

(3B) *Payroll tax* is based on historical experience.

(3C) *Rent* is according to the lease, Exhibit II, and includes real estate property tax.

(3D) *Depreciation* is according to the following schedule:

Method Item	Cost	Life	Salvage	Depreciation
S.L. Slapinator	$15,000	10 yrs.	$4,000	$ 1,100
S.L. Assembly Equipment	20,000	10 yrs.	3,000	1,700
S.L. Improvements	10,000	8 yrs.	2,000	1,000
S.L. Furniture	5,000	8 yrs.	1,000	500
Present equipment as per income statement 7/30/83				6,000
Total annual depreciation				$10,300

(3E) *Interest is for $200,000,* 6 year, 10% SBA Loan. Annual principal *and* interest payments are $44,460.

NOTE ON ALL EXPENSES PROJECTED
All expenses that are not noted above are based on historical costs.

(4) *Income tax* is based on 45% of net profit to pay state and federal income taxes.

(5) *Principal loan repayment* is based on $200,000, 10%, 6 year SBA Loan. Interest portion is included in operating expense (Footnote 3E).

(6) *Monthly sales* are seasonally adjusted according to the *Department of Commerce Survey of Current Business,* Industrial Production for Business Equipment Index (copy in Exhibit II).

(7) *Monthly collections* are based on a 63-day receivable period that the company experienced as per the 7/30/83 financial statements. The following chart illustrates the sales and corresponding collections for each month:

	Jan.	Feb.	March	April	May	June
Sales	53,840	54,408	55,534	56,204	56,522	46,748
Collections:						
Period 1	5,374*	5,402*	5,423	5,384	5,441	5,553
Period 2	48,622*	48,812*	48,456*	48,967	49,981	50,584
Total collections	53,996	54,214	53,879	54,351	55,422	56,137

	July	Aug.	Sept.	Oct.	Nov.	Dec.
Sales	57,438	53,310	53,664	53,840	54,158	54,334
Collections:						
Period 1	5,620	5,562	5,675	5,744	5,331	5,366
Period 2	50,870	51,073	51,694	47,979	48,298	48,456
Total collections	56,490	56,725	57,369	53,723	53,629	53,822

*Receipts from previous periods whose sales were in the previous year.

(8) *Operating expense* used in the monthly cash flow is less depreciation, a noncash expense.

(9) *Loan disbursements* are for:

Equipment	$35,000
Furniture	5,000
Leasehold improvement	10,000
Debt repayment	42,550
Iventory	60,000
Prepayments	1,450

Personal Data: The following résumés are of John Your, Tath Tacki, and Ed Syrup, partners with 20% or more ownership of Yourcompany.

Résumés

John Your
85 Ole Fifty-Five
Chevy, Minn.
Phone: 411/333-3333

Born:	September 14, 1944 in Torrance, Calif.
Marital status:	Married with one child, age seven
Education	Notre Dame University, B.A., Psychology, 1967
Experience:	1977 to present—President, Yourcompany

1970 to 1977	Comptroller, Software Development Company Thompson, Wis.
1964 to 1970	Auditor, Arthur Anderson, CPAs, 200 Englewood Ave. Denver, Colo.

Tath Tacki
1222 Fromp
Chevy, Minn.
Phone: 411/333-2222

Born:	April 1, 1947 in Duluth, Minn.
Marital status:	Single
Education:	Southern Minnesota University, B.A. Physical Education, 1969
Experience:	1977 to Present—Part time bookkeeper at Yourcompany
	1969 to Present—Field Supervisor, Revenue Service, Chevy, Minn.

Ed Syrup
7211 Last Street
Chevy, Minn.
Phone: 411/222-333

Born:	July 4, 1948 in Van Nuys, Calif.
Marital status:	Widower with five children
Education:	Ohio State University, BA in Chemistry, 1972
Experience:	1975 to present—Manager of Gilpin Hilton, Chevy, Minn.
	1972 to 1975—Night Desk Manager, Gilpin Hilton, Englewood, Colo.

Personal Data: The following is a personal financial statement for John Your, Tath Tacki, and Ed Syrup as of 7/30/83 and accompanying footnotes:

Financial Statements:

	John Your	Tath Tacki	Ed Syrup
Assets			
Cash	$ 6,00	3,000	13,000 (1)
C.S. Value Life Insurance	3,000	1,500	2,400
Stock and securities	4,000	3,500	-0- (2)
Real estate	15,000	110,000	90,000 (3)
Auto	15,000	7,000	1,500 (4)
Stamp collection	-0-	-0-	18,000
Total assets	$178,000	125,000	121,900

Liabilities			
Charge accounts payable	2,000	500	-0- (5)
Auto note payable	7,000	3,700	-0- (4)
Other notes payable	-0-	2,500	1,600 (6)
Real estate	60,000	80,000	60,000 (3)
Total liabilities	69,000	86,700	60,600
Net Worth	$109,000	38,300	64,300
Total liabilities and net worth	$178,000	125,000	124,900

Footnotes to Personal Financial Statements:

(1) Cash for John Your is $4000 in savings (account #14-628) and $2000 in checking (#384-16) at Gold Bank, Jewel, Min. Tacki has $1000 in checking (#44-55) and $2000 in savings (#456-78) at Universe Bank, Chevy, Minn. Syrup has $11,000 in saving (#987-66 and #12-789) at Supermin S&L and $2000 in checking at Gold Bank, Jewel, Minn. (#386-29).

(2) Stock and securities represents shares of S-T-S Development company for both your (100 shares) and Tacki (87 shares).

(3) Real Estate is according to the following schedule:

Owner	Address	Purchased	Year	Market Value	Balance Owed	Held by
Your	85 Ole Fifty-Five Chevy, Minn.	$75,000	1977	$150,000	$60,000	Supermin Chevy, Minn.
Tacki	1222 Frompt Chevy, Minn.	$90,000	1979	110,000	$80,000	Trollop S&L Jewel, Minn.
Syrup	7211 Last St. Chevy, Minn.	$70,000	1979	90,000	$60,000	Supermin S&L Jewel, Minn.

(4) Autos are: Your—'65 Mercedes 280SL balance owed to Gold Bank, Jewel, Minn. is $7000; Tacki—'75 Chevette and 1980 Gilbert Patriot, balance owed to Gilbert Finance, Oxnard, California is $3700; Syrup—'76 Datsun 210.

(5) Your owes $1500 to Mastercharge (#234-2345-6785) and $500 to Visa (#4567-88979-0887). Tacki owes $1500 to Visa (#3452-09476-9854).

(6) Other notes payable include $2500 that Tacki owes to John Metatarsel, 23 Meg Rd., Blinkin, Alaska, and $600 Syrup owes to Larry's Stamps, 23 Bullitin Blvd., Chevy, Minn.

Collateral: The following is a summary of property offered as collateral by Yourcompany and its owners for the proposed loan:

Business Assets:		
Equipment	$225,000	
Leasehold improvements	36,000	
Office furniture	29,000	
Inventory	130,000	
Total business assets		$420,000

Personal Assets:

Net Worth of Your, Tacky, and Syrup residences (market value minus balance owed on mortgage)	130,000
Total Collateral Pledged	$550,000
Plus: Life Insurance on applicants for the benefit of the lender	$200,000

Pro-Forma Balance Sheet: The following is a comparative and proforma balance sheet is at the time of the loan disbursement.

YOURCOMPANY
Comparative and Pro-Forma Balance Sheet

	7/30/83	At Disbursement
Current assets:		
Cash	$ 10,000	$ 55,000
Accounts receivable	115,164	115,164
Inventory	70,000	130,000
Deposits	1,750	3,200
Total current assets	$196,914	$303,364
Fixed assets:		
Equipment	190,000	225,000
Office furniture	24,000	29,000
Improvements	26,000	36,000
Less: Accumulated depreciation	(83,000)	(83,000)
Total fixed assets	$157,000	$207,000
Total assets	$353,914	$510,364
Current liabilities		
Trade payable	$ 86,000	$ 86,000
Current portion—Note	6,350	24,460
Total current liabilities	$ 92,350	$110,460
Long-term note payable	$ 37,200	$175,540
Total liabilities	$129,550	$286,000
Equity	224,364	224,364
Total liabilities and equity	$353,914	$510,364
Ratios		
Current	2.13	2.74
Debt-to-Worth	0.57	1.27

Appendix Three
SBA Publications

sma 71

Small Marketers Aids
U.S. Small Business Administration

Checklist for Going into Business

Thinking of starting a business? Ask yourself these questions.

You want to own and manage your own business. It's a good idea—provided you know what it takes and have what it takes.

Starting a business is risky at best. But your chances of making it go will be better if you understand the problems you'll meet and work out as many of them as you can before you start.

Here are some questions to help you think through what you need to know and do. Check each question if the answer is YES. Where the answer is NO, you have some work to do.

September 1977 Revision

BEFORE YOU START

How about YOU?

Are you the kind of person who can get a business started and make it go? (Before you answer this question, use the worksheet on pages 4 and 5.) ____

Think about *why* you want to own your own business. Do you want to badly enough to keep you working long hours without knowing how much money you'll end up with? ____

Have you worked in a business like the one you want to start? ____

Have you worked for someone else as a foreman or manager? ____

Have you had any business training in school? ____

Have you saved any money? ____

How about the money?

Do you know how much money you will need to get your business started? (Use worksheets 2 and 3 on pages 6 and 12 to figure this out.) ____

Have you counted up how much money of your own you can put into the business? ____

Do you know how much credit you can get from your suppliers—the people you will buy from? ____

Do you know where you can borrow the rest of the money you need to start your business? ____

Have you figured out what net income per year you expect to get from the business? Count your salary and your profit on the money you put into the business. ____

Can you live on less than this so that you can use some of it to help your business grow? ____

Have you talked to a banker about your plans? ____

How about a partner

If you need a partner with money or know-how that you don't have, do you know someone who will fit—someone you can get along with? ____

Do you know the good and bad points about going it alone, having a partner, and incorporating your business? ____

Have you talked to a lawyer about it? ____

How about your customers?

Do most businesses in your community seem to be doing well? ____

Have you tried to find out whether stores like the one you want to open are doing well in your community and in the rest of the country? ____

Do you know what kind of people will want to buy what you plan to sell? ____

Do people like that live in the area where you want to open your store? ____

Do they need a store like yours? ____

If not, have you thought about opening a different kind of store or going to another neighborhood? ____

WORKSHEET NO. 1

Under each question, check the answer that says what you feel or comes closest to it. Be honest with yourself.

Are you a self-starter?

- ☐ I do things on my own. Nobody has to tell me to get going.
- ☐ If someone gets me started, I keep going all right.
- ☐ Easy does it. I don't put myself out until I have to.

How do you feel about other people?

- ☐ I like people. I can get along with just about anybody.
- ☐ I have plenty of friends—I don't need anyone else.
- ☐ Most people irritate me.

Can you lead others?

- ☐ I can get most people to go along when I start something.
- ☐ I can give the orders if someone tells me what we should do.
- ☐ I let someone else get things moving. Then I go along if I feel like it.

Can you take responsibility?

- ☐ I like to take charge of things and see them through.
- ☐ I'll take over if I have to, but I'd rather let someone else be responsible.
- ☐ There's always some eager beaver around wanting to show how smart he is. I say let him.

How good an organizer are you?

- ☐ I like to have a plan before I start. I'm usually the one to get things lined up when the group wants to do something.
- ☐ I do all right unless things get too confused. Then I quit.
- ☐ You get all set and then something comes along and presents too many problems. So I just take things as they come.

How good a worker are you?

- ☐ I can keep going as long as I need to. I don't mind working hard for something I want.
- ☐ I'll work hard for a while, but when I've had enough, that's it.
- ☐ I can't see that hard work gets you anywhere.

Can you make decisions?

- ☐ I can make up my mind in a hurry if I have to. It usually turns out O.K., too.
- ☐ I can if I have plenty of time. If I have to make up my mind fast, I think later I should have decided the other way.
- ☐ I don't like to be the one who has to decide things.

Can people trust what you say?

- ☐ You bet they can. I don't say things I don't mean.
- ☐ I try to be on the level most of the time, but sometimes I just say what's easiest.
- ☐ Why bother if the other fellow doesn't know the difference?

Can you stick with it?

- ☐ If I make up my mind to do something, I don't let *anything* stop me.
- ☐ I usually finish what I start—if it goes well.
- ☐ If it doesn't go right away, I quit. Why beat your brains out?

How good is your health?

- ☐ I *never* run down!
- ☐ I have enough energy for most things I want to do.
- ☐ I run out of energy sooner than most of my friends seem to.

Now count the checks you made.

How many checks are there beside the *first* answer to each question? ____

How many checks are there beside the *second* answer to each question? ____

How many checks are there beside the *third* answer to each question? ____

If most of your checks are beside the first answers, you probably have what it takes to run a business. If not, you're likely to have more trouble than you can handle by yourself. Better find a partner who is strong on the points you're weak on. If many checks are beside the third answer, not even a good partner will be able to shore you up.

Now go back and answer the first question on page 2.

WORKSHEET NO. 2

ESTIMATED MONTHLY EXPENSES			
Item	**Your estimate of monthly expenses based on sales of $ ________ per year**	**Your estimate of how much cash you need to start your business** (See column 3.)	**What to put in column 2** (These figures are typical for one kind of business. you will have to decide how many months to allow for in your business.)
	Column 1	Column 2	Column 3
Salary of owner-manager	$	$	2 times column 1
All other salaries and wages			3 times column 1
Rent			3 times column 1
Advertising			3 times column 1
Delivery expense			3 times column 1
Supplies			3 times column 1
Telephone and telegraph			3 times column 1
Other utilities			3 times column 1
Insurance			Payment required by insurance company
Taxes, including Social Security			4 times column 1
Interest			3 times column 1
Maintenance			3 times column 1

Legal and other professional fees			3 times column 1
Miscellaneous			3 times column 1
STARTING COSTS YOU ONLY HAVE TO PAY ONCE			Leave column 2 blank
Fixtures and equipment			Fill in worksheet 3 on page 12 and put the total here
Decorating and remodeling			Talk it over with a contractor
Installation of fixtures and equipment			Talk to suppliers from who you buy these
Starting inventory			Suppliers will probably help you estimate this
Deposits with public utilities			Find out from utilities companies
Legal and other professional fees			Lawyer, accountant, and so on
Licenses and permits			Find out from city offices what you have to have
Advertising and promotion for opening			Estimate what you'll use
Accounts receivable			What you need to buy more stock until credit customers pay
Cash			For unexpected expenses or losses, special purchases, etc.
Other			Make a separate list and enter total
TOTAL ESTIMATED CASH YOU NEED TO START WITH		$	Add up all the numbers in column 2

GETTING STARTED

Your building

Have you found a good building for your store? ____

Will you have enough room when your business gets bigger? ____

Can you fix the building the way you want it without spending too much money? ____

Can people get to it easily from parking spaces, bus stops, or their homes? ____

Have you had a lawyer check the lease and zoning? ____

Equipment and supplies

Do you know just what equipment and supplies you need and how much they will cost? (Worksheet 3 and the lists you made for it should show this.) ____

Can you save some money by buying secondhand equipment? ____

Your merchandise

Have you decided what things you will sell? ____

Do you know how much or how many of each you will buy to open your store with? ____

Have you found suppliers who will sell you what you need at a good price? ____

Have you compared the prices and credit terms of different suppliers? ____

Your records

Have you planned a system of records that will keep track of your income and expenses, what you owe other people, and what other people owe you? ____

Have you worked out a way to keep track of your inventory so that you will always have enough on hand for your customers but not more than you can sell? ____

Have you figured out how to keep your payroll records and take care of tax reports and payments? ____

Do you know what financial statements you should prepare? ____

Do you know how to use these financial statements? ____

Do you know an accountant who will help you with your records and financial statements? ____

Your store and the law

Do you know what licenses and permits you need? ____

Do you know what business laws you have to obey? ____

Do you know a lawyer you can go to for advice and for help with legal papers? ____

Protecting your store

Have you made plans for protecting your store against thefts of all kinds—shoplifting, robbery, burglary, employee stealing? ____

Have you talked with an insurance agent about what kinds of insurance you need? ____

Buying a business someone else has started

Have you made a list of what you like and don't like about buying a business someone else has started? ____

Are you sure you know the real reason why the owner wants to sell his business? ____

Have you compared the cost of buying the business with the cost of starting a new business? ____

Is the stock up to date and in good condition? ____

Is the building in good condition? ____

Will the owner of the building transfer the lease to you? ____

Have you talked with other businessmen in the area to see what they think of the business? ____

Have you talked with the company's suppliers? ____

Have you talked with a lawyer about it? ____

MAKING IT GO

Advertising

Have you decided how you will advertise? (Newspapers—posters—handbills—radio—by mail?) ____

Do you know where to get help with your ads? ____

Have you watched what other stores do to get people to buy? ____

The prices you charge

Do you know how to figure what you should charge for each item you sell? ____

Do you know what other stores like yours charge? ____

Buying

Do you have a plan for finding out what your customers want? ____

Will your plan for keeping track of your inventory tell you when it is time to order more and how much to order? ____

Do you plan to buy most of your stock from a few suppliers rather than a little from many, so that those you buy from will want to help you succeed? ____

Selling

Have you decided whether you will have salesclerks or self-service? ____

Do you know how to get customers to buy? ____

Have you thought about why you like to buy from some salesmen while others turn you off? ____

Your employees

If you need to hire someone to help you, do you know where to look? ____

Do you know what kind of person you need? ____

Do you know how much to pay? ____

Do you have a plan for training your employees? ____

Credit for your customers

Have you decided whether to let your customers buy on credit? ____

Do you know the good and bad points about joining a credit-card plan? ____

Can you tell a deadbeat from a good credit customer? ____

A FEW EXTRA QUESTIONS

Have you figured out whether you could make more money working for someone else? ____

Does your family go along with your plan to start a business of your own? ____

Do you know where to find out about new ideas and new products? ____

Do you have a work plan for yourself and your employees? ____

Have you gone to the nearest Small Business Administration office for help with your plans? ____

If you have answered all these questions carefully, you've done some hard work and serious thinking. That's good. But you have probably found some things you still need to know more about or do something about.

Do all you can for yourself, but don't hesitate to ask for help from people who can tell you what you need to know. Remember, running a business takes guts! You've got to be able to decide what you need and then go after it.

Good luck!

U. S. GOVERNMENT PRINTING OFFICE: 1978 O - 273-975

WORKSHEET NO. 3

LIST OF FURNITURE, FIXTURES, AND EQUIPMENT

Leave out or add items to suit your business. Use separate sheets to list exactly what you need for each of the items below.	If you plan to pay cash in full, enter the full amount below and in the last column.	If you are going to pay by installments, fill out the colunms below. Enter in the last column your downpayment plus at least one installment.			Estimate of the cash you need for furniture, fixtures, and equipment
		Price	Downpayment	Amount of each installment	
Counters	$	$	$	$	$
Storage shelves, cabinets					
Display stands, shelves, tables					
Cash register					
Safe					
Window display fixtures					
Special lighting					
Outside sign					
Delivery equipment if needed					
TOTAL FURNITURE, FIXTURES, AND EQUIPMENT (Enter this figure also in worksheet 2 under "Starting Costs You Only Have To Pay Once," page 7.)					$

Copies of this Aid are available free from field offices and Washington headquarters of the Small Business Administration. Aids may be condensed or reproduced. They may not be altered to imply approval by SBA of any private organization, product, or service. If material is reused, credit to SBA will be appreciated. Use of funds for printing this publication approved by the Office of Management and Budget. March 20, 1975.

Management Aids for Small Manufacturers
U.S. Small Business Administration

A Venture Capital Primer for Small Business

by **LaRue Tone Hosmer**
Professor and Chairman
Policy and Control
Graduate School of
Business Administration
The University of Michigan
Ann Arbor, Michigan

Summary

First Printed
August 1978

Small businesses never seem to have enough money. Banks and suppliers, naturally, are important in financing small business growth through loans and credit, but an equally important source of long term growth capital is the venture capital firm. Venture capital financing may have an extra bonus, for if a small firm has an adequate equity base, banks are more willing to extend credit.

This Aid discusses what venture capital firms look for when they analyze a company and its proposal for investment, the kinds of conditions venture firms may require in financing agreements, and the various types of venture capital investors. It stresses the importance of formal financial planning as the first step to getting venture capital financing.

What Venture Capital Firms Look For

One way of explaining the different ways in which banks and venture capital firms evaluate a small business seeking funds, put simply, is: Banks look at its immediate future, but are most heavily influenced by its past. Venture capitalists look to its longer run future.

To be sure, venture capital firms and individuals are interested in many of the same factors that influence bankers in their analysis of loan applications from smaller companies. **All** financial people want to know the results and ratios of past operations, the amount and intended use of the needed funds, and the earnings and financial condition of future projections. But venture capitalists look much more closely at the features of the product and the size of the market than do commercial banks.

Banks are creditors. They're interested in the product/market position of the company to the extent they look for assurance that this service or product can provide steady sales and generate sufficient cash flow to repay the loan. They look at projections to be certain that owner-managers have done their homework.

Venture capital firms are owners. They hold stock in the company, adding their invested capital to its equity base. Therefore, they examine the existing or planned products or services and the potential markets for them with extreme care. They invest only in firms they believe can rapidly increase sales and generate substantial profits.

Why? Because venture capital firms invest for long-term capital gains, not for interest income. A common estimate is that they look for **three to five times their investment** in five or seven years.

Of course venture capitalists don't realize capital gains on all their investments. Certainly they don't make capital gains of 300% to 500% except on a very limited portion of their total investments. But their intent is to find venture projects with this appreciation potential to make up for investments that aren't successful.

Venture capital is a risky business, because it's difficult to judge the worth of early stage companies. So most venture capital firms set rigorous policies for venture proposal size, maturity of the seeking company, requirements and evaluation procedures to reduce risks, since their investments are unprotected in the event of failure.

Size of the Venture Proposal. Most venture capital firms are interested in investment projects requiring an investment of $250,000 to $1,500,000. Projects requiring under $250,000 are of limited interest because of the high cost of investigation and administration; however, some venture firms will consider smaller proposals, if the investment is intriguing enough.

The typical venture capital firm receives over 1,000 proposals a year. Probably 90% of these will be rejected quickly because they don't fit the established geographic, technical, or market area policies of the firm—or **because they have been poorly prepared.***

The remaining 10% are investigated with care. These investigations are expensive. Firms may hire consultants to evaluate the product, particularly when it's the result of innovation or is technologically complex. The market size and competitive position of the company are analyzed by contacts with present and potential customers, suppliers, and others. Production costs are reviewed. The financial condition of the company is confirmed by an auditor. The legal form and registration of the business are checked. Most importantly, the character and competence of the management are evaluated by the venture capital firm, normally via a thorough background check.

*Figure 1

Elements of a Venture Proposal

Purpose and Objectives — a summary of the what and why of the project;

Proposed Financing — the amount of money you'll need from the beginning to the maturity of the project proposed, how the proceeds will be used, how you plan to structure the financing, and why the amount designated is required;

Marketing — a description of the market segment you've got now or plan to get, the competition, the characteristics of the market, and your plans (with costs) for getting or holding the market segment you're aiming at;

History of the Firm — a summary of significant financial and organizational milestones, description of employees and employee relations, explanations of banking relationships, recounting of major services or products your firm has offered during its existence, and the like;

Description of the Product or Service — a full description of the product (process) or service offered by the firm and the costs associated with it in detail;

Financial Statements — both for the past few years and pro forma projections (balance sheets, income statements, and cash flows) for the next 3-5 years, showing the effect anticipated if the project is undertaken and if the financing is secured (This should include an analysis of key variables affecting financial performance, showing what could happen if the projected level of revenue is not attained.);

Capitalization — a list of shareholders, how much is invested to date, and in what form (equity/debt).

Biographical Sketches — the work histories and qualifications of key owners/employees;

Principal Suppliers and Customers

Problems Anticipated and Other Pertinent Information — a candid discussion of any contingent liabilities, pending litigation, tax or patent difficulties, and any other contingencies that might affect the project you're proposing;

Advantages — a discussion of what's special about your product, service, marketing plans or channels that gives your project unique leverage.

These preliminary investigations may cost a venture firm between $2,000 and $3,000 per company investigated. They result in perhaps 10 to 15 proposals of interest. Then, second investigations, more thorough and more expensive than the first, reduce the number of proposals under consideration to only three or four. Eventually the firm invests in one or two of these.

Maturity of the Firm Making the Proposal. Most venture capital firms' investment interest is limited to projects proposed by companies with some operating history, even though they may not yet have shown a profit. Companies that can expand into a new product line or a new market with additional funds are particularly interesting. The venture capital firm can provide funds to enable such companies to grow in a spurt rather than gradually as they would on retained earnings.

Companies that are just starting or that have serious financial difficulties may interest some venture capitalists, if the potential for significant gain over the long run can be identified and assessed. If the venture firm has already extended its portfolio to a large risk concentration, they may be reluctant to invest in these areas because of increased risk of loss.

However, although most venture capital firms will not consider a great many proposals from start-up companies, there is a small number of venture firms that will do only "start-up" financing. The small firm that has a well thought-out plan and can demonstrate that its management group has an outstanding record (even if it is with other companies) has a decided edge in acquiring this kind of seed capital.

Management of the Proposing Firm. Most venture capital firms concentrate primarily on the competence and character of the proposing firm's management. They feel that even mediocre products can be successfully manufactured, promoted, and distributed by an experienced, energetic management group.

They look for a group that is able to work together easily and productively, especially under conditions of stress from temporary reversals and competitive problems. They know that even excellent products can be ruined by poor management. Many venture capital firms really invest in management capability, not in product or market potential.

Obviously, analysis of managerial skill is difficult. A partner or senior executive of a venture capital firm normally spends at least a week at the offices of a company being considered, talking with and observing the management, to estimate their competence and character.

Venture capital firms usually require that the company under consideration have a complete management group. Each of the important functional areas — product design, marketing, production, finance, and control — must be under the direction of a trained, experienced member of the group. Responsibilities must be clearly assigned. And, in addition to a thorough understanding of the industry, each member of the management team must be firmly committed to the company and its future.

The "Something Special" in the Plan. Next in importance to the excellence of the proposing firm's management group, most venture capital firms seek a distinctive element in the strategy or product/market/process combination of the firm. This distinctive element may be a new feature of the product or process or a particular skill or technical competence of the management. But it **must** exist. It **must** provide a competitive advantage.

Provisions of the Investment Proposal

What happens when, after the exhaustive investigation and analysis, the venture capital firm decides to invest in a company? Most venture firms prepare an equity financing proposal that details the amount of money to be provided, the percentage of common stock to be surrendered in exchange for these funds, the interim financing method to be used, and the protective covenants to be included.

This proposal will be discussed with the management of the company to be financed. The final financing agreement will be negotiated and generally represents a compromise between the management of the company and the partners or senior executives of the venture capital firm. The important elements of this compromise are: ownership, control, annual charges, and final objectives.

Ownership. Venture capital financing is not inexpensive for the owners of a small business. The partners of the venture firm buy a portion of the business's equity in exchange for their investment.

This percentage of equity varies, of course, and depends upon the amount of money provided, the success and worth of the business, and the anticipated investment return. It can range from perhaps 10% in the case of an established, profitable company to as much as 80% or 90% for beginning or financially troubled firms.

Most venture firms, at least initially, don't want a position of more than 30% to 40% because they want the owner to have incentive to keep building the business. If additional financing is required to support business growth, the outsiders' stake may exceed 50%, but investors realize that small business owner-managers can lose their entrepreneurial zeal under those circumstances. In the final analysis, however, the venture firm, regardless of its percentage of ownership, really wants to leave control in the hands of the company's managers, because it is really investing in that management team in the first place.

Most venture firms determine the ratio of funds provided to equity requested by a comparison of the present financial worth of the contributions made by each of the parties to the agreement. The present value of the contribution by the owner of a starting or financially troubled company is obviously rated low. Often it is estimated as just the existing value of his or her idea and the competitive costs of the owner's time. The contribution by the owners of a thriving business is valued much higher. Generally, it is capitalized at a multiple of the current earnings and/or net worth.

Financial valuation is not an exact science. The final compromise on the owner's contribution's worth in the equity financing agreement is likely to be much lower than the owner thinks it should be and considerably higher than the partners of the capital firm think it might be. In the ideal situation, of course, the two parties to the agreement are able to do together what neither could do separately: **1**) the company is able to grow fast enough with the additional funds to more than overcome the owner's loss of equity, and **2**) the investment grows at a sufficient rate to compensate the venture capitalists for assuming the risk.

An equity financing agreement with an outcome in five to seven years which pleases both parties is ideal. Since, of course, the parties can't see this outcome in the present, neither will be perfectly satisfied with the compromise reached.

It is important, though, for the business owner to look at the future. He or she should carefully consider the impact of the ratio of funds invested to the ownership given up, not only for the present, but for the years to come.

Control. Control is a much simpler issue to resolve. Unlike the division of equity over which the parties are bound to disagree, control is an issue in which they have a common (though perhaps unapparent) interest.

While it's understandable that the management of a small company will have some anxiety in this area, the partners of a venture firm have little interest in assuming control of the business. They have neither the technical expertise nor the managerial personnel to run a number of small companies in diverse industries. They much prefer to leave operating control to the existing management.

The venture capital firm does, however, want to participate in any strategic decisions that might change the basic product/market character of the company and in any major investment decisions that might divert or deplete the financial resources of the company. They will, therefore, generally ask that at least one partner be made a director of the company.

Venture capital firms also want to be able to assume control and attempt to rescue their investments, if severe financial, operating, or marketing problems develop. Thus, they will usually include protective covenants in their equity financing agreements to permit them to take control and appoint new officers if financial performance is very poor.

Annual Charges. The investment of the venture capital firm may be in the final form of direct stock ownership which does not impose fixed charges. More likely, it will be in an interim form—convertible subordinated debentures or preferred stock. Financings may also be straight loans with options or warrants that can be converted to a future equity position at a pre-established price.

The convertible debenture form of financing is like a loan. The debentures can be converted at an established ratio to the common stock of the company within a given period, so that the venture capital firm can prepare to realize their capital gains at their option in the future. These instruments are often subordinated to existing and planned debt to permit the company invested in to obtain additional bank financing.

Debentures also provide additional security and control for the venture firm and impose a fixed charge for interest (and sometimes for principal payment, too) upon the company. The owner-manager of a small company seeking equity financing should consider the burden of any fixed annual charges resulting from the financing agreement.

Final Objectives. Venture capital firms generally intend to realize capital gains on their investments by providing for a stock buy-back by the small firm, by arranging a public offering of stock of the company invested in, or by providing for a merger with a larger firm that has publicly traded stock. They usually hope to do this within five to seven years of their initial investment. (It should be noted that several additional stages of financing may be required over this period of time.)

Most equity financing agreements include provisions guaranteeing that the venture capital firm may participate in any stock sale or approve any merger, regardless of their percentage of stock ownership. Sometimes the agreement will require that the management work toward an eventual stock sale or merger. Clearly, the owner-manager of a small company seeking equity financing must consider the future impact upon his or her own stock holdings and personal ambition of the venture firm's aims, since taking in a venture capitalist as a partner may be virtually a commitment to sell out or go public.

Types of Venture Capital Firms

There is quite a variety of types of venture capital firms. They include

- **Traditional partnerships**—which are often established by wealthy families to aggressively manage a portion of their funds by investing in small companies;

• **Professionally managed pools**—which are made up of institutional money and which operate like the traditional partnerships;

• **Investment banking firms**—which usually trade in more established securities, but occasionally form investor syndicates for venture proposals;

• **Insurance companies**—which often have required a portion of equity as a coniition of their loans to smaller companies as protection against inflation;

• **Manufacturing companies**—which have sometimes looked upon investing in smaller companies as a means of supplementing their R & D programs (Some "Future 500" corporations have venture capital operations to help keep them abreast of technological innovations); and

• **Small Business Investment Corporations (SBIC's)**—which are licensed by the Small Business Administration (SBA) and which may provide management assistance as well as venture capital. (When dealing with SBIC's, the small business owner-manager should initially determine if the SBIC is primarily interested in an equity position, as venture capital, or merely in long-term lending on a fully secured basis.)

In addition to these venture capital firms there are individual private investors and finders. Finders, which can be firms or individuals, often know the capital industry and may be able to help the small company seeking capital to locate it, though they are generally not sources of capital themselves. Care should be exercised so that a small business owner deals with reputable, professional finders whose fees are in line with industry practice. Further, it should be noted that venture capitalists generally prefer working directly with principals in making their investments, though finders may provide useful introductions.

The Importance of Formal Financial Planning

In case there is any doubt about the implications of the previous sections, it should be noted: **It is extremely difficult for any small firm—especially the starting or struggling company—to get venture capital.**

There is one thing, however, that owner-managers of small businesses can do to improve the chances of their venture proposals at least escaping the 90% which are almost immediately rejected. In a word—**plan.**

Having financial plans demonstrates to venture capital firms that you are a competent manager, that you may have that special managerial edge over other small business owners looking for equity money. You may gain a decided advantage through well-prepared plans and projections that include: cash budgets, pro forma statements, and capital investment analyses and capital source studies.

Cash budgets should be projected for one year and prepared monthly. They should combine expected sales revenues, cash receipts, material, labor and overhead expenses, and cash disbursements on a monthly basis. This permits anticipation of fluctuations in the level of cash and planning for **short term** borrowing and investment.

Pro forma statements should be prepared for planning up to 3 years ahead. They should include both income statements and balance sheets. Again, these should be prepared quarterly to combine expected sales revenues; production, maketing, and administrative expenses; resultant profits; product, market, or process investments; and supplier, bank, or investment company borrowings. Pro forma statements permit you to anticipate the financial results of your operations and to plan **intermediate term** borrowings and investments.

Capital investment analyses and capital source studies should be prepared for planning up to 5 years ahead. The investment analyses should compare rates of return for product, market, or process investment, while the source alternatives should compare the cost and availability of debt and equity and the expected level of retained earnings, which together will support the selected investments. These analyses and source studies should be prepared quarterly so you may anticipate the financial consequences of changes in your company's strategy. They will allow you to plan **long term** borrowings, equity placements, and major investments.

There's a bonus in making such projections. They force you to consider the results of your actions. Your estimates must be explicit; you have to examine and evaluate your managerial records; disagreements have to be resolved—at least discussed and understood. Financial planning may be burdensome, but it's one of the keys to business success.

Now, making these financial plans will not guarantee that you'll be able to get venture capital. Not making them, however, will virtually assure that you won't receive favorable consideration from venture capitalists.

For Further Information

Readers who wish to explore venture capital financing in more depth may be interested in the reference below (and in the contents of its bibliography): *Guide to Venture Capital Sources* (4th edition). 1977. Stanley M. Rubel, editor. Capital Publishing Corporation, 10 South La Salle Street, Chicago, IL 60603.

You may also find other Small Business Administration management publications of use for financial planning. Complete lists of these publications are available without charge from **SBA, P.O. Box 15434, Forth Worth, TX 76119.** Ask for **SBA-115A** and **SBA-115B.** SBA publications describing the SBIC program may be obtained from any SBA field office or by writing **SBA, Washington, DC 20416.**

Copies of this **Aid** are available free from field offices and Washington headquarters of the **Small Business Administration.** Aids may be condensed or reproduced. They may not be altered to imply approval by SBA of any private organization, product, or service. If material is reused, credit to SBA will be appreciated. Use of official mailing indicia to avoid postage is prohibited by law. Use of funds for printing this publication approved by the Office of Management and Budget, March 20, 1975.

MARKETING CHECKLIST for small retailers

By GEORGE KRESS and R. TED WILL – Professors of Marketing

College of Business, Colorado State University, Fort Collins, Colorado

FIRST PRINTED
JUNE 1974

REPRINTED
NOVEMBER 1978

This *Aid* is a checklist for the owner-manager of a small retail business. The questions cover areas that undergird retail marketing as well as deal with obvious aspects like customer analysis, buying, pricing, and promotion. You can use it to evaluate your current status and, perhaps, to rethink certain decisions.

If your retail firm is to be successful over the long run, it must satisfy the needs and desires of its present and/or potential CUSTOMERS. Sound BUYING means knowing where to buy, what to buy, how much to buy, and how to place an order. This requires familiarity with old and new products, adequate amounts of the right stock on hand, and selecting and working with suppliers in ways that benefit the store. In PRICING, you need to understand the market forces affecting your business, plan the price policies that you will follow, and know whether your pricing policies meet State and Federal regulations.

You need to be familiar with various types of PROMOTION and when, where, and how to use them. In addition, a credit program or other special customer services can be attractions.

Under the heading of MANAGEMENT goes the establishment both of long- and short-range goals. How you set up your organization and how you communicate with your employees are crucial factors in the accomplishment of your objectives. Of equal importance to good management is the ability to keep and make use of accurate FINANCIAL RECORDS. It also pays to examine your INSURANCE coverage in various areas.

In answering the following questions, you will be reminded of what you may still need to do to round out all marketing aspects of your business.

CUSTOMER ANALYSIS

Who are your target customers and what are they seeking from you?	**Yes**	**No**
Have you estimated the total market you share with competition?	☐	☐
Should you try to appeal to this entire market rather than a segment(s)?	☐	☐
If you concentrate on a segment, is it large enough to be profitable?	☐	☐
Have you looked into possible changes taking place among your target customers which could significantly affect your business?	☐	☐
Can you foresee changes in the makeup of your store's neighborhood?	☐	☐
Are incomes in the community apt to be stable?	☐	☐
Is the community's population subject to fluctuation or seasonal?	☐	☐
Do you stress a special area of appeal, such as lower prices, better quality, wider selection, convenient location, or convenient hours?	☐	☐
Do you ask your customers for suggestions on ways to improve your operation?	☐	☐
Do you use "want slips"?	☐	☐

Do you belong to your trade association?	☐	☐
Do you subscribe to important trade publications?	☐	☐
Have you considered using a consumer jury or consumer questionnaire to aid you in determining customer needs?	☐	☐
Do you visit market shows and conventions to help anticipate customer wants?	☐	☐
Do most of your customers buy on weekends?	☐	☐
Do sales increase in the evening?	☐	☐
Does the majority of your customers prefer buying on credit?	☐	☐

BUYING

Have you a merchandise budget (planned purchases) for each season?	**Yes**	**No**
Does it take into consideration planned sales for the season?	☐	☐
Does it achieve a planned stock turnover?	☐	☐
Have you broken it down by departments and/or merchandise classifications?	☐	☐
Have you a formal plan for deciding what to buy and from whom?	☐	☐
Have you a system for reviewing new items coming onto the market?	☐	☐
Have you considered using a basic stock list and/or a model stock plan in your buying?	☐	☐
Are you using some sort of unit control system?	☐	☐
Do you keep track of the success of your buying decisions in previous years to aid you in next year's buying?	☐	☐
Do you attempt to consolidate your purchases with two or three principal suppliers?	☐	☐
Have you a useful supplier evaluation system for determining their performance?	☐	☐
Have you established a planned gross margin for your firm's operations and are you buying so as to achieve it?	☐	☐

PRICING

Have you established a set of pricing policies?	**Yes**	**No**
Have you determined whether to price below, at, or above the market?	☐	☐
Do you set specific markups for each product?	☐	☐
Do you set markups for product categories?	☐	☐
Do you use a one-price policy rather than bargain with customers?	☐	☐
Do you offer discounts for quantity purchases, or to special groups?	☐	☐
Do you set prices so as to cover full costs on every sale?	☐	☐
Have you developed policy regarding when you will take markdowns and how large?	☐	☐
Do the prices you have established earn planned gross margin?	☐	☐
Do you clearly understand the market forces affecting your pricing methods?	☐	☐

Do you know which products are slow movers and which are fast?	☐	☐
Do you take this into consideration when pricing?	☐	☐
Do you know which products are price sensitive to your customers, that is, when a slight increase in price will lead to a big dropoff in demand?	☐	☐
Do you know which of your products draw people when put on sale?	☐	☐
Do you know the maximum price customers will pay for certain products?	☐	☐
If the prices on some products are dropped too low, do buyers hesitate?	☐	☐
Is there a specific time of year when your competitors have sales?	☐	☐
Do your customers expect sales at certain times?	☐	☐
Have you determined whether a series of sales is better than one annual clearance sale?	☐	☐
Do you know what role you want price to play in your overall retailing strategy?	☐	☐
Are you influenced by competitors' price changes?	☐	☐

Are there restrictions regarding prices you can charge?	**Yes**	**No**
Do any of your suppliers "fair trade" their product by setting a minimum standard at which it can be sold?	☐	☐
Does your State have fair trade practice acts which require you to mark up your merchandise by a minimum percentage?	☐	☐
Are there any State regulations on how long "close-out" sales can be advertised?	☐	☐
Are you sure you know all the regulations affecting your business, such as two-for-one sales and the like?	☐	☐
Do you issue "rainchecks" to customers when sale items are sold out so they can purchase later at sale price?	☐	☐

PROMOTION

Are you familiar with the strengths and weaknesses of various promotional methods?	**Yes**	**No**
Have you considered how each type might be used for your firm?	☐	☐
Do you know which of your items can be successfully advertised?	☐	☐
Do you know which can best be sold through personal selling?	☐	☐
Do you know which can best be sold by demonstrations?	☐	☐
Do you know when it is profitable to use institutional advertising?	☐	☐
Do you know when product advertising is better?	☐	☐
Do you know which of the media (radio, television, newspapers, yellow pages, handbills) can most effectively reach your target group?	☐	☐
Do you know what can and cannot be said in your ads (Truth in Advertising requirements)?	☐	☐
Can you make use of direct mail?	☐	☐
Is a good mailing list available?	☐	☐
Are your promotional efforts fairly regular?	☐	☐
Do you concentrate them on certain seasons?	☐	☐
Are certain periods of the week better than others?	☐	☐

Is there available financial or technical assistance which you can use to enhance your promotional efforts?	**Yes**	**No**
Can you get help from local newspapers, radio, or television?	☐	☐
Are cooperative advertising funds available from suppliers?	☐	☐
Do you tie your local efforts to your suppliers' national program?	☐	☐
Do you join with other merchants in area-wide programs?	☐	☐
Have you looked for guidelines or ratios to estimate what comparable firms are spending on promotion?	☐	☐
Do you study the advertising of other successful retail firms, as well as of your competitors?	☐	☐
Have you some way of measuring the success of the various promotional programs you are using?	☐	☐

Are your products displayed to maximize their appeal within the store?	**Yes**	**No**
Do you know which of your items have unusual eye appeal and can be effective in displays?	☐	☐
Have you figured out the best locations in the store for displays?	☐	☐
Are you making use of window displays to attract customers?	☐	☐
If you use multitiered display stands or gondolas, do you know which shelves are the best sellers?	☐	☐
Have you a schedule for changing various displays?	☐	☐
Do you display attention-getting items where they will call attention to other products as well?	☐	☐
Do you know which items are bought on "impulse" and therefore should be placed in high traffic areas?	☐	☐
Where price is important, do you make sure the price cards are are easy to read?	☐	☐
Do your suppliers offer financing of accounts receivable, floor planning, and so forth?	☐	☐

Do you know what type of credit program (if any) you should offer?	**Yes**	**No**
Does the nature of your operation require some type of credit for your customers?	☐	☐
Have you discussed credit operations with your local credit bureau?	☐	☐
Would a credit program be a good sales tool?	☐	☐
Is a credit program of your own desirable?	☐	☐
Have you looked into other programs of credit cards?	☐	☐
If you set up your own credit program, do you know what standards you should use in determining which customers can receive credit, for what time periods, and in what amounts?	☐	☐
Do you know all of the costs involved?	☐	☐
Will the interest you charge pay for these costs?	☐	☐
Do you know about the Fair Credit Reporting Act?	☐	☐
Are you familiar with the Truth-in-Lending legislation?	☐	☐
Have you determined a safe percentage of your business to have on credit that won't jeopardize paying your own bills?	☐	☐
Have you discussed your credit program with your accountant and attorney?	☐	☐

Do you offer some special customer services?	**Yes**	**No**
If you offer delivery service, do you own your vehicles?	☐	☐
Have you considered leasing them instead?	☐	☐
Have you thought about using commercial delivery service?	☐	☐
Do you charge for delivery?	☐	☐
If not, do you know how to work the delivery expenses into the selling price of your products?	☐	☐
Have you a policy for handling merchandise returned by customers?	☐	☐
Have you considered certain obligations to your community, in terms of charitable contributions, donations for school functions, ads in school yearbooks?	☐	☐
Do you participate in activities of your chamber of commerce, merchants' association, better business bureau, or other civic organizations?	☐	☐

MANAGEMENT

Have you developed a set of plans for the year's operations?	**Yes**	**No**
Do your plans provide methods to deal with competition?	☐	☐
Do they contain creative approaches to solving problems?	☐	☐
Are they realistic?	☐	☐
Are they stated in such a way that you know when they have been achieved?	☐	☐
Have you a formal plan for setting aside money to meet any quarterly tax payments?	☐	☐

Are you organized effectively?	**Yes**	**No**
Are job descriptions and authority for responsibilities clearly stated?	☐	☐
Does your organizational structure minimize duplication of effort and maximize the use of each employee's skills?	☐	☐
Do employees understand how they will be rated for promotion and salary increases?	☐	☐
Does your wage schedule meet the local rate for similar work and retain competent employees?	☐	☐
Would you or some of your employees profit by taking business education courses offered at local schools?	☐	☐
Will training help your employees achieve better results?	☐	☐
Do your experienced employees help train new and part-time employees?	☐	☐
Have you provided for good working conditions?	☐	☐
Do you use positive personal leadership techniques like being impartial, giving words of encouragement and congratulations, and listening to complaints?	☐	☐
Are you familiar with the Fair Labor Standards Act as it applies to minimum wages, overtime payments, and child labor?	☐	☐
Do you avoid all forms of discrimination in your employment practices?	☐	☐
Do you have a formal program for motivating employees?	☐	☐
Have you taken steps to minimize shoplifting and internal theft?	☐	☐

Have you an effective system for communicating with employees?	**Yes**	**No**
Are they informed on those plans and results that affect their work?	☐	☐
Do you hold regular meetings that include all personnel?	☐	☐
Do your employees have their own bulletin board for both material you need to post and items they wish to post?	☐	☐
Have the "rules and regulations" been explained to each employee?	☐	☐
Does each employee have a written copy?	☐	☐
Is each employee familiar with other positions and departments?	☐	☐
Do you have an "open door" policy in your office?	☐	☐

FINANCIAL ANALYSIS AND CONTROL

Have you established a useful accounting system?	**Yes**	**No**
Do you know the minimum amount of records you need for good control?	☐	☐
Do you know all the records you should keep to aid you in meeting your tax obligations on time?	☐	☐

Do your SALES records give you the key information you need to make sound decisions?	**Yes**	**No**
Can you separate cash sales from charge sales?	☐	☐
Can sales be broken down by department?	☐	☐
Can they be broken down by merchandise classification?	☐	☐
Do they provide a way to assess each salesperson's performance?	☐	☐

Do your INVENTORY records give you the key information you need to make sound decisions?	**Yes**	**No**
Do they show how much you have invested in merchandise without the necessity of a physical inventory?	☐	☐
Do you know the difference between inventory valuation at cost and at market?	☐	☐
Can you tell which one shows a loss in the period earned?	☐	☐
Can you tell which one conserves cash?	☐	☐
Do you understand the pros and cons of the cost method of inventory accounting versus the retail method?	☐	☐
Have you found an accounting method that shows the amount of inventory shortages in a year?	☐	☐

Do your EXPENSE records give you the key information you need to make sound decisions?	**Yes**	**No**
Do you know which expense items you have the greatest control over?	☐	☐
Are the records sufficiently detailed to identify where the money goes?	☐	☐
Can you detect those expenses not necessary to the successful operation of your business?	☐	☐

Do you effectively use the information on your profit and loss statement and balance sheet?	**Yes**	**No**
Do you analyze monthly financial statements?	☐	☐
Can you interpret your financial statements in terms of how you did last year and whether you met this year's goals?	☐	☐
Do your financial statements compare favorably with other similar businesses in terms of sales, cost of sales, and expenses?	☐	☐
Are you undercapitalized?	☐	☐
Have you borrowed more than you can easily pay back out of profits?	☐	☐
Can you see ways to improve your profit position by improving your gross margin?	☐	☐
Do you use the information contained in your financial statements to prepare a cash budget?	☐	☐

INSURANCE

Have you adequate insurance coverage?	**Yes**	**No**
Do you have up-to-date fire coverage on both your building equipment and inventory?	☐	☐
Does your liability insurance cover bodily injuries as well as such problems as libel and slander suits?	☐	☐
Are you familiar with your obligations to employees under both common law and workmen's compensation?	☐	☐
Do you spread your insurance coverage among a number of agents and take the risk of overlapping coverage or gaps which may raise questions as to which firm is responsible?	☐	☐
Has your insurance agent shown you how you can cut premiums in areas like fleet automobile coverage, proper classification of employees under workmen's compensation, cutting back on seasonal inventory insurance?	☐	☐
Have you looked into other insurance coverage, such as business interruption insurance or criminal insurance?	☐	☐
Do you have some fringe benefit insurance for your employees (group life, group health, or retirement insurance)?	☐	☐

U. S. GOVERNMENT PRINTING OFFICE : 1978 O - 277-945

Copies of this Aid are available free from field offices and Washington headquarters of the Small Business Administration. Aids may be condensed or reproduced. They may not be altered to imply approval by SBA of any private organization, product, or service. If material is reused, credit to SBA will be appreciated. Use of funds for printing this publication approved by the Office of Management and Budget, March 20, 1975.

Glossary

Accelerated depreciation. A method of depreciation that charges off more of the original cost of the fixed assets in the earlier years than in the later years of the asset's service life.

Account. A recording unit used to reflect the changes in assets, liabilities or owners' equity.

Account receivable. An amount that is owed to the business, usually by one of its customers, as a result of the ordinary extension of credit.

Accounting period. The period of time over which an income statement summarizes the changes in owners' equity; usually, the period is one year.

Accrual basis. The measurement of revenues and expenses, as contrasted with receipts and expenditures.

Accrued expense. A liability arising because an expense occurs in a period prior to the related expenditure.

Accumulated depreciation. An account showing the total amount of depreciation of an asset that has been accumulated to date.

Acid-test ratio. The ratio obtained by dividing quick assets by current liabilities.

Allowance for doubtful accounts. The amount of estimated bad debts that is subtracted from accounts receivable on the balance sheet.

Amortization. The process of writing off the cost of intangible assets; similar to depreciation.

Asset. An item which is owned by the business and has a value that can be measured objectively.

Auditing. A review of accounting records by independent, outside public accountants.

Bad debts. The estimated amount of credit sales that will not be collected.

Balance. The difference between the totals of the two sides of an account.

Balance sheet. A financial statement which reports the assets and equities of a company at one point in time. Assets are listed on the left and equities on the right.

Bond. A written promise to repay money furnished the business, with interest, at some future date, usually five or more years hence.

Capital stock. A balance sheet account showing the amount that was assigned to the shares of stock at the time they were originally issued.

Capital turnover. A ratio obtained by dividing annual sales by investment.

Cash basis accounting. An accounting system that does not use the accrual basis.

Closing. The transfer of the balance from one account to another account.

Common stock. Stock whose owners are not entitled to preferential treatment with regard to dividends or to the distribution of assets in the event of liquidation; usually, common stockholders control the company.

Cost accounting. The process of identifying manufacturing costs and assigning them to inventory in the manufacturing process.

Cost concept. Assets are ordinarily valued at the price paid to acquire them.

Cost of goods sold. The cost of the merchandise sold to customers.

Credit. The right-hand side of an account or an amount entered on the right-hand side of an account.

Creditor. A person who lends money or extends credit to a business.

Current assets. Assets which are either currently in the form of cash or are expected to be converted into cash within a short period of time (usually one year).

Current liabilities. Obligations which become due within a short period of time (usually one year).

Current ratio. The ratio obtained by dividing the total of the current assets by the total of the current liabilities.

Days' receivables. The number of days of sales that are tied up in accounts receivable.

Debt. The left-hand side of an account or an amount entered on the left-hand side of an account.

Debt capital. The capital raised by the issuance of bonds.

Debt ratio. The ratio obtained by dividing debt capital by total capital.

Deferred revenue. The liability that arises when a customer pays a business in advance for a service or product. It is a liability because the business has an obligation to render the service or deliver the product.

Depletion. The process of writing off the cost of a wasting asset.

Depreciation. The process of recognizing a portion of the cost of an asset as an expense during each year of its estimated service life.

Direct labor or material. The labor or material that is used directly on a product.

Dividend. The funds generated by profitable operations that are distributed to the shareholders.

Double-declining balance method. An accelerated method of depreciation.

Double-entry system. A characteristic of accounting in which each transaction recorded causes at least two changes in the account.

Dual-aspect concept. The accounting concept which assumes that the total assets of a company always equal the total equities.

Earnings. Another term for net income.

Earnings per share. A ratio obtained by dividing the total earnings for a given period by the number of shares of common stock outstanding.

Entity concept. The accounting concept which assumes that accounts are kept for business entities, rather than for the persons who own, operate, or are otherwise associated with the business.

Entry. The accounting record made for a single transaction.

Equities. Claims against assets that are held by owners or by creditors.

Equity capital. The capital raised from owners.

Expenditure. An amount arising from the acquisition of an asset.

Expense. A decrease in owners' equity resulting from operations.

FIFO. The first-in, first-out inventory method which assumes that the goods that enter the inventory first are the first to be sold.

Fixed assets. The tangible properties of relatively long life that are generally used in the production of goods and services, rather than being held for resale.

Going-concern concept. The accounting concept which assumes that a business will continue to operate indefinitely.

Goodwill. An intangible asset; an amount paid for a favorable location or reputation.

Gross margin. The difference between sales revenue and cost of goods sold.

Income statement. A statement of revenues and expenses for a given period.

Interim statements. Financial statements prepared for a period of less than one year.

Inventories. Goods being held for sale, and material and partially finished products which will be sold upon completion.

Inventory turnover. Tells how many times inventory was totally replaced during the year; calculated by dividing the average inventory into cost of goods sold.

Investments. Securities that are held for a relatively long period-of-time and are purchased for reasons other than the temporary use of excess cash. They are noncurrent assets.

Journal. A record in which entries are recorded in chronological order.

Lease. An agreement under which the owner of property permits someone else to use it.

Ledger. A group of accounts.

Liability. The equity or claim of a creditor.

LIFO. The last-in, first-out inventory method which assumes that the last goods purchased are the first to be sold.

Liquid assets. Cash and assets which are easily converted into cash.

Liquidity ratios. The relationship of obligations soon coming due to assets which should provide the cash for meeting these obligations.

Manufacturing overhead. All manufacturing costs that are not direct material or direct labor.

Market value. The amount for which an asset can be sold in the marketplace.

Marketable securities. Securities that are expected to be converted into cash within a year; a current asset.

Matching concept. Costs are matched against the revenue of a period.

Materiality concept. Disregard trivial matters; disclose all important matters.

Money measurement concept. Accounting records show only facts that can be expressed in monetary terms.

Mortgage. A pledge of real estate as security for a loan.

Net book value. The difference between the cost of a fixed asset and its accumulated depreciation.

Net income. The amount by which total revenues exceed total expenses for a given period.

Net loss. The amount by which total expenses exceed total revenues for a given period.

Nominal account. An income statement account that is closed at the end of the period to a balance sheet account.

Noncurrent liability. A claim which does not fall due within one year.

Note receivable. An amount owed that is evidenced by a promissory note.

Obsolescence. A loss in the usefulness of an asset because of the development of improved equipment, changes in style, or other causes not related to the physical condition of the asset.

Operating expenses. Costs associated with sales and administrative activities as distinct from those associated with production of goods or services.

Overhead rate. A rate used to allocate overhead costs to products.

Owners' equity. The claims of owners against the assets of a business.

Paid in capital. An amount in excess of the par or stated value of stock that is paid by investors.

Par value. The specific amount printed on the face of a stock certificate.

Partnership. An unincorporated business with two or more owners.

Period costs. Costs associated with general sales and administrative activities.

Permanent capital. Debt and equity capital.

Perpetual inventory. An individual record of the cost of each item in inventory.

Physical inventory. The counting of all merchandise currently on hand.

Posting. The process of transferring transactions from the journal to the ledger.

Preferred stock. Stock whose owners receive preferential treatment with regard to dividends or with regard to the distribution of assets in the event of liquidation.

Prepaid expenses. Services and certain intangibles purchased prior to the period during which their benefits are received; treated as assets until they are consumed.

Price-earnings ratio. A ratio obtained by dividing the average market price of the stock by the earnings per share.

Product costs. Costs associated with the manufacture of products.

Profit. See net income.

Profit margin. Net income expressed as a percentage of net sales.

Proprietorship. An unincorporated business with a single owner.

Quick assets. Current assets other than inventory and prepaid expenses.

Real account. An account with a balance after the closing process has been completed; it appears on the balance sheet.

Realization concept. An accounting concept which assumes that revenue is recognized when goods are delivered or services are performed, in an amount that is reasonably certain to be realized.

Recognize. The act of recording a revenue or expense item in a given accounting period.

Residual value. The amount for which a company expects to be able to sell a fixed asset at the end of its service life.

Retained earnings. The increase in the shareholders' equity as a result of profitable company operations.

Return. The amount earned on invested funds during a period.

Return on shareholders' investment. A ratio obtained by dividing the return by the average amount of shareholders' investment for the period.

Revenue. An increase in owners' equity resulting from operations.

Security. An instrument such as a stock or bond.

Service life. The period of time over which an asset is estimated to be of service to the company.

Shareholders. The owners of an incorporated business.

Solvency. The ability to meet long-term obligations.

Stated value. The amount that the directors decide is the value of no-par stock.

Statement of changes in financial position. A financial statement explaining the changes that have occurred in asset, liability, and owners' equity items in an accounting period.

Stock split. An exchange of the number of shares of stock outstanding for a larger number.

Straight-line method. A depreciation method which charges off an equal fraction of the cost of a fixed asset over each year of its service life.

Taxable income. The amount of income subject to income tax, computed according to the rules of the Internal Revenue Service.

Transaction. A business event that is recorded in the accounting records.

Treasury stock. Previously issued stock that has been bought back by the company.

Write down. To reduce the cost of an item, especially inventory, to its market value.

Years'-digit method. An accelerated method of depreciation.

Index